Tom Wolfe's America

TOM WOLFE'S AMERICA

Heroes, Pranksters, and Fools

Kevin T. McEneaney

Westport, Connecticut
London

Library of Congress Cataloging-in-Publication Data

McEneaney, Kevin T.
   Tom Wolfe's America : heroes, pranksters, and fools / Kevin T. McEneaney.
      p.   cm.
   Includes bibliographical references and index.
   ISBN 978–0–313–36544–7 (alk. paper)
      1. Wolfe, Tom—Criticism and interpretation.   2. Wolfe, Tom—Political and social
views.   3. United States—In literature.   4. Social values in literature.   5. Manners
and customs in literature.   6. Popular culture—United States—History—20th century.
7. United States—Social life and customs—20th century.   I. Title.
   PS3573.O526Z77   2009
   818′.5409—dc22   2008051908

British Library Cataloguing in Publication Data is available.

Library of Congress Catalog Card Number: 2008051908
ISBN: 978–0–313–36544–7

First published in 2009

Praeger Publishers, 88 Post Road West, Westport, CT 06881
An imprint of Greenwood Publishing Group, Inc.
www.praeger.com

Printed in the United States of America

The paper used in this book complies with the
Permanent Paper Standard issued by the National
Information Standards Organization (Z39.48–1984).

10 9 8 7 6 5 4 3 2 1

To Sandy

CONTENTS

PREFACE

This book provides an explanation of how the journalism, essays, and novels of Tom Wolfe work. It lays the foundation for a greater understanding of his writings. Although it offers a critical perspective, that organism remains rooted in the common sense of judgment and taste employed by Aristotle and Samuel Johnson, avoiding the various fashionable philosophical tools employed at the post-graduate level, approaches to which Wolfe himself has vociferously objected. Each of Wolfe's books receives separate treatment, keeping cross-treatment to a minimum, while connecting threads between his book projects are illuminated.

Although Wolfe's work and stature continues to be highly visible, academic scrutiny of his work remains markedly thin. I have chosen to put an emphasis on the literary qualities of his journalism and fiction as they relate to Wolfe's sociological perspective on American society. In the tradition of the gadfly, Wolfe's work attempts to raise questions about social trends, patriotism, religion, as well as manners and mores amid the larger trajectory of American history and society. The influence of French, English, and past American literature on Wolfe's work is immense and I provide some explanations of how he employs these influences in an original way that make statements about American society. The general arc of Wolfe's career moves from youthful enthusiasms to elderly critic, yet much of his work is built conceptually upon the foundations of late nineteenth-century thought in Germany. Wolfe conspicuously displays himself as both a stylist and thinker and while his greatest influence has been on the history of American journalism, the latter part of his career has been dedicated to the American novel and the revival of realism in the arts.

Although Wolfe courts a wide public audience, attempting both a popular and sophisticated salon following, he forges his work with great clarity, a lively accessibility, and even impish humor that entertains with wit and probing irony.

Yet the subtle way in which he works with ideas and literary references are not as straightforward as the common reader might presume. As a matter of principle, Wolfe avoids the philosophically arcane, preferring the tradition of common sense and larger historical vision that one finds in the humanitarian tradition of Montaigne, de Tocqueville, or Thomas Jefferson. Wolfe himself shows a fond predilection for the quick sketch and in many instances I have sketched out ideas or themes that other students may more fully develop. My treatment of Wolfe's journalism falls along more appreciative lines while my analysis of his fiction explicates Wolfe's peculiar and unique use of ironic counterpoint. I have also emphasized how Wolfe's satiric strain relates to his understanding of morality, both private and public. Like many post-World War II thinkers, Wolfe's presentation runs along dualistic lines and he dramatizes this division through a prankish humor that has had wide appeal.

Wolfe has assiduously courted a popular image of himself as a social dandy, yet he has been fiercely private about his personal and family life; a short biographical chapter begins the book to give some context to this most unusual thinker and American social commentator. Although I disagree on the extremity of Wolfe's political perspective, I arrive at the conclusion that Tom Wolfe is one of the most significant post-modern practitioners of American letters in the last fifty years.

I wish to thank two people in particular for their generous help: David Stanford for making numerous valuable suggestions on the Ken Kesey chapter and Martha L. Moffett for her observant comments on the manuscript as a whole. Suzanne Staszak-Silva, my editor, has beamed with the warm sunshine of encouragement.

CHAPTER 1

THE MANHATTAN VIRGINIAN

For the Snark was a Boojum, you see.
—Lewis Carroll, *The Hunting of the Snark*

On May 10, 2006, Tom Wolfe delivered the 35th Jefferson Lecture in the Humanities at the historic 1931 art deco Warner Theatre in Washington, D.C. Established in 1972, the Jefferson Lecture, funded by the National Endowment for the Humanities, claims it is the highest honor the federal government bestows on distinguished intellectuals for their public achievements in the humanities. Previous lecturers included Bernard Bailyn, Saul Bellow, Cleanth Brooks, Gwendolyn Brooks, Erik Erikson, John Hope Franklin, Henry Louis Gates, Jr., Donald Kagan, David McCullough, Arthur Miller, James McPherson, Toni Morrison, Walker Percy, Vincent Scully, Stephen Toulmin, and Robert Penn Warren. For the young Virginian who aspired to play baseball in the major leagues, Wolfe now had his place confirmed in the major league of American letters.

Thomas Kennerly Wolfe was born in Richmond, Virginia, on March 2, 1931, to Thomas Kennerly Wolfe and Helen Hughes Wolfe, who taught her son to sketch and appreciate literature. His sister was born five years later. The young Wolfe took ballet and tap dancing lessons. Wolfe's grandfather had fought as a Confederate rifleman in the Civil War. Wolfe's father had a doctorate from Cornell University; he taught agronomy at Virginia Polytechnic while his real income came from two large farms and his directorship of a farmer's cooperative that became a Fortune 500 company. Wolfe recalls his father as the writer of numerous books on farming and as the editor of *The Southern Planter*.[1] Wolfe's interest in dressing in custom tailored clothing appears to have come from his observation of his father's habits. In 1984, Tom was inducted with his "Southern

Planter meets Saville Row"[2] style into the 1988 Vanity Fair Best Dressed Men Hall of Fame.[3] As an only son, Wolfe enjoyed a happy childhood of genteel privilege in the landscape of the rolling Shenandoah hills.

As a child, Wolfe was interested in the power of genius and he had a precocious interest in history. At nine, Wolfe embarked upon a biography of Napoleon; at thirteen he produced a sketchbook portrait of Mozart's life.[4] Later in life, he had one-man exhibitions of his sketches at two New York galleries, the Maynard Walker in 1965 and the Tunnel Gallery in 1974. He also had the pleasure of publishing an oversize book of satiric sketches, *In Our Time* (1980).

Wolfe was raised a Presbyterian and attended public school until the seventh grade when he was enrolled in St. Christopher's, an Episcopalian high school in Richmond where at first he felt like an outside commuter, but he became the student council president and worked on the school's newspaper, becoming its chief editor in his last year. His regular column, "The Bullpen," focused primarily on sports and was often accompanied by his sketches. Wolfe did well in his study of Latin, graduating in 1947 with "nineteen sons of the conservative Richmond elite."[5] He chose the then all-male college of Washington and Lee over Princeton, perhaps because Washington and Lee was closer to home or had a more vigorous program in journalism, a program that had been founded by General Lee himself when he became president of the college after the Civil War.

However, Wolfe chose to major in English rather than journalism. He began writing fiction under the tutelage of George Foster and he was one of three founders of the national literary magazine *Shenandoah* (which still endures) where he served on the board and where his first short stories appeared in the first two issues. In "Shattered" a freshman football player dreams of being hero-worshipped by the whole school, but his knees are shattered in the first game.[6] (Wolfe would return to this same theme of a young provincial shattered by romantic illusions, which he derived from Balzac's *Lost Illusions*, when he came to write his greatest novel, *I Am Charlotte Simmons*.) Wolfe continued to pursue journalism by working on the college newspaper, becoming its sports editor. During college Wolfe always wore a hat and often carried an umbrella, dressing in "tough guy" dark shirts and dark suits.[7]

In his junior year (1949) Wolfe met a newly hired instructor who had published a collection of war poems, *The Face of Jang* (1945). Marshall Fishwick became the most influential mentor in Wolfe's life. The young Fishwick had just received his doctorate from Yale in American Studies. Fishwick, a native Virginian from Roanoke, became a pioneer in what today is called Studies in Popular Culture; he was the cofounder of the Popular Culture Association, the founder *The Journal of American Culture* and the journal *International Popular Culture*, and the author of more than twenty books. Fishwick's courses were a hectic blend of literature, art, architecture, and artifacts from a wide spectrum of American popular culture. Later in life, Wolfe penned a foreword for his former teacher's book, *Popular Culture in a New Age* (2003). In an interview occasioned by that publication, Fishwick said of Wolfe:

I was teaching at Washington and Lee University and met Tom Wolfe. He was one of my students. Tom was a gifted writer and I recognized that. He wrote a wonderful term paper for me in which he described the place as a zoo full of zebras. From the first, he was a very astute and interesting observer of America. At my behest, he went to Yale for American Studies. I was able to help him get in. He's always said that I shaped him twice. Once at Washington and Lee and once at Yale. We've been in close touch ever since. He's been kind enough to do Forewords for some of my books. I count him as a personal friend.[8]

Fishwick had relished the precocity of Wolfe's undergraduate thesis, *A Zoo Full of Zebras: Anti-Intellectualism in America*, anticipating in some ways Richard Hofstadter's classic study, *Anti-Intellectualism in American Life* (1963). Fishwick observed, "He saw through the façade of the small, elite college and demonstrated that everyone was of the same pattern."[9] Wolfe and Fishwick remained lifelong friends, so that any future biographer will most likely find great interest in their correspondence whenever that becomes available, especially since Fishwick (who passed away in 2006) remained the liberal Virginian while Wolfe became the conservative Virginian. Fishwick had an optimistic vision about America that included the study of heroes. A lifelong interest in heroes resulted in five books on heroism: *Virginians on Olympus, The Hero: Myth and Reality, The Hero: American Style, Heroes of Popular Culture,* and *The Hero in Transition.* A meditation on heroism was to be become one of Wolfe's trademark themes, particularly evident in his longer works of journalism like *The Right Stuff* for which in 1979 he was awarded the American Book Award, the Howard Vussell Award for prose style from the National Institute of Arts and Letters, and the Columbia Journalism Award.

At Washington and Lee, Wolfe was able to combine his interest in fiction, journalism, and popular culture while shining as a student, graduating in 1951 *cum laude.* After college he pursued a professional baseball career for a year, pitching in a semipro league, but gave it up in the spring of 1952 when he didn't make the New York Giants, being dropped after three days of tryouts. Wolfe "made a decent showing: three innings, three men on base, no runs scored. Good screwball, nice sinker, not much heat. 'If somebody had offered me a Class D professional contract,' says the prospect... 'I would have gladly put off writing for a couple of decades.'"[10] With that door closed and with Fishwick's strong recommendation, Wolfe departed gleefully went north to Yale to get the same degree in American Studies that Fishwick received, arriving much like those southern gentlemen whom Henry Adams unexpectedly befriended at Harvard.[11] Fishwick's dissertation was entitled *A New Look at the Old Dominion*[12] which was later revised and published in 1959, a few years after he published his first book, *General Lee's Photographer: The Life and Work of Michael Miley* (1954). Wolfe, as a journalist and a writer with a sociological proclivity, has championed the educational value of photographs and reproductions of historical paintings; he proudly sat in the White House audience in 2008 as Laura Bush announced the "Picturing America" initiative, a federally sponsored program that provides free on-line images of American paintings and photographs for schools.[13]

At Yale, Wolfe read Hegel, Darwin, Max Weber, Joachim Wach, Friedrich Nietzsche, Sir James Fraser, Alexis de Tocqueville, Arnold Toynbee, Thorstein Veblen, and further readings in American, French, and Russian literature. He studied under Cleanth Brooks, one of the stars of the New Criticism movement in literature, which championed close textual readings as a self-enclosed world. The trend of the time was to supplement close readings with analysis of style and structure rather than link the work to social commentary. Such an approach ran counter to what Fishwick had taught Wolfe, and all his life Wolfe has remained steadfast in his commitment to a wider and more populist view of literature with a more interactive cultural relationship, attacking a narrower Marxist constructs of class analysis and the more recent French literary schools that put texts under the microscope of linguistic or philosophic principles.

While Wolfe appears to have enjoyed his course work in graduate school, he has expressed a certain degree of frustration: he was not able to stand out because "everybody was eccentric in graduate school."[14] Like most students, he discovered dissertation work to be painful drudgery, but managed to complete the work by haunting the dusty stacks at Yale's well-stocked library. Wolfe's 1957 dissertation, *The League of American Writers: Communist Activity Among American Writers, 1929–1942*, gives no hint of Wolfe's later polished style, being written in "the same stilted, passive language as so many dissertations."[15] The focus on the social dynamics of political history among literary circles in his dissertation allowed Wolfe to avoid the kind of abstract theory he has loathed all his life, and which later led to his denunciation of contemporary theorists like Michel Foucault, Jacques Derrida, Stanley Fish, and Judith Butler, an academic scenario which he characterized as "The battle of the Fools versus the Young Turks."[16]

Wolfe worked for a few months as furniture mover in Manhattan and unhappily descended into a brief bohemian fling as he sent out letters seeking employment. He was offered a teaching job at a Midwestern university, but instead decided to take a job penning obituaries for the *Springfield Union* (Massachusetts). By choosing a newspaper, Wolfe showed his desire to follow in the footsteps of Stephen Crane, Mark Twain, and Ernest Hemingway. Starting from the bottom of the trade, he worked his way up into becoming a reporter for the paper; when his resume had been beefed up by diligent and successful reporting, he found a job at *The Washington Post* as their Latin American correspondent late in 1959, but his first beat there was covering local news in the District of Columbia. At the *Post* he wrote an illustrated comic commentary on President Eisenhower's 1959 world tour that was notably successful. For his coverage of the Cuban revolution, he won an award from the Washington Newspaper Guild in 1961; the Guild also bestowed upon him a second award that same year for his humor, in homage to his amusing sketches.[17]

Landing a job in New York City in 1962 as a reporter for the *New York Herald Tribune* by sending a portfolio of clips, Wolfe rubbed shoulders with the working-class legend Jimmy Breslin, who became a mentor and lifelong friend.

When he first arrived in the city, he bought a white silk-tweed suit to wear in the summer, which he continued to wear through the fall and winter. Since the white suit, common in the South but uncommon in the north, made him stand out, he continued to wear it.[18] Subsequent interviewers persisted in asking Wolfe about his attire because just such a white suit was the sartorial trademark of Mark Twain.

At the *Tribune* Wolfe was first assigned to the city desk where he reported on the rent strike of New York University students as well as the disappearance of a Mafia boss. His articles were distinguished by his minute attention to atmosphere and detail.[19] Shifting to feature articles, Wolfe's tabloid writing style evolved in prolific experiments that later came to be labeled the New Journalism. At the *New York Herald Tribune*, Clay Felker was both an encouraging and indulgent editor and upon his death in 2008 Wolfe said: "Clay was the greatest idea man of any editor I've ever known.... And so I can't tell you how many stories I did and for which I was duly praised, which were really Clay's ideas."[20]

During a printer's strike at New York newspapers, Wolfe began to write features for *Esquire* magazine, which proved more hospitable to the new kind of journalistic approach that accepted the involvement of the reporter in the story line itself. After the strike Wolfe turned more of his attention to feature writing, at which he excelled. Felker gave Wolfe time off to write the book that defined an age, *The Electric Kool-Aid Acid Test* (1968), which documented important aspects of the 1960s in American culture, just as his subsequent books would do for succeeding decades. Unlike most of Wolfe's books that occasioned numerous rewrites, that work was written according to deadline and received no revision.[21] From 1978 to 1981 Wolfe was a contributing artist at *Harper's* magazine where some of his sketches appeared. In an interview from that era he declared: "I own no summer house, no car, I wear tank tops when I swim, long white pants when I play tennis, and I'm probably the last man in America to still do the Royal Canadian Air Force exercises."[22]

Amid the serial publication of *Bonfire of the Vanities* in *Rolling Stone* magazine (July 1984 to August 1985), Longwood University bestowed upon Wolfe in 1984 the coveted Dos Passos Award. In 1986, Wolfe attempted to complete revisions of his first novel on a computer, but gave up in frustration, returning to his old manual typewriter on which he types triple-spaced in order to leave space for revisions and corrections, some samples of which are available at the *Paris Review* Web site. After the publication of his best-selling novel *The Bonfire of the Vanities* (1987), Wolfe described the writing process in a 1966 interview:

> To me the great joy of writing is discovering. I started out as a journalist. I still love the adventure of going out and reporting on things I don't know about. When I wrote "The Bonfire of the Vanities" I headed out as a reporter into areas I knew nothing about the South Bronx, Wall Street and the court system. That was exciting. Most writers are told to write about what they know. There's nothing wrong with that, but it's rather limiting to put that kind of boundary around one's writing.[23]

After publishing *Bonfire* to great acclaim, Wolfe was included in the prestigious *Paris Review* series of interviews. When asked what makes a good novel, Wolfe responded:

> To me, it's a novel that pulls you inside the central nervous system of the characters . . . and makes you feel in your bones their motivations as affected by the society of which they are a part. It is folly to believe that you can bring the psychology of an individual successfully to life without putting him very firmly in a social setting.[24]

In his 1998 novel *A Man in Full*, the writing of which was interrupted in 1996 by a heart attack and quadruple bypass surgery, Wolfe returned to his Southern roots, writing about plantations, quail hunting, and the lingering legacy of slavery, suburban mansions, strip malls, gilded banks, ghettoes, and speculative urban sprawl. In an unusually frank and peripatetic article-interview with *The New York Times* journalist Peter Applebome, Wolfe recalled his childhood bedtime prayer:

> First, I thanked God for having been born in America, which was obviously the greatest country on earth. I was pretty dead right on that. And in what was obviously the greatest state, because more Presidents came from Virginia than anywhere else. And from the greatest city in the greatest state in the greatest country, because it was the capital of Virginia. Just think of all the people not fortunate enough to be born in Richmond, Va.

Applebome goes on to observe:

> Mr. Wolfe strayed from the steamy Eden of his youth, but his friends say that to understand his work—the (dare one say?) cavalier detachment from the passing parade; the acerbic skewering of most elements of modernism from art to architecture; the conservatism about politics, art and race; the withering disdain for what he calls the think-alike "intellectual etiquette" of liberal Manhattan—one need only think of Wolfe not as dandy or New Journalist or satirist, but as Virginian.[25]

In this charming and casual article Applebome unmasks the mystique about Wolfe the charming poseur to arrive at the central mystery of his history and personality.

At the age of 47 in 1978, on the eve of his great success with *The Right Stuff* (1979), Wolfe married 35-year-old Sheila Berger, a Jewish girl from the Bronx who was 23 when Wolfe first met her while he was working at the *Tribune*, and at that time the art director for *Harper's* magazine. Making New York City their home, Wolfe committed himself to domestic life, renouncing the hectic life of a roving reporter.

When Wolfe returned his attention to his early love, the writing of fiction, he initially encountered a six-month writer's block before making headway on his first novel.[26] That novel, *The Bonfire of the Vanities*, eventually became his most popular book. Most recently he occupied a twelve-room suite in Manhattan's Carlyle Hotel on the Upper East Side.[27] Tom and Sheila had two children: Alexandra in 1980 and Tommy in 1985. Alexandra graduated from Duke University and Tommy from Trinity College, Connecticut. Alexandra is a reporter for *The Wall Street Journal.*

Wolfe has been awarded honorary doctorates by a number of schools, including the School of Visual Arts, Manhattanville College, and Johns Hopkins University. Quninnipiac College awarded him its Presidential Award in 1993. On November 2, 1998, he was featured on the cover of *Time* magazine, dressed all in white. An art poster of the cover was made for fans.

Two movies have been made from his books: *The Right Stuff* (1983), a modest success that won four Oscars; about *The Bonfire of the Vanities* (1990) he has showed little enthusiasm and most people thought it a disaster—he had nothing to do with the movie, yet he diligently viewed *Bonfire* three times, but never could get himself to like it.[28] Wolfe appeared as an actor in *Superstar, Life and Times of Andy Warhol* (1990), penned the film script and narrated the six-part The Video McLuhan (1996), and wrote the film script for the historical comedy *Almost Heroes* (1997). Wolfe appears as a talking head interviewed in the documentary *Gonzo: The Life and Work of Dr. Hunter S. Thompson* (2008).[29]

While Wolfe was born in Virginia and received his formative education there, he has traveled widely about the country for journalistic assignments, interviews, or lectures, priding himself in his split identity of being both a Southerner from Richmond and an urbane, successful New Yorker. He sees himself as being a cultural representative from a Southern capital, Richmond, as well as the Northern cultural capital, New York.

Jann Wenner, the editor and publisher of *Rolling Stone* magazine, characterizes Wolfe as "a sponge for popular culture."[30] The theme of splitting subjects, personalities, the history of ideas, or the psyche of American culture runs through Wolfe's work as a persistent, electric, and illuminating dialectic. Wolfe locates himself amid this dialectic with a cavalier detachment and a floating Lewis Carroll-like Cheshire smile, a Virginian prankster living in Manhattan astride the turbulent sociology of the American decades he has explicated, dramatized, and recorded with earthy humor, sublime eloquence, and memorable phrases.

CHAPTER 2

JOURNALISM AND HYPERBOLE

> When a gross instance of Snobbishness happens, why should not the indig-
> nant journalist call the public attention to that delinquency too?
> —William Makepeace Thackeray, *The Book of Snobs*

Wolfe's first book, *The Kandy-Kolored Tangerine-Flake Streamline Baby*, published
by the prestigious publishing house Farrar, Straus, and Giroux, whose collection
of Nobel laureates remains second to none, appeared in July of 1965, a bottom
priority release period in the year, usually referred to as "summer reading list"
because of its low visibility in terms of reviews and promotion. The book garnered
mostly positive but mixed reviews with petty reservations, such as that of Emile
Capouya from the *Saturday Review* who objected to the hyperbolic quality of
Wolfe's style as "exclamatory and goes on too long"—an objection that now
appears prosaic.[1] The book marries seemingly whimsical journalistic sketches
galvanized by storylike techniques to quirky content; some of these pieces were
first published in *Esquire* magazine. The essays examine American culture—
high and low—with an autobiographical camera eye, at once nearly innocent
but indefatigably cool, as it records a chorus of New Yorkers on some mythical
Sunday afternoon. There are also some alternate settings of various American
locales, like the title piece from a Los Angeles custom car show and some pieces
on car racing, gambling, and boxing, which function as a roaring bass line to this
brilliant assembly of Manhattanites who know how to knock off a quirky and
trendy solo, even if they are just singing about their knack for hailing a cab. It's
a kind of high-class, hip, operatic *Sound of Music* with the island of Manhattan
in the foreground with the rest of America cast as the plains and mountains in
the background. One could conceivably argue that Saul Steinberg's famous cover
illustration for *The New Yorker* on March 29, 1976, with a view of Manhattan from

Ninth Avenue in a close-up with the rest of America as accidental background takes its cue from the architecture of Wolfe's essay collection, although the humor of Steinberg's illustration resides in the closed-mindedness of an island mentality afflicting most New Yorkers who are committed to the snooty pride of congestion, high rents, and loud noise.

The real significance of Wolfe's book lies in the larger questions the collection raises: What are the appropriate topics of journalism? How do journalists cover stories? How does the seemingly trivial achieve a symbolic importance when it is put into a cultural context that brackets either the situation or the people described? How much license does a reporter have to represent a particular character or manner of speaking? Why do such odd or even obscure topics have resonance for our larger social identity? This larger question of "Who are Americans?" Wolfe investigates through the theme of what constitutes an American hero, as well as the diversity of social situations he investigates, or rather dramatizes. Perhaps such literary technique as well as abrupt switches in point of view during the course of a piece confused reviewers and blinded them to the larger structure of the book—the very surface of Wolfe's prose danced and dazzled.

The twenty-two essays are divided up into diverse categories: The New Culture Makers; Heroes and Celebrities; A Metropolitan Sketchbook (he includes twenty pen-and-ink cartoons of his own); Status Strife and High Life; Love and Hate New York Style. The subjects of status, wealth, and celebrity will remain central features of Wolfe's subsequent writings. There are some portraits of lower-class culture, but the book concentrates on the upper class. The single take on the middle class in the book, "Loverboy of the Bourgeoisie," set in the Edwardian room of the Plaza Hotel, provides an amusing send-up of the actor Cary Grant's coy approach to suave seduction. The middle class has little to offer in the way of exciting material for a writer of Wolfe's caliber. Wolfe's technique often relies on anecdotal collage and the quick portrait sketch.

The book sports an introduction that has often been cited as the credo of a new journalistic movement. In the introduction Wolfe daringly attacks "the somnambulistic totem newspapers in America,"[2] comparing them to the dog ears the Mahili clan in Bengal carry around. This kind of savvy and savage over-the-top anthropological ridicule was later to be taken up by the so-called gonzo journalists like Hunter S. Thompson and Warren Hinkle. The deadening dullness of most newspapers is presented as a screaming headache. It is as if news stories proclaim that there is normalcy and freedom everywhere in America, but news reporters themselves are abnormally kept in chains, tethered to the editor's post, lest they write something interesting or insert their own point of view into what should be an impersonal documentation of ritual and trivial nonsense.

Even though *The Herald Tribune* where he worked was the most experimental newspaper in New York, he felt stifled, and he had draft notes for an article about custom cars that was "outside the system of ideas," the first long piece he would attempt. He talked to a managing assistant editor, Byron Dobell, at *Esquire* magazine who agreed to look at the piece. In a fit of panic Wolfe froze and faced momentary writer's block, telling Dobell that he couldn't write the piece. Dobell replied that if Wolfe sent him his notes, he would get someone else to write the article because they already had the expensive plate illustrations of the cars already produced. Wolfe then recounts his manic Kerouac-like fit of all-night writing in 1963, hammering out a forty-eight page "Dear Byron" letter to Dobell that he brought to the *Esquire* office at 9:30 A.M. Dobell appended an alliterative title to it and ran Wolfe's long memorandum as an essay. In the Introduction Wolfe goes on to note that World War II drastically changed America and that change came in the way of how money was re-shaping American society and creating its own High Society centered in New York with Las Vegas as America's outpost Versailles, built in an isolated place, just as Louis XIV, the Sun King, constructed, but that Las Vegas was free-form Americana, and that meant vroom!—only a new kind of free-form journalism could capture and mimic what was happening to the country at large.

A central focus of the roving camera lens in the book is the sociology of American culture as consumer fetishism as well as what constitutes an American icon or idol, which is still a popular topic today. These unusual sketches have an amusing satiric edge, for on the one hand, his handheld camera has a naive eye that searches out the symbolic truth behind shadowy illusions, while on the other hand, we know that our tour guide to American consumerism is the hippest tomcat ever to stroll through an alley of garbage cans or dangle his scarf in an upper-crust coat room before sipping champagne. This was all back in the days when JFK Airport was named Idlewild Airport and beatniks lived on Avenue B. Yet the subject of the rich in America has not changed very much and it is this dominant motif in the collection of essays that has stamped the book with such droll longevity.

The book's opening essay, "Las Vegas," dwells on the proletarian psychology of a gambling haven modeled on Monte Carlo's black-tie-only casino. As narrator, the reporter revels in the city's glum fascination with tasteless neon glitz. The essay, which climaxes appropriately in a sanitarium, brims with mordant black humor and pathetic lost souls inhabiting their own self-inflicted inferno. The dementia that Wolfe delves into has continued to careen in the tumbleweed desert.

On the genteel end of monetary speculation the art world is cattily assailed in "The Saturday Route," which evokes an auction wherein staggering sums are casually dispensed, yet the real reason for the ritual flaunting of money is to nail the most recent gossip of what is happening in London. A new chronicler of Low Rent, The Whacked Out, and High Society has arrived in his own custom-built prose, and yet Wolfe later recalls his writing of this particular piece to be just one item of his seven-days-a-week Grub Street stint at *The Herald Tribune* when he worked on more than one piece at the same time, dictating on the phone from Vegas the last third of "Clean Fun at Riverhead,"[3] which provides a brief, bemused account of the origin and history of the demolition car derby out on Long Island. The inventor of this peculiar sport, which became for a while a national phenomenon, assures any concerned reader who wonders about any of this car-bashing activity that it is all perfectly safe and that no one has ever been injured.

During the course of the longest essay in the book, which examines the tradition of distilled whiskey in the hills of North Carolina, "The Last American Hero," Vance Packard is resentfully maligned by Junior Johnson, a young bootlegger (with a respectable bootlegging genealogy) who is after the cold and sober truth, devoid of tabloid exploitation. This telling moment indicates that Vance Packard, a popular writer of sensational sociological tomes about the superficial nature of American society, is a dated back number and virtual ignoramus when compared to our new eyewitness-on-the-scene—Packard's hip, more astute, and less predictable replacement has arrived in a glow of word-smithy glory, able to both capture and mimic (as narrator) the varied dialects of American slang, whether high or low. In this essay Wolfe gives the reader an implicit promise that he will not be guilty of the lurid promotional sensationalism that accompanies Packard's books. The bootleg hero of this essay, a national hero because he was a NASCAR champion later busted for illegal distillation of moonshine, learned to drive by smuggling whiskey for his father; Jonson manages to escape from his portrait without being framed by irony. The essay contains interesting digressions on dogs, stock car racing, and how Detroit came to market its automobiles. This is the essay in which Wolfe notes that he discovered what he calls the downstage voice, "as if characters downstage from the protagonist himself were talking."[4] Wolfe admires the independence, eloquence, and workaholic devotion of an insomniac jack-of-all trades: coopersmith, distiller, carpenter, plumber, salesman, and fugitive—the varied expertise that produces something people really want: booze and thrilling entertainment.

The delightful essay on Cassius Clay (later Muhammad Ali), the second assigned piece he received from *Esquire* but actually published before the custom cars article, "The Marvelous Mouth," recounts blow by blow descriptions of the boxer's comic pantomimes on Sonny Liston, but zooms in for a close-up on how the ebullient folk hero treats no-class autograph hounds, especially those guilty of unconscious racism. He notes with admiration Clay's adroit ability to mimic an assortment of Southern accents, both white and black, and even Clay's comic ability to make fun of his own Louisville accent (the same Kentucky hometown as Hunter S. Thompson). Wolfe shrewdly notes that Clay is more respectful of people who admire what he has done rather than his witty ability to be an improvisational showman. Although the essay begins with some glancing irony concerning the passing of time that is directed at Clay's entourage, the essay itself remains a pleasant run of straight journalism and it stands out in the book collection as one of the few essays in which Wolfe does not attempt to be cleverer than his subject.

In the title article on custom cars Wolfe remains fascinated by the surface of clothes, slang, and music, but his real focus remains on the custom car as an artifact that has no utilitarian value and hence qualifies as a work of high esoteric art, appreciated somewhat ironically only by lower-class cult fans; the hero he dutifully limns, Dale Alexander (who coined the book's title), struggles as a devoted artist in complete obscurity and near poverty, a proletarian martyr in the annals of those one-of-kind status cars now so beloved by the idle rich. Some of these custom car innovations like flaring tail fins were later appropriated by Detroit. One senses that an aspect of Wolfe's admiration lies in the hero's single-minded devotion to his craft and his nonstop workaholic lifestyle. It is interesting that although Wolfe flaunts his credentials as the chronicler of High Society (and he achieves this quite casually and most impishly in "The New Art Gallery Society" essay), the book's three main heroes, devoid of debilitating hang-ups, arrive by way of the lower class, and all three are continuous talkers who could charm a mockingbird sitting on a picket fence into imitating them.

"The Girl of the Year" offers a manic prose poem on the chic mod scene in the underground Manhattan art world: in the space of a few short paragraphs Wolfe adopts three different narrating points of view: a model, those looking at her, and his own voice. In response to such adroit pyrotechnics, one reviewer insultingly accused Wolfe of being a chameleon an insult that Wolfe took as a great compliment.[5] Wolfe dishes out a brief nod to the innovations of Andy Warhol and features a cameo appearance by strutting Mick Jagger as it skewers the frenetic pace of ambitious models on the scent of the latest diva metamorphosis; Wolfe characteristically sends it all up in smoke with a leering conclusion that indicates the momentary superficiality of a scene at the fashionable Brasserie: "Girl of the Year? Listen, they will *never* forget."[6] The italics underline the sardonic irony.

"The Fifth Beatle" provides a genial, thumbnail biopic of the legendary disc jockey Murray the K, concluding with a bevy of teenage girls waiting, with trembling breasts, for the sacred tablet script of his autograph that will uplift them to seventh heaven. While Wolfe could be cute in a proletarian mode of popular culture with regard to the collection of status symbols, he could also be witty about the upper crust. In "The Nanny Mafia" he reports that the "nannies' hold on the East Side comes first from the fact that they keep holding up status values to their masters."[7] Nannies are also expert at social networking. An early sketch like this one manages to be light and wittily supercilious: their masters assure nannies are served champagne at their charge's birthday parties and that the sun shines properly on little Bobby's bangs.

The success of "A Sunday Kind of Love" resides in its ability to capture the plainly incidental and to deflate small pleasures with whimsy and nostalgia. Wolfe records the relaxed ambiance of a nearly depopulated Manhattan Sunday afternoon as he unobtrusively inserts status symbols into his collage of Gothamites dawdling away the sunshine in the smell of coffee or strolls through Central Park. He imagines a couple listening to an E. Power Biggs organ record *as if* on a psychedelic high, taking in the most commonplace objects with radiance and significance, citing Aldous Huxley and alluding to his essay *The Doors of Perception* (1954), the book after which the band "The Doors" were named. He concludes with the pronouncement of an advertiser who says of New York Sundays: "'Now that was love,' says George, 'and there has never been anything like it. I don't know what happens to it. Unless it's Monday. Monday sort of happens to it in New York.'"[8] The very lack of ambition in this piece, as it exudes charm and sunshine, ignores the difficult social realities of life that Wolfe will address in his later writings; here poetic delight discovers visual pleasure in Gotham's spires that rise "over the landscape in silhouette like ikons representing all that was great, glorious and triumphant in New York"[9]—it reads like an infectious form of patriotic good will that endures as a testament to the ordinary pleasures of life on a day away from the grind of work. In this snapshot of how successful professional couples without children dawdle away Sunday afternoons, the foreground glows in an ebullient and artificial aesthetic, yet in the background an ambiguous satiric tone lingers like a ghost: Pablo Picasso and Paul Klee are decoratively mentioned—painters Wolfe will later attack in *The Painted Word* (1975).

"The First Tycoon of Teen" presents the boy wonder Phil Spector, a multimillionaire before the age of twenty-three, who became an instant financial guru to all the big names in the rock-and-roll business, in his happier boy-wonder days. Wolfe frames the whole piece with the theme of raindrops falling, but switches the point of view in this piece as the novelist Henry James understood it: entering into the mind of the character. He preens his feathers:

> I began the article not only inside his mind but with a virtual stream of consciousness. One of the news magazines apparently regarded my Spector story as an improbable feat, because they interviewed him and asked him if he didn't think this passage was merely a fiction that appropriated his name. Spector said that, in fact, he found it quite accurate. This should have come as no surprise, since every detail in the passage was taken from a long interview with Spector about exactly how he had felt at the time."[10]

The sketch headlines the *wunderkind* with his fists full of dollars and a rolodex of who's who in the rock industry, but concludes with a tone of pregnant irony: "Phil Spector tamps his frontal lobes and closes his eyes and holds his breath. As long as he holds his breath, it will not rain, there will be no raindrops, no schizoid water wobbling, sideways, straight back, it will be an even, even, even, even, even, even, even world."[11] The godlike fillip of those seven evens reads today as a muted but certainly unintended prophecy of the garden before the fall—Phil Spector's golden frontal lobes being not always in control. (Spector was tried for the murder of an actress in his house; he admitted committing the murder accidentally, yet his lawyer managed to retrieve an acquittal from the jury.) Unlike most of Wolfe's subjects, Wolfe and Spector remained quite close friends for a long time[12] and Spector cited Wolfe as his favorite contemporary author in *Vanity Fair's* Proust Questionnaire on November 8, 2000.[13]

"The Luther of Columbus Circle" provides an analytical dissection of the American billionaire Huntington Hartford with sympathetic pot shots at the limited social roles the wealthy have at their disposal because of America's thin cultural tradition. Wolfe notes Plato's overarching agreement with the English Puritan tradition; yet despite the tone of bemused ridicule toward the Puritan tradition and the eccentricities of the very rich at which the reader gleefully rubbernecks— the essay tilts toward a respectful acknowledgement of independent self-reliance and appreciation of what was best about the nineteenth century British gentleman and the Protestant work ethic as embodied in Rudyard Kipling's verse—Kipling being branded as moralistically crude by the British upper class as early as the 1920s. The reader is expected to laugh at the quotations from corny Kipling, yet there is the underlying sense that Kipling may have the last laugh on the reader. Such ironic doubling of perspective becomes a signature of Wolfe's essays wherein he surfaces as a slumming voyeur in love with money or squalor, yet an aloof enough historian or adroit enough anthropologist to let the reader know he's above any such considerations, other than being the most informative and witty observer in the bizarre and primitive society that he is reporting from, as if he's from another century.

"The Voices of Village Square" supplies an unexpected essay during the Christmas season on the disembodied voices floating out the cell block windows at the Women's House of Detention, 10 Greenwich Avenue. Amid the hectoring abuse of the insane and the abuse of the narrator himself toward the reader, Wolfe proclaims the building to resemble a Yale power plant, and the subject itself retains more originality than the attempted hyper-wit of the writing. Without entering the building Wolfe tries to write a comic sketch about the unpredictable atmosphere of the Village, but madness is really not comic material at all. On the other end of the social scale, "The Woman Who Has Everything" gives a portrait of a rich and spoiled woman undergoing the melodramatic trials of the divorced life—not surprisingly, the mild humor here is more jaundiced, dated, and sexist. Nonetheless, Joe David Bellamy chose these satiric forays as two of Wolfe's best comic essays for the Tom Wolfe Reader, *The Purple Decades*, in 1982.

"The Secret Vice" offers a sartorial essay on the importance of hand-tailored clothing, concentrating on real buttonholes and underarm scythes in men's suits. The essay concludes by mocking President Lyndon Johnson, the champion of the poor, for requesting a London tailor for six suits to make him look like a British diplomat. An essay that began with an explanation of the inadequacies of manufactured clothing closes with a deriding political dig.

"The Big League Complex" is a gentle spoof of the egotistical pretentions of New Yorkers with regard to "status points," from Gargantuan-cursing street bums to chauffeurs discussing the running time of operas—status permeating even the lowest levels of Manhattan society, such is the inbred snobbishness of the island itself. Although this last essay raises petty bragging rights in an amusing skit concluding with a near-operatic duet; it is not an ephemeral clinker like the essays on insane women, rich or poor, although the implicit observation that one can gather from these two essays on the insanity of women is that from an anthropological point of view the only difference between these pathetic women consists of their bank accounts. That somewhat bizarre but highly calculated reference to anthropology in the first paragraph of the book's introduction gives a hint that as a journalist Wolfe prefers to write about unknown circles or peculiar niches of people; this justifies his gravitation to both high and low culture while avoiding the middle class. Wolfe conjures his chameleon-like persona as the consummate winking magician with his collage slideshow of Americana up for auction: clothing, boxing, cars, music, movies, museums, hip locales, dog walking, reputations, hairdos, doormen, drop-outs, the ivy-league buttonhole, nannies, even the Central Park Zoo itself.

The immediacy of Wolfe's style of writing bridges and appropriates from the upper and lower classes of American life, while occasionally indulging in a free-form poetic prose that mimics the excitement of his subject. We get large chunks of American vernacular slang from the horse's mouth: whether in a backwoods illegal distillery in North Carolina or at an East Side art auction, combined with an occasional pyrotechnical paroxysm of breathless parataxis that conveys a peculiar American enthusiasm which highlights all that's *new*; a variety of scattered witty and pithy salon phrases that would grace any museum art opening; and a ragbag assortment of in-your-face gimmicks, like the first sentence of the book which stutters that low class word *hernia*, not thrice, but fifty-seven times in a variety of typefaces as if it's a self-mocking concrete poem.

Unconventional typography and dramatic punctuation will become signature traits of his freewheeling journalistic beat, something Wolfe himself says he discovered by roaming the library stacks at Yale as a graduate student and discovering a dissident circle of Russian writers called the Brothers Serapion— Evgeny Zamyatin (author of *We*, later loosely imitated by George Orwell in *1984*), being their leader and Maxim Gorky playing a significant role in their founding—who employed wanton and nearly reckless punctuation, "anything to stimulate the rushes and abrupt swings of actual thought."[14] The Serapion group from Petrograd championed the primacy of art over ideology, which later becomes the consistent theme of Wolfe's criticism of literature, art, and architecture. The title Serapion Brothers comes from the Gothic Romantic E.T.A. Hoffmann's four-volume collection of stories under that name, the collection purportedly being the work a group of friends who met regularly.[15]

Wolfe's seemingly slapdash manner of writing (it's not that) appears some-what verbosely anecdotal while hyped by improbable and flippant segues: Two lovers passionately kissing at rush hour are compared to a fat man "crossing the English channel in a barrel"[16] (288) and the Romantic revolutionary William Wordsworth—the greatest sonneteer in English after Shakespeare and the man who restored to English poetry he natural spoken diction that enlivens Shake-speare's work—is snootily derided as displaying a "delicatessen owner's love of minute inventory"[17] in his poetic metaphors (take *that*, lower-class poets and shameless commoners kissing on the street!). Yet despite the odd diamond-cravat lapse (the putting down of Rousseau or Shakespeare at an upper-class social event remains to this day a salon sport, if not cliché), Wolfe's pranks manage to shock the reader out of bourgeois complacency. Pranks were indeed popular in late 1960s culture throughout America before they were replaced by the culture of fear.

In terms of Wolfe's language, everything is embraced with a populist Whit-manlike panorama of language—from lower-class cliché to upper-class under-stated wit—and as readers, he really lets us know so winsomely that he has arrived, that he can skewer and make fun of everyone, even the very cream of the society that he loves to admire and mock, both because they and the lower classes are not (like Vance Packard middle-class page turners) capable of being shocked. Like Walt Whitman, Wolfe is fond of composing effective on-the-spot lists that contain euphonic resonance and hyperactive energy.

As a carnival barker and salon entertainer, Wolfe's persona offers a remarkable performance, though some might grumble that passages in the book exhibit a sophomoric, self-indulgent humor. The book presents a fundamentally comic performance that raises questions about where America's new prosperity is taking the country. But any book that *performs* and *illustrates* the central metaphoric elements from Plato's Allegory of the Marketplace (in the *Apology* when Socrates takes a stroll) and converts these elements to a popular bestseller about the texture, unself-conscious pride, and off-the-cuff ambiance of American consumerist culture deserves the front row seat the book so effortlessly achieved, both in the popular and critical arena.

Although the middle class offers little in the way of subject matter, the book achieved great popularity among middle-class readers because they could identify with Wolfe's witty satire on the upper class and could empathize with the real working-class heroes he extols in the essays, which implies that there's an open American idol contest waiting to ripen and that if this new kind of journalism catches on you may find out that there is an American hero living in your own home town. Ironic wit with some discussions of high culture is served up for the upper class, while popular entertainment and odd-ball subjects relieves the boredom of the middle class; the result is that the book sells very well and appeals to the voyeur instinct of the middle class who would like to know what the upper classes are really up to.

Wolfe's arrival on the scene, as both charmer and sly cultural commentator, if not the journalist as maverick anthropologist, remains nothing short of spectacular in the annals of American journalism, although in terms of income it would be some time before Wolfe could really say that he was successful. In a general sense—in terms of humor and keen eye for the outrageous and telling detail— his antecedent is another Southern commentator who furthered his education up north and began his career as a satiric travelogue journalist, Samuel Clemens, more commonly known as the steamboat captain Mark Twain.

Wolfe not only hurdles the bar, but leaps and says gee-whiz, look, this is child's play, and what can you not expect from a writer and observer as gifted as I? After all, who better than someone with a doctorate from Yale in American Studies would know that two of America's greatest authors, Stephen Crane and Mark Twain, launched their humble careers in letters as underestimated workaholic journalists tacking their sails both with and against the baffling currents of America's blustery winds? Wolfe himself has recently admitted the influence of Stephen Crane on the period of this book's composition:

> I finally reached New York, which was my goal. I worked on *The New York Herald Tribune* and then came a strike in 1962. All the papers were on strike and the strike lasted for months. Just to make a living, I began freelance magazine writing and then became interested in what was eventually called the New

Journalism, which was very, very similar to the journalism Stephen Crane did in the 1890s.

I just wrote an afterword for a Penguin edition of Stephen Crane's *Maggie, A Girl of the Streets*. Crane was most famous for a novel, *The Red Badge of Courage*. But most of his career was journalism. He loved getting material as a journalist. Before he wrote *Maggie, A Girl of the Streets*, he spent night after night in the 1890s version of the homeless shelters—namely, the flophouses, seventeen cents a night or less which was probably where he got tuberculosis, which he died of at the age of twenty-eight.

He did many pieces in which he stuck to the facts, like any conventional journalist, but wrote using the techniques of the short story and the novel. They are very specific techniques, incidentally.

I hadn't read any Stephen Crane at the time, but his kind of work was beginning to be done in the early 1960s. I noticed it first in Gay Talese and Jimmy Breslin. I said, "*Hey*, this is exciting." By the time I got into it, I was not even thinking about novels any longer. Up to this day, I think that the experimental nonfiction that was done in the sixties, seventies, a little bit in the eighties was the most exciting new direction in literature in this country in the second half of the twentieth century.[18]

Yes, Wolfe was out there, like Stephen Crane, wearing down his shoe leather— mostly in Manhattan, but getting out a bit elsewhere, too. Not only was Wolfe's first book of journalism a notable success by any standard, it put the wider journalistic community on notice that it had fallen into an abysmal lethargy worse than John Bunyan's Slough of Despond; here was a new member of a clique that would give the profession a new look and change its practices. Wolfe recounts how he felt at the time:

I had the feeling, rightly or wrongly, that I was doing things no one had ever done before in journalism. I used to try to imagine the feeling readers must have had upon all this carrying on and cutting up in a Sunday supplement. I liked that idea. I had no sense of being a part of any normal journalistic or literary environment. Later I read the English critic John Bayley's yearnings for an age when writers had Pushkin's sense of "looking at all things afresh," as if for the first time, without the constant intimidation of being aware of what other writers have already done. In the mid-1960s that was exactly the feeling I had.[19]

Few books manage to change both the direction and technique of a profession, yet *The Kandy-Kolored Tangerine-Flake Streamline Baby* was one such book, as was Truman Capote's *In Cold Blood*, according to the critic and sociologist Dan Wakefield.[20]

Flush with the immodest success of his new book, and secure with this approach in profiling little-known groups, Wolfe knew that he was going somewhere with his theme of status, pronounced he says at Yale by his professors as STAY-tus (the English pronunciation with a long a) rather than the more commonly used American pronunciation of STAT-us (with a short a vowel). Wolfe recalled his postgraduate days at Yale and credited "sociology professor John Sirjamaki with awakening his interest in the science of human interaction and the then-new concept of 'status'": "I arrived with the standard liberal arts student's disdain for the social sciences," Wolfe said. "But I couldn't have written a book like *The Right Stuff* had I not become interested in [sociologist] Max Weber and status structures."[21] That observation also applies to Wolfe's earlier work.

It is the concept of social status that firmly anchors Wolfe's second book, *The Pump-House Gang* (1968), where he applies his new journalistic techniques, high and low. While Wolfe's first book is often cited as one of the pioneering works of the New Journalism; the principles of the New Journalism, as he later codified them, are clearer in *The Pump-House Gang*. According to Wolfe, the four characteristics of the New Journalism are: 1) provide a clear scene-by-scene construction rather than general narrative; 2) establish a point of view in a character's head, as a reader might find in a Henry James novel; 3) employ extended dialogue that brings out the character; 4) itemize status details like dress, décor, accents, the way people treat other people, etc.[22] While New Journalists like Jimmy Breslin, Gay Talese, Hunter S. Thompson, and later Norman Mailer practiced the first three items, it became Wolfe's signature to dwell on the last item on the list, and in the final analysis it is that which set him apart from the other writers in the elite movement to resuscitate journalism. There is some concern for status in the writings of Joan Didion, but in the end she is more interested in the nexus between individual psychology and social pathology.[23]

When on January 6, 1969, the twenty-two-year-old Julie Baumgold wrote the cover story for *New York* magazine on private schools in the New York City area, the publisher George Hirsh was incredulous at such a phenomenally successful issue on education by an unknown writer. Running into Wolfe, he asked him why it was such a success. Wolfe replied: "Well, of course, George! It's about status, and status is the number one concern of New Yorkers."[24] Yet Wolfe was to take the theme of status to the nation at large.

The influence of Max Weber on Wolfe remains especially focused on manifestations of style: "Status groups, Weber contended, are the creators of all new styles of life."[25] Wolfe adapted this perception to particular subjects that other reporters were not covering. He displayed an ability to identify such subjects and adroitly investigate them. Wolfe has never shied from acknowledging the influence of Weber:

> Weber was well known in academia for his essay "The Protestant Ethic and the Spirit of Capitalism," written after he toured the United Sates in 1904. It was the origin of the unfortunately non-Protestant cliché, "the work ethic." He introduced the terms "charisma" and "charismatic" in their current usage; also "bureaucracy," which he characterized as "the routinization of charisma." He coined the term "style of life," which was converted into the compound noun "lifestyle" and put to work as the title of a thousand sections of newspapers across the United States. But what caught my imagination was the single word "status." In a very short, very dense essay called "Class, Status, and Party" he introduced an entirely new concept.

I was by no means the first person to get excited over Weber's "status." The concept was well known within the field of sociology, although it was more often expressed in such terms as "social class," "social stratification," "prestige systems," and "mobility." Six years later Weber's terms "status-seeking" and "status symbols" began showing up in the press. Soon they were part of everyday language.[26]

Although many writers employed the concept of status, perhaps Tom Wolfe was more responsible than any other writer in making status not only central to everyday language in America but also a tool of analysis in his investigations of subcultural niches in America.

The title essay of *The Pump-House Gang* satirizes a small homeless surfer gang by that name; they live by their wits and are driven by a cultural nihilism stemming from a plentiful society; a worship of youthful spontaneity is their central act of faith. The point of view is Puritan disdain for these social dropouts and Wolfe takes us along with them on a foray into the Los Angles Watts riot in order to dramatize their narcissism, ignorance, and reckless sense of blind adventure. Wolfe concedes that they have a low-wattage wit, but the curious thing he notices is that within their own social hierarchy they are driven by rigid perceptions of status that are not altogether clear to themselves because such status depends upon improvising the appropriate cool reaction to events that have not yet happened and so they meditate on the "mysterioso" factor in life. Here at the very bottom fringes of society status rules the group and though they are all aware of this, their lack of articulated rules enables childish mentalities.

"The Mid-Atlantic Man" recounts the parable of an Englishman who once committed a petty but public sartorial blunder (wearing a Cambridge scarf to the wrong social club) that holds him back amid the gossip of English society. To escape the frustrations of the social order in England (the upper class will never forgive his middle-class background or accent and therefore he cannot rise), he flees to America and becomes mildly successful in the advertising business. But he doesn't really *like* Americans, even as he tries to lose his accent; he successfully adopts the odious slang clichés of the business. At a business luncheon a boss who is departing on vacation obscenely insults him before his peers, most probably because he still has traces of an English accent. That's too much for him, and he decides to pack up and return to England where he plans to move his advertising skills into the English upper class, but upon arrival back in England not even the lower-class menials will do the slightest thing he asks—presumably because he now has traces of America in his accent! From a single sartorial gaff he has become a mid-Atlantic man, a man from nowhere! This is much like the Princess with the Pea under her mattress; we are now in Storyville rather than the world of journalism, but the point is that small rules of status in the way we talk or dress determine whether we are successful or not—a truism wittily delineated in this rambling parable. Of course, the psychology of this piece empowers the American middle class to think that *they* at least are not like this.

"Bob & Spike" provides a Horatio Alger-like anecdote to "The Mid-Atlantic Man." Bob had no money, but he married Ethel ("Spike") from the Upper West side whose family had some money. Bob had a small business that "went down the chute" but with Ethel's family backing him he started a taxi business in the Bronx which became wildly successful. The couple had an apartment in mid-town Manhattan that overlooked the Museum of Modern Art. Bob was interested in art but the prices of brand name modern artists were out of his reach. On a whim he bought some art from an unknown struggling artist, Jasper Johns, and he rose in the social world by buying the New Realism—this is the fairy tale of making it in New York come true. Wolfe calls Bob and Spike "folk heroes" because they improved their status and wealth through their smarts and good luck. The outsider artists would gather at Bob and Spike's parties and gaze down at the Museum of Modern Art in superiority, derision, and a touch of envy, knowing that they were both excluded and ahead of the times, but that at some point in the future the Museum would beg to buy their work at inflated prices. Bob and Spike are valorized for their chic behavior once they were invited into the upper crust of art owners and become the good Heroes of Status. Bob and Spike are obviously close friends of Tom's and this Cinderella paean bounces with infectious contagion.

These three entries in the book are quite good and they appear appropriately in *The Purple Decades* anthology. Many of *The Pump-House Gang*'s sketches merely attempt wit and humor; there is no architecture to the collection, although the themes of status and fashion appear like billboards throughout the book. Wolfe's proclivity for lists has an even greater flamboyance and presence and at times the reader feels as if the lists are rapids to be run in a foam-flecked river. "The Noonday Underground" spoofs the latest London Mod fashions by indicating that the more things appear to change, the more the bourgeois retain their grip on fashion. "The Put-Together Girl" profiles a stripper who swells her breasts with silicone injections as it simultaneously illustrates what was probably an accurate indication of her mental abilities. "The Mild Ones" offers a silhouette of a motorcycle enthusiast who has dropped a V-8 engine onto his cycle; the piece dramatizes the desire of the American male to become a speed machine, in the sense that a religious acolyte might aspire to become a saint. "The Hair Boys" chronicles the fashions of hairdos amid the hot-rod culture of Los Angeles; it features a digression on the diarist Samuel Pepys and the accidental history that originated the crease in men's trousers: Queen Victoria's eldest son Albert (later Edward VII) had his white flannels ruined in a downpour, so he stopped and bought some ready-mades that had long lain in a shop drawer.

In "What if He is Right?"—the longest and best essay in the collection— Wolfe limns a simultaneous profile and deconstruction of Marshall McLuhan, the Canadian savant who formulated the observation that "the medium is the message" into the maxim "Print gave tribal man an eye for an ear."[27] This might be the most academic essay Wolfe has ever penned, yet although it is nearly scholarly, the essay is personally reflective in the sense that Montaigne's amateur but probing essays focus on both self and society. Wolfe provides an informal and friendly portrait of a man who has no notion of sartorial dress but sparks aflame with concepts that are nearly anthropological. Wolfe concludes that McLuhan is really a "theoretical cognitive psychologist," comparing his autobiography to that of Sigmund Freud and psychoanalyzing his ideas as stemming from his education at Cambridge in popular culture and from elements of his personal life, including McLuhan's conversion to Roman Catholicism. Self-indulgently but adeptly, Wolfe interjects a couple of his own poems on the American pastime of armchair psychoanalysis.

McLuhan's astigmatic monomania amid the circus of advertising and academia preoccupies and fascinates Wolfe. He's bemused by the way some of McLuhan's oracular pronouncements confuse people, even though they are based upon elementary observations. Wolfe thinks that someone like McLuhan can become an unlikely celebrity only because we live in the period of confusion that Nietzsche and Max Weber predicted; for Nietzsche this was "the death of God" and for Weber it was the "demystification of the world,"[28] and that McLuhan, like Freud, delineated our basic experiences (for Freud it was sex, for McLuhan it was advertising) in obvious lowlife terminology, which is what enraged academics. Wolfe goes on to debunk any scientific basis for either Freud or McLuhan—he treats both as fashionable pop sages making common-sense heyday amid sensory confusion (for Freud, sex replacing God; for McLuhan the appearance of new stimulating media like television replacing causal linear thinking). Although Wolfe demythologizes McLuhan as he explicates him, he does so in such a condensed and empathetic way that Wolfe was later asked to write an introduction to a posthumous collection of McLuhan's essays, probably because Wolfe was one of the few popular writers who actually understood McLuhan. Wolfe's grasp of Weber's sociology and his background foundation from his former mentor Fishwick gave him the perspective to understand the maverick academic of pop culture.

"King of Status Dropouts" profiles Hugh Hefner of *Playboy* magazine and his adolescent self-indulgence as a peculiar form of heartland wisdom. Although in terms of wealth, Hefner must be rated at the zenith of Chicago moguls, city society turns its back on him and Hefner turns his back upon the world, striking a chic and reclusive hedonist poise in his bathrobe and pajamas as he makes his bed his business office while working on The Philosophy: "The Philosophy imputes deep moral purpose to his enterprises, legitimizes them, in Weberian terms, just as the libraries helped Andrew Carnegie feel better about the whole thing. But so what? Just inches away, at all times, are the dials and wonders of The House."[29] To a reporter who worked with pen and paper, such technological worship must have appeared both bizarre and adolescent.

With double-entendres and the use of neologism (Weberian), Wolfe satirizes Hefner's philosophy as the sociological reification of personal proclivities. The amusing and stark contrast of books and sex, altruism and selfishness, brings focus to Wolfe's central hobbyhorse: that the Protestant work ethic, based upon self-sacrifice and concern for the common good, may have contributed to the amassing of wealth in the West, but we now inhabit a vastly different sociological terrain that is not confined to either coast. Vanished are the ascetic roots of the capitalist economy as well as any sense of Freudian guilt. As Nietzsche, who did not consider the English to be a philosophical people, predicted, the general drift is toward Godless nihilism. Here Hefner's homespun philosophy of the wealthy dandy fixated only on his sex drive remains a naïve mockery of philosophy itself. While Weber writes about religious affiliation as it relates to social stratification in *The Protestant Work Ethic and the Spirit of Capitalism*, Wolfe meditates on monetary wealth, the manner of speaking and dress, and general social code as it relates to social stratification. Hefner's nonacceptance by the Chicago elite and his solitary defiance becomes a pioneering model for the *nouveau riches* to pursue their own brand of "liberating" solipsism "in the privacy of their own home."[30] Such American navel-gazing as pseudo-philosophy will resurface later as a theme in the novel *A Man in Full*.

The remaining pieces in the book remain ephemeral exercises in wit and humor. "Tom Wolfe's New Book of Etiquette" satirically explicates the vulgarisms admitted by the status elite into their behavior and vocabulary; Wolfe amusingly explicates the history of kissing in the Persian Empire via Herodotus. "The Private Game" takes the reader into the demimonde of a gambling club in London as it evokes the ambiance of Edgar Allan Poe's "The Masque of the Red Death." Set in Los Angeles' Little Venice, "The Life & Hard Times of a Teenage Society Girl," portrays a crowd of English snobs whose informal *patois* Wolfe cleverly manages to imitate; the piece sympathetically satirizes Dollies, those middle-class society girls who climb the social ladder, yet it paints a darker, predatory picture of a privileged elite accustomed to a lifetime of sneering.

"The Automated Hotel" checks in with a witty complaint about the inefficiency of hotel management, while "The Shokkkkkk of Recognition" (the title parodies a landmark anthology of Civil War writings edited by Edmund Wilson) delivers a supercilious piece on the value of art and celebrity stardom that features Natalie Wood. "Sliding Down into the Behavioral Sink" laments with a sociologist the "bombed-out" condition of 1960s Harlem, its claustrophobic conclusion evoking Bob Dylan's "Stuck Inside of Mobile with the Memphis Blues Again" from Bob Dylan's first electric album, *Blonde on Blonde* (1966).

The general theme of the essays (and sketches as each piece is illustrated by a Wolfe cartoon) in *The Pump-House Gang* is that status effects *everyone*, whether we are aware of it or not, whether we deny it or not, and those who are aware of it and can overcome any genealogical, sociological, personal, or other handicap and *rise* in status have triumphed through the Protestant work ethic, as Max Weber astutely observed, and *this* is what has made this country so interesting and more susceptible to change than, for example, England, which is the message behind the leitmotif of English themes in the volume. To improve one's status remains heroically and patriotically American. So it would seem that Wolfe's preoccupation with status eventually led him to the more ambitious project of *The Right Stuff* (1979), but for the moment Wolfe was working on the slightly more ambiguous task of chronicling some other writers in the counterculture movement with *The Electric Kool-Aid Acid Test* (1968), which was Wolfe's first extended narrative and published on the same day as *The Pump-House Gang*. Wolfe claims that he had the idea for *The Electric Kool-Aid Acid Test* in his head for about eighteen months, but that the actual writing of it took only about four months.[31]

CHAPTER 3

PRANKSTER RIDDLES

It made no difference to him what the project, event, or experiment was, Ken only knew life, happiness, joy, and standing on the edge.
—Bill Walton, *Spit in the Ocean* #7

According to Wolfe's later retrospective, the Prankster psychedelic movement "whose waves are still felt in every part of the country, in every grammar school even, like the intergalactic pulse"[1] would ripple throughout Western culture. Others would tweak it and even perfect it in various ways—to which Kesey would invariably reply: "They know *where* it is, but they don't know *what* it is."[2]

Yet how did a New York features writer arrive at describing the psychedelic age on the West Coast? On the lookout for material to write a novel, Wolfe initiated a short assignment on Ken Kesey, which became a long assignment, and the long assignment became an obsession that turned into a docudrama novel employing fictional techniques. Ed McClanahan first got Wolfe interested in Kesey by sending him carbon copies of letters Kesey had written to the novelist Larry McMurtry, who with McClanahan, Ken Babbs, Robert Stone, and Kesey had been students of Wallace Stegner's at Stanford. Wolfe persuaded his editor, Clay Felker, to buy him a ticket to Mexico for a profile on Kesey in exile, but by the time Wolfe was to depart, Kesey had smuggled himself back into the San Francisco area and had been arrested for popping up in public (playing the Scarlet Pimpernel), including a television appearance with the San Francisco personality Roger Grimsby (Plummer 149).[3]

In the summer of 1966, two years after the fabled bus trip, Wolfe visited Ken Kesey in jail, speaking to him by phone through plate glass. Wolfe was fascinated by Kesey's personality and wanted to do the piece; he stayed in the San Francisco area for a month doing interviews, publishing a three-part series for *The Herald Tribune* in January and February of 1967 with photos of the Merry Pranksters and Ken Kesey, who resembled a younger Marlon Brando. While Wolfe was somewhat satisfied with the first piece and less so with the two follow-ups, he could not but notice Ken Kesey's disappointed and resigned acquiescence to some minor publicity instead of a real story. Kesey had objected that the coverage was too distant, too cold, too traditional, and never revealed what the Merry Pranksters had experienced from *within* and the palpable effect they had on *others.*[4]

Kesey had been expecting from Wolfe embedded, partisan publicity for his new project, which began as a pilgrimage to both the 1964 World's Fair out on Long Island and to Kesey's own launch party in Manhattan for his new novel, *Sometimes a Great Notion.* The celebrated experiments with drugs on the trip and after eventually culminated in Kesey's martyrdom to a six-month hard labor sentence, for the possession of a small amount of marijuana, at an honor camp in the woods not far from his La Honda home.[5] Brooding over Ken Kesey's reaction—after all, Kesey was one the pioneer fathers of this new bohemian movement that embraced technology ("hippie,"a label Kesey loathed, was originally a derisive term for a wannabe hip cat[6]) as well as a young roaring lion of the American novel whom legendary editor Malcolm Cowley was backing. There's also the fact that Kesey's entourage numbered notable writers and artists: the novelist Ed McClanahan, best known for his amusing memoirs *Famous People I Have Known* (1985) and *O the Clear Moment* (2008); Stewart Brand, author of *The Whole Earth Catalogue* (1968); poet Robert Hunter, lyricist for The Grateful Dead; Mountain Girl (Carolyn Adams); Ken Babbs, chronicler, novelist, and publicist for the movement; novelist Robert Stone, a friend from Stanford, who had been with Ken Kesey and Neal Cassady in Mexico and briefly drove with them in New York; photographer Ron "Hassler" Bevirt. Other writer friends from Stanford not on the bus included novelist Larry McMurtry, a supportive bystander involved in the Stark incident; the poet and essayist Wendell Berry; novelists Gurney Norman and Ernst Gaines; the short story writer and essayist Tillie Olsen, as well as others.

Yet all these people were predominantly West Coast figures. They probably saw Wolfe as a fellow rebel; after all, in 1965 he was the author of two satiric pieces that attacked *The New Yorker* magazine, an East Coast culture magazine from which West Coast writers were virtually barred, although Westerners had been welcomed by its former editor, Harold Ross. As a giant slayer of East Coast pretention, Wolfe brought antiestablishment credentials to the Pranksters—the infamous episode of the *New Yorker* affair (see Chapter 6) remains as much prank as it is social and literary critique. The Pranksters themselves certainly thought Wolfe was strange in his tailored suits and polished shoes, but they saw him as an anti-establishment ally in their attack on suburban culture. Yet they did not appear to consider that the prank might be on them and not the cultural establishment. They were confident of bringing Wolfe *into their movie.*

To complete the book Wolfe had to go back West for a month and gather more material, tracking down Pranksters, interviewing them, reading Kesey's diaries and correspondence, and viewing uncut film footage of the 1964 bus trip, some of which is now available on DVD. As Wolfe was about to tackle the book, his father became ill and was hospitalized with heart problems. Wolfe retired to his home in Virginia to be near his father where he buckled down and wrote the book chronicling the ecstatic birth of a new movement while he somberly meditated on death. As a professional journalist, Wolfe wanted to document what he recognized as a vanguard movement in the arts; in his previous pieces he had compulsively resorted to irony. How could he be both dramatic and noncommittal toward a group of talented writers he admired but wasn't sure that he agreed with?

As noted, both *The Pump House Gang* and *The Electric Kool-Aid Acid Test* were published the same day. The latter book furthers the techniques employed in the former book's title essay where Wolfe becomes a fellow traveler, a genial sidekick, trying to capture not merely the conversations and attitudes of his companions during a wild escape-fray into the notorious Watts riots in Los Angeles, but the very motivations and thought-processes of his cast of characters. This was something he had tried in his article on Phil Spector, but Wolfe would enhance this approach on a larger canvas with a more varied cast, employing shorter scene slides and converting punctuation into nearly another character in the book through its constant dramatic implications that imply the process of what characters thought; it is as if punctuation itself takes on the role of the chorus in a Greek tragedy.

For the technique of sliding empathetic view back and forth between a large cast of characters Wolfe had an example before him in Kesey's most recent novel, *Sometimes a Great Notion* (1964).[7] Wolfe employs a truncated format of this technique which appears as nearly collage—its fast-paced austerity mimetically capturing a breathless ecstasy. Wolfe's compulsive leaning toward droll satire would not completely disappear, but since he respected these writers and their aims in shaking up the literary and cultural establishment, Wolfe's satire and defense of high culture would be much more muted, fading into sly distortions, eliminating exculpatory evidence, letting his own editorial point of view nearly vanish into the shadows of a second reading—an effort few readers would probably attempt, but what did that matter if the masses devoured the surface without digesting the material? As in "The Pump-House Gang" essay, Wolfe would at first remain the slumming representative of high culture charting a lower class fashionable trend as if he were an anthropologist fresh from the labyrinthine stacks of Yale Library, a library, by the way, that was traditionally more inclusive than most important libraries in acquiring new material documenting the current changes in American literature.

The Electric Kool-Aid Acid Test chronicles two journeys, one to New York City in the East via the South and another journey southward through the landscape of Mexico; in this respect resembling the structure of Jack Kerouac's *On the Road* (1957); the last third of the book describes the public acid tests that Kesey and the Merry Pranksters performed.

The first chapter, "Black Shiny FBI Shoes," delineates the cultural conflict between the hipsters and the law in terms of sartorial footwear. The corporate world and the FBI wear black leather shiny shoes, while hipsters prefer hand-tooled Mexican, over-ankle moccasins. The presentation of Ken Kesey is that of a talented writer done in by drugs and surrounded by a whacked-out assortment of somewhat talented eccentrics who have gone "*mysto*"[8] in much the same way that the Pump House Gang has plunged into the ineluctable horizon of the "mysterioso" enigma. Wolfe refers to the Pranksters as the Flag People as if they are an exotic tribe from an off-the-map corner of America. When Wolfe asks Kesey in jail why he has given up writing, Kesey replies: "I'd rather be a lightening rod than a seismograph,"[9] which might be a variation of Frederich Nietzsche's line in the Prologue of *Thus Spake Zarathustra*: "Lo, I am the herald of the lightning, and a heavy drop out of the cloud: the lightning, however, is the *Superman*."[10] Kesey, whom everyone casually called The Chief, often dressed in the camp costume of Captain Marvel.

In the second chapter of the book Wolfe hangs around the 1939 Harvester bus being prepped for the crosscountry continental ride—the trip had been conceived on a drive George Walker and Ken Kesey took after the launching party for *One Flew Over the Cuckoo's Nest* in New York City.[11] The chapter shockingly concludes with a repeated refrain cursing God, first spoken by the educated Ron Hassler, but then taken up as a menacing mantra by a Hell's Angel gang member by the name of Freewheeling Frank. Frank functions as the gutter street-flapper to the assortment of counterculture intellectuals, thus the title of that second chapter, "The Bladder Totem" (alluding to Swift[12]) which began with a rant about the difficulties these fringe "gypsies" had in copping a pee within an urban neighborhood. Nietzsche's prophecy of social deterioration and malaise, once the lower classes lose their discipline and minimal education,[13] slyly moves from potential to act in the form of a nihilistic Hell's Angels biker obscenely cursing God, thus breaching Nietzsche's echoed advice from Plato's *Republic* in *Beyond Good and Evil* that the lower classes be shielded from atheism.[14]

Chapter Three, "The Electric Suit," refers to Kesey's proclaiming that he had a revelation about rejecting LSD to "go beyond acid" and that in this revelation inspired by a cast of the *I-Ching* he "had a second skin, of lightning, of electricity, like a suit of electricity, and I knew it was in us to be superheroes and that we could become superheroes or nothing."[15] This statement not only echoes Nietzsche but also recalls the culturally transformative metaphor of electricity employed throughout *The Education of Henry Adams* (1918) whereby a new kind of society, possibly atheistic, emerges from the dynamo that produces electricity. Wolfe had opened the chapter with the expectation of a "fluorescent yahoo of incalculably insane proportions"[16] for Kesey's out-of-jail reception, but is surprised by the matter-of-fact, casual reception accorded Kesey. In Swift a yahoo is a human animal covered in excrement and ignorance and Wolfe's use of the word indicates his elitist disdain for the grungy attire of the Pranksters.

A scene is then painted wherein a reporter appears like the devil tempting Jesus and Kesey rejects the idea of worldly leadership as he remains staunch in his rejection of declaring acid a sacrament with which to lay the foundation for a new religion like those of Zoroaster or Jesus of Nazareth, yet Wolfe presents Kesey as a mystic St. Paul on the move across America. Wolfe concludes with a surreal prose poem collage that resembles John Bunyan's Dismal Swamp, but the setting is on "poor abscessed Harriet Street" in a dilapidated warehouse immersed in an eclectic mantra of Eastern mysticism in the middle of "poor old Formica polyethylene 1960's America."[17] With the manic driving energy of an impromptu list poem, Wolfe sympathetically manages to capture the cosmic, dialectic struggle the Pranksters will confront. Wolfe wants to present the point of view of both his protagonists and the mainstream culture—his compulsive satire cuts both ways. He abhors the synthetic conformity of a polyethylene mass culture, yet he can't help but see the hipsters as a quixotic cult, even as the hipsters attempt to shed the "game" of religion or any philosophy amid their ersatz ragbag of Eastern talismans as they plunge headlong into the mysteries of chance.

"What Do You Think of My Buddha?" attempts in a more serious and lengthy manner to give a rounder portrait of Kesey and his recent history, yet the very title of the chapter poses a question so that the reader is presented with a riddle rather than thesis. Such a clever approach engages the reader and at times comes close to limning sympathetic chronicle, ending with a journalistic hook: Kesey's re-incarnation of himself in his "Low Rent Versailles, over the mountain and through the woods" with "a considerable new message . . . the blissful counter-stroke."[18] Yet the trajectory of Wolfe's biography begins in condescending derision of Kesey's middle-class background with proletarian roots, mocking the theme of Kesey's *feelings* and his drug experiences, as well as the postwar boomer demographic that produced a wunderkind not yet weaned from tabloid comics. In a rather bizarre passage Wolfe equates Kesey's days at his Perry Lane address with the Arcadia of Wolfe's lost childhood, citing his favorite childhood book, *Honey Bear* by Dixie Willson, as well as the illustrations of Arthur Rackham. Mellowing his sarcasm, Wolfe describes the history of LSD and early drug experiments in more neutral terms as he warms to the theme of portraying clinical psychologists as mechanical idiots, but on the whole this chapter remains a diffident, patronizing chronicle—a brief sketch of some background information the reader should know as the narrator confesses deep ambivalence. The chapter title's more literal meaning signposts the established culture's blindness toward creative expression and Eastern themes, yet Mountain Girl denies that the Pranksters were ever into the Buddha, saying: "We've never had a clue as to what the Buddhists might be up to."[19] Wolfe had employed Buddha as in the American slang sense—an exotic leader.

In the next chapter Wolfe indulges in some mocking doggerel, almost in comic-book style, comparing Kesey and his band to Western gunslingers as Wolfe indulges in adolescent fantasies of the West. Like the author of *Jason and the Argonauts*, Wolfe assembles the cast of superheroes that will be on the bus, but he demythologizes Kesey's perceived reputation as a backwoodsman and nature lover: Kesey does not see nature but his narcissistic fantasies of nature; he prefers experiments with electronics to botanical explorations; and, as implied in the previous chapter, he is a circus showman intent on manipulating people, the narrative example here being the writer Robert Stone, reluctantly and pointlessly summoned to Kesey's rural retreat in the exercise of a group prank that tests the telepathic will of the Pranksters.

The "journey to the East" is revealed to be the blissful counterstroke to the dead end the Western tribe of "outlaws" has reached. The sixteenth century Chinese epic *Ch'eng-en Wu* (*The Journey to the West*) by Hsi-yu Chi may perhaps be evoked by this counterstroke: In the rambling Chinese epic, a small band of travelers set out to bring back some ancient Buddhist texts from India; the epic contains fabulous stories of magic and folklore which *test* the group's devotion and determination in various ways. Eventually, the merry band completes its mission and brings the scrolls back to China. Kesey's group will go east to create aural and video texts that will be assembled after Kesey's death; these "texts" will document the cultural torpor of America and reveal the unleashing creative power of LSD in random experiments among the populace; their vehicle will be a magic psychedelic school bus. In a more prosaic sense they are going to fetch the first copies of Kesey's new novel, *Sometimes a Great Notion*, from the Manhattan launching party. The lengthy Chinese allegory that combined folk tales of the supernatural with poetry became a cult beatnik classic because of its impish humor, led by the antics of an impulsive but sometimes wise monkey kept in check by the holy monk Tripitaka, the epic being available in a superb but abridged translation by Arthur Waley under the title *Monkey* (1942). The atheistic Wolfe does not appear to be aware of this Eastern literary parallel as he tries at first to comically frame Kesey's group as innocent bandits rather than spiritual seekers of texts beyond texts. Wolfe will continue the use this theme of outlaw bandits as a ballad refrain motif in the book.[20]

Later in the book, Wolfe will cite Hermann Hesse's *Journey to the East* (1932), a well-thumbed slim volume he noticed on the shelf in Kesey's library, which describes an Eastern journey by a Gnostic League of brothers who enter the world of dreams and "move Time and Space about like scenes in a theater."[21] This roving band of brothers brings the past, the future, and all fictions into the mystic present:

> When something precious and irretrievable is lost, we have the feeling of having awakened from a dream. In my case this feeling is strangely correct, for my happiness did indeed arise from the same secret as the happiness in dreams; it arose from the freedom to experience everything imaginable simultaneously, to exchange outward and inward easily, to move Time and Space about like scenes in a theatre. And as we League brothers traveled throughout the world . . . we creatively brought the past, the future, and the fictitious into the present moment.[22]

While Hesse's book is certainly the more inspiring script in a general sense and became the inspiration for Thomas Pynchon's *Against the Day* (2006), the Chinese epic with its riotous immersion in popular culture and outrageous fantasy offers more enlightened parallels. It is hard not to see similarities in the principal cast of seekers in the Chinese epic: Kesey as Tripitaka, Cassady as Monkey, Sandy as Sandy, and Pigsy as Mountain Girl whose slang language and earthy humor provide comic resonance. The rollicking and prankish humor of the Chinese epic (especially in the character Monkey) is also in sync with the outrageous improvisations of the Pranksters amid their quest to find a higher truth, for Monkey operates in an invisible world of self-generated archaic and telepathic wisdom not accessible to his questing partners—he is the embodiment of the prank.

Wolfe's preoccupation with moral warnings against the effects of drugs characterized the three-part series on Ken Kesey, Dr. Timothy Leary, and Dr. Richard Alpert (who later called himself Baba Ram Das), which originally appeared in *The World Journal Tribune* of January and February of 1967; the portraits read very much like Wolfe's essay "The Pump House Gang," lending a lurid tabloid sensationalism to the use of LSD. Wolfe's Puritanical prejudice against the use of drugs colors and even distorts the end of Chapter Six and the beginning of Chapter Seven. As Wolfe presents the narrative, Stark Naked (whom none of the Pranksters really know) goes crazy when they reach Texas. Wolfe leaves her running off into the desert, a wild maniac, as if the Pranksters were carelessly ruthless in their exploitation of drugs—there's no reaction at all from the Pranksters on this situation and no reaction from the host Larry McMurtry in Wolfe's version: no one at all appears to care about a nudist who freaked out on too much LSD, and in a mimetic sense the reader is not asked to care much because Stark was merely a peripheral sideshow, or rather a peepshow in Wolfe's narrative, as he does little to explain her character, except that she sits around naked with a blanket over her and she misses her young child. Since the reader wants to board the bus of the narrative, the reader is encouraged to chalk it up to the uncaring nature of these Pranksters on a mission, but Larry McMurtry rebuts Wolfe's narrative in a memoir article.[23] McMurtry explains that it was the Pranksters themselves and not the Texas neighbors who were shocked by the nude scene in front of his house; in spite of his solicitude and care, she escaped from his house at night into the arms of the police. McMurtry tells how with the help of his lawyer and her boyfriend (all of them named Larry with attendant confusions); he succeeded in releasing her from the asylum and reuniting her with her boyfriend. All of these efforts must have run up a considerable bill. The narrator's perspective of neither Kesey nor the Pranksters not caring about Stark remains prejudiced for sensational purposes. Such carelessness was antithetical to their sensibility. Their cult message, if you want to call it that or present it as that (which is what Wolfe does in the book) was always about caring for others in the moment and not being sidetracked by goals which would become obstacles. McMurtry vowed to take care of Stark and he was as good as his word.

"Unauthorized Acid," Chapter Seven, begins with the Pranksters callously inured to the harm they cause other people in their dispensing of drugs, but shifts to emphasize Ken Kesey's dual role as master Prankster and healing organizer of people and events as the magic school bus whirs through the heat of Alabama. The chapter becomes bracketed by very stern homilies on the danger of excessive drug use as it profiles Sandy Lehmann-Haupt's experiences, attempting to describe the fragility of his ego within his deranged senses from his experiential point of view. In interviews with Wolfe, Sandy, Wolfe's chief source for the book as a whole, was particularly helpful to Wolfe in providing one of the key but fragile first person perspectives that animate the book as Wolfe.[24]

The next couple of chapters attempt to put the reader inside the bus as if the reader is part of the gonzo ride; these chapters are virtually free of Wolfe's partisan editorial perspective. We thrill to Kesey riding atop the bus down the Blue Ridge Mountains with Neal Cassady at the wheel without applying the brake, the two in fearless mystic synchronization. They roll into New York City where Robert Stone joins them and they have a great party with an anonymous character, probably notorious Crypto Terry from Provincetown,[25] passing himself off as the writer Terry Southern and successfully pranking the Pranksters!

The high jinks of the prank constituted a significant status boast as part of the bohemian world of writers, especially the Beat writers. One of the more famous literary pranks of the period was the one the poet Gregory Corso played upon Maurice Girodias who was notorious for publishing pornography as well as great writers like Samuel Beckett, Henry Miller, William Burroughs, Jean Genet, Vladimir Nabokov, and Chester Himes. For a pornography series Corso quickly dashed off the novel *The American Express* (1961) and later said: "I thought it was funny writing a book with one kiss in it for a dirty book company."[26] A merry Girodias had hoped that the American Express lawyer would press a threatened lawsuit yet that never happened. The element of play and the ludicrous embroiled the literary world then in a kind of false propaganda that writers took pride in creating and disseminating.

The appropriately short chapter on the Prankster's visit to Timothy Leary in Millbrook called "The Crypt Trip"—as if they were getting a preview of a horror flick, which is how this episode functions in Sandy's psyche—becomes the Ken Babbs prank tour while Leary gives the boisterous group the cold shoulder, but a Leary follower manages to ambush the vulnerable Sandy for personal exploitation. Wolfe manages to convey the infectious enthusiasm of the Merry Pranksters while hinting of a secretive and somewhat sinister atmosphere surrounding Leary.[27] In these chapters Wolfe effectively accomplishes his goal of giving the bus ride from the inside perspective of the Pranksters. These chapters are as near as Wolfe will go at the moment in terms of Prankster advocacy and he does manage to get their take on the snobbish and elitist Timothy Leary, yet Leary's crowd probably took a dim view of the way the Pranksters announced themselves by lobbing red and green smoke bombs as they drove through the estate's portcullised gateway.

"Dream Wars" concludes the continental bus trip (without Neal Cassady who left in another vehicle) back to Kesey's La Honda home in California, depicting some raunchy behavior at the Calgary Stampede (perhaps the last genuine cowboy event in North America), but the chapter's focus shifts to poor Sandy's nervous breakdown and the failed attempts at therapy the Pranksters offer, with Kesey taking the solicitous lead and trying to turn Sandy around. Kesey puts in a great effort but does not succeed; Sandy is eventually taken off the bus by the cops, but with Sandy's help later Wolfe provides a good description of an extended bad trip about someone who has "freaked out." The word "freak" is so common today in slang—I even found it in the fourth grade among my children some years ago—that it might be instructive to recall that a freak was originally someone who had taken a number of acid or mescaline trips and was familiar with what a bad trip was, but managed to come out the other side and cope with life in a positive way; "freaky" referred to those strange moments of nonverbal telepathy, group memory, or group synchronization, or past lives evoked by such trips, and it was jokingly used sometimes in counterpoint to give an elevated reference to the mundane world enmeshed in the matrix of repression. In general, the word freak as a stand-alone designated an outsider to mainstream culture. But language moves on; overuse and misuse debases it, so that language must be constantly renewed.

Wolfe does an excellent job in the next chapter, "The Unspoken Thing," in describing this place of the unspoken among the Pranksters and the wondrous happenings of religious revelation. The reader is presented with the riddle of the chapter heading to solve. Wolfe's account runs to autobiographical musings in the manner of Michel Montaigne. Such meditation provides historical sweep, and Wolfe's probing ruminations don't really fall into place until he conjures up Max Weber's "possession of the deity."[28] That's a fine phrase, yet Wolfe's confusion is such that as an intellectual he can't place what he has witnessed firsthand among the Pranksters until he can locate it in the framework of his Yale education on the history of religions. He falls back upon Joachim Wach's paradigm (1944) on the founding of religions, quoting Wach at length. This brings some clarity, but something else bothers Wolfe: if the experiences of Kesey and the Pranksters are similar to the wisdom of Jesus or St. Paul or Zoroaster or Gautama, why did Kesey not found a new religion? He certainly could have! Why does Kesey remain a low-key secularist amid divine possession and strange minor miracles in the experience of the group? In the framework of a current doyen of American studies, Sacvan Berkovitch, why does not Kesey establish a new church, view his group as "American Israelites, the sole reliable exegetes of a new, last book of scripture"[29]? Kesey had the experience, the reputation, and certainly the charisma to do so.

The very fact that this bothers Wolfe at all displays his lack of understanding of what he's been bearing witness to. The effects of LSD to repress the frontal lobes of the brain, where the brain's control center is located, remain so radical that any movement in that direction—or any direction whatever—appears to be a cartoon of itself, a self-parody, a camp event in which the game of rules and order have already been worn out in routine before they can even be enacted. Under LSD, "the boundaries between the experiencing self and the outer world more or less disappear.... A portion of the self overflows into the outer world, into objects, which begin to live, to have another, deeper meaning."[30] The Beats, from their experience of marijuana, centered their humor on the goof, the spurious self-parodying jail rap wending in ridiculous loops, mocking the narrowly legalistic concepts that justified social injustice, repression, and racial prejudices.

The Pranksters, however, lived in the loop of the prank, which emerges not from perceiving hypocritical incongruities in society, but from the deep anarchy of LSD which can be double edged: either illuminating freedom or maddening paranoia (which was why Timothy Leary, acting as a self-appointed High Priest of LSD, was leery of casual use, emphasizing the importance of an artificial salon setting, whereas the Pranksters had first grounded their trips in rural nature with a Wordsworthian sensibility—something, by the way, that Wolfe despised and that Albert Hofmann, the discoverer of LSD who warned against a casual use of it, consistently proclaimed. Hofmann (who befriended Timothy Leary, Allen Ginsberg, and Aldous Huxley) once declared to the psychiatrist Stanislav Gof: "Through my LSD experience and my new picture of reality, I became aware of the wonder of creation, the magnificence of nature and of the animal and plant kingdom."[31] Much of Hofmann's thinking was ecological: He thought that a deeper awareness of nature would help curb mankind's compulsive destruction of nature. Such a background, rooted in the LSD experience of nature, gave the Pranksters the confidence to explore the improvisational chaos of the street. It also explains their proselytizing zeal to spread the use of LSD.

In the context of paranoia (the bad trip), the mind dwells upon the omnipotence of social structures and social conditioning to inhibit the functions of one's own mind, thus inducing a circular fear of both society in general and people in particular, whom one perceives as out to mock or destroy one's ego. In the context of anarchy (the good trip), the mind instantly perceives the limitations of all structures, even if those structures can be momentarily helpful, yet those moments appear so evanescent that such structures appear to be childish games—in fact, games appear to be the actual principle of human behavior and the greatest game of all is language which is why the LSD (or peyote) experience appears to the initiate to be outside of language, never mind tribal or social customs and their attendant mind-sets. Because an enlightened Prankster trips beyond all the corners of the possible game mentality he becomes electrically attuned to the trivial aspects of games, allowing him to arrive at "Tootling the multitudes," as Wolfe entitled Chapter Eight. On a literal level the tootling consisted of using the bus horn on from the platform roof. Pranksters can see the games and be beyond all games, yet indulge in the prank of letting other people know the Prankster can spot their game, knowing that the other can never see the Prankster is beyond being subjected to any game other than the supercilious and indulgent whim of the moment, which includes both the past and the future. The Prankster's ego is malleable to whatever situation because there is no script (and his or her ego has dissolved) and there never has been a script because they inhabit the unspoken place. Nearing despair at elucidation, Wolfe resorts to the analogy of riddles in the discipline of Zen Buddhism, which is the best anyone can do with a subject beyond words. In his memoir *Prime Green* Robert Stone described

Kesey's quest as an attempt to invent an applied spirituality as a libertarian shaman:

> Kesey was listening for some inner voice to tell him more precisely what role history and fortune were offering him. Like his old teacher Wallace Stegner, like his friend Larry McMurtry, he had the western artist's respect for legend. He felt his own power and he knew that others did, too. Certainly his work cast its spell. But, beyond the world of words, he possessed the thing itself, in its ancient mysterious sense. 'His charisma was transactional,' Vic Lovell, the psychologist to whom Kesey dedicated *Cuckoo's Nest,* said to me when we spoke after Ken's death. He meant that Kesey's extraordinary energy did not exist in isolation—it acted on and changed those who experienced it. His ability to offer other people a variety of satisfactions ranging from fun to transcendence was not especially verbal, which is why it remained independent of Kesey's fiction, and it was ineffable, impossible to describe exactly or to encapsulate in a quotation.[32]

As a teacher, Kesey was not a narcissist nor interested in self-glorification.

Timothy Leary's approach moved toward starting a new religion around LSD. He took *The Tibetan Book of the Dead* in the Evans-Wentz translation to be the new scripture for America, writing books using that text to explain the gaming limitations of popular American culture, gently mocking those limitations, and encouraging people to drop out of those games to pursue a contemplative life of inaction and meditation. Hermann Hesse's Gnostic novels were also on Leary's recommended reading list. But Leary's approach of withdrawal had little momentum in a culture empowered by the dynamics of technology and economics—this was something that Kesey and the Pranksters understood quite well in a casual manner. Besides, when people got deep and serious the Pranksters usually thought that this was an indication of superficiality or delusion. Years later at a 92nd Street YMHA talk in Manhattan, during a posthumous panel tribute to Ken Kesey that also included Ed McClanahan, Robert Stone, and David Stanford (Kesey's longtime editor), Tom Wolfe once more indicated that Kesey could have, if he wished, founded a religious cult that might have been as successful as the Mormons.[33]

This refusal of priesthood on the part of Kesey appears to have haunted Wolfe because he was one of the few who understood the enormity of what Kesey had done and its popular potential. Instead of donning the robes of the High Priest like Timothy Leary and becoming a guru, Kesey went back home to work his farm and write, much like the example of his Stanford writing companion Wendell Berry. While Kesey continued to write on his farm, he never continued in the mainstream genre of his first two novels. Although *Last Go Round* (1994), written with his lifelong friend Ken Babbs, remains an excellent novel, it suffered in its general reception and reputation from being a genre novel, a Western. Likewise, *Caverns* (1990) provided an adventure yarn, while *Sailor Song* (1992) offered a science fiction novel. Kesey also wrote screenplays, plays, and a children's book; he continued to work with various happenings like *Where's Merlin?* during his

1998 trip to England. After Kesey's first great novels, his exploration of other genres became an impediment to marketing his work within an identifiable niche.[34]

Always skeptical about being manipulated by *feelings*, Wolfe proceeds to discuss the feeling of synchronicity as a psychological experience with reference to Jung's theories: that archetypal patterns reflect the micro-macrocosm dialectic and that sometimes people—like the theologian Meister Eckhart, the philosopher Hume, the physicist Einstein, or the Indian mystic Mahavira—through some quirk of metabolism and intellect (or drugs) can discern a larger pattern outside of ordinary perception (Hume with cause and effect, Einstein with space equals time) that impinges on the notion of free will. So the Pranksters entered the vatic Otherworld where the great mystics and geniuses tread. Wolfe notes that their response evoked two important mottoes: *"Go with the flow"* and *"Put your good where it will do the most!"*[35] The primary precept comes from the contemplative tradition of Buddhism, the second from the active Judeo-Christian tradition of doing good works. The Pranksters called the opening of the doors to the Otherworld *kairos*, a Greek word meaning at the right or opportune time. The word was important to the Sophists and Aristotle; it appears in Mark's Gospel at 1:15 and was a significant term in recent existential theology.[36]

Confessing puzzlement with the Pranksters use of the *I-Ching*, Wolfe discovers some help from Jung and realizes that the *I-Ching* is the supreme book of the *now* moment: The quality of how the casting coins fall is tied to the pattern of the now moment and telepathic aspects of group synchronization—that is, the attempt to provide a group interpretation of the coins allows the group to focus on their communal project at hand, furthering their harmony as the group pursues their goals relating to the prophetic coins—it becomes a form of group meditation that provides calm and focus. Wolfe mildly ridicules the Pranksters' evening discussion, comparing them to a summer camp Boy Scout Honor Council, as he registers his horror of a few joints being passed around: "saliva-liva-lava-liva."[37] (149) Kesey then speaks of the lag sound system they have which creates time distortions and sensory lags in our perceptions of time with the end result that our lives are a *movie* of our lives which we edit. Creativity is breaking though the personal, social, and historical lags which hold us back, especially because of the yawning lags between our emotions and intellect. Then Neal Cassady chimes in (the time frame here is not clear but this appears to be a round-up after the completion of the magic bus trip) with a Zen riddle and his disciple Bradley picks up the thread about God being the bottled-up red animal inside us, except that those who can't perceive this think that God is dead (a critique of Nietzsche). Babbs talks about how people are trapped inside the movie of their lives, but that they usually are not aware of the script for the movie or who has written it. And various Prankster movies of their lives are reviewed, with Kesey concluding with a summation of how our movies prevent us from moving into the present, how our hang-ups debilitate us from controlling our own movie, and that reality is like a player piano plunking a wonderful song never heard before, and until you get your fingers moving in sync with it and start singing that marvelous song with your own words, you won't have a chance to control the piano, and you will not be able to *"extend the message to all people,"*[38] an explicitly evangelical injunction. After Wolfe's somewhat patronizing introduction to the group session, Wolfe does an excellent job of navigating through the elliptical segues and analogies in the conversation to convey the sliding and swerving manner of hip group discourse—its model being ensemble jazz—with its associational improvisation and ad-hoc plunge into the *kairos* wisdom of the moment.

Wolfe depicts a model rap session that includes all the players around the camp fire, as if he's presenting a Platonic gestalt model of how this whole group rap goes down, and how the group becomes welded to a missionary zeal for working change in the consciousness of society. Yet the nighttime setting with the flickering flames also suggests that these disembodied voices searching for truth might inhabit Plato's Cave of Illusion where they cannot discern the shadows from reality, especially those drug-induced shadows of illusion where they wallow while they engage in a groupthink. Wolfe is clearly not one of these people to whom a believable message has arrived. He's not taking a toke of the joint being passed around the campfire but recording it. This exotic tribe has their analogies and mythologies which he tries to learn and explicate, but he has his own educated analogies and groomed skepticism from studying American culture and the history of religions at Yale. He's a savvy reporter working with a difficult linguistic argot amid arcane, unspoken mystic loops and *déjà-vu* time lags which he cannot always explain, but not yet a convert about to imbibe drugs as he hangs out with the natives, nor does he take their rituals very seriously, other than attempt an explanation of how their metafictions work for them in a magical way, nor will he give credence to something as exotically Eastern as the *I-Ching*. If Neal Cassady is the mystic oracle and Ken Kesey the lighting rod shaman conducting a public drug experiment in consciousness, Wolfe functions as the wandering scholar composing improvised poetic prose riffs that capture this peculiar moment in the history of American culture while providing elegant, rational explanations derived from the texts of Western wisdom to better comprehend the bizarre Day-Glo puzzles of a landscape no reporter has ever set foot in. Yet Wolfe himself never baldly states his thesis like an academic, he only intimates the riddle of "the unspoken thing," which is that all group discourse under LSD must be positive—paranoia, fear, the possibility of freaking out must never be broached because they are the ultimate taboo.

This chapter, "The Unspoken Thing," is the longest chapter in the book and in many ways the heart of the book: a peculiar combination of mimetic understanding and scholarly research, it is the most sensitive, concise, and eloquent chapter in the book, and in these pages Wolfe reveals his mind as most open, searching, and discriminating in his quest for truth, even though he hints that he cannot buy the whole fascinating story he's relating. Wolfe has put much thought into a chapter which transcends the conventions and expectations of mere journalism. Instead of traditional one-dimensional journalism, Wolfe provides a dual perspective: that of the tribal natives and that of the visiting anthropologist amid a phantasmagoria of the mystical unspoken *now* during a nighttime group session. The reader is presented with riddles of the Prankster experience as well as riddles of the prankster journalist. For naïve readers excited by the descriptions of drugs or sex or even feelings, the joke is on them—for Wolfe is at bottom an upper-class writer interested in patterns of intellect.

For the Pranksters the prank is a religious lesson of illumination (usually nonverbal when directed at others who have not been enlightened by LSD), much like the literary fable or the now-moment parables that Jesus of Nazareth compulsively resorted to; the prank is designed to shame narrow consciousness or open the consciousness of the subject to unforeseen possibilities of thought or behavior. For Wolfe, the literary prank consists of appearing as a modest reporter just doing his job, while he quietly melds into the background like a chameleon to create a prism of irony. If the Pranksters have a time-lag sound system that humorously mocks linear time, Wolfe modestly hints at the Western tradition of philosophy to create an ironic echo chamber of ideas. While the Pranksters struggle to find free will by entering the *kairos* moment, Wolfe lets the now moment fly by so that it can be reframed by later revision which illuminates, in Shakespeare's memorable phrase, the "remembrance of things past." Yet despite the hindsight the past offers the historian, he cannot penetrate the telepathic moment, or the telepathic mechanism of how those on LSD communicate. Later, Kesey was to sum up the acid experience:

> I believe that with the advent of acid, we discovered a new way to think, and it has to do with piecing together new thoughts in your mind. Why is it that people think it's so evil? What is it about it that scares people so deeply, even the guy that invented it, what is it? Because they're afraid that there's more to reality than they have confronted. That there are doors that they're afraid to go in, and they don't want us to go in there either, because if we go in we might learn something that they don't know. And that makes us a little out of their control.[39]

Wolfe had met the Pranksters on a number of occasions, but he was never travelling on the bus (although he wants to capture the *feeling* of being on the bus for the reader): he did interviews, hung out with them a bit, consulted the diaries made available to him, looked at film footage to get his costume effects right, and then composed his own drama, masking it as sensational journalism. The Pranksters have their drugs to trip on and their mystic, evangelical quest; Wolfe has his pen to paint with and mental library to trip with. Yet what fascinates Wolfe the most is the lack of logic surrounding the "unspoken thing"—that is, the Pranksters often communicate in ways beyond logic through telepathic thinking and this is something that no outsider can understand, a mystical nonverbal event beyond the ordinary and approaching the border of the miraculous where the historian of ideas and religions finds a stumbling block. Yet somehow Wolfe manages to get the drift of the mystery and describe how it operates.

With Chapter Eleven we enter the magic woods of Germanic folk legend and eavesdrop on the Pranksters at their mystic best; our Yale don presents his retrospective analysis with anthropological aplomb. During La Honda daylight we confront ordinary problems. "The Bust" begins with a pseudo-ballad of the outlaw Pranksters, "yahooing worse than gunslingers"[40] as if Wolfe's composing a mock-epic Western. Wolfe frames a minor downfall of the Pranksters like a Greek tragedy—they are brought down by their own *hubris*: "By now the Pranksters had built up so much momentum they began to feel immune even to a very obvious danger, namely, the cops."[41] Previously, Wolfe had described some run-ins with the cops, the most notable ones being in New Orleans and the Calvary stampede, but it is now clear that these escapades functioned as comic anticipation and foreshadowing for the eventual tragedy, but at the moment the Pranksters are more than a match for the cops and the forthcoming bust amounts to little. The Pranksters know the cops are watching, learn their names, and make signs welcoming them by name to La Honda. The Pranksters are clean but Kesey is predictably framed and the result makes him an instant celebrity in San Francisco where all intellectuals smoke weed. Wolfe, keeping a low reportorial profile, no longer needs to provide his own ironies—the storyline itself provides them.

Wolfe sheds his doctoral robes and returns to describing *things*, trying to limn the Prankster's behavior as individuals acting in the social gestalt of Kesey's commune, employing the perspective of an artist visitor to do this, then attempts to get a female take on the Kesey commune by profiling Mountain Girl, an eighteen-year-old dropout from a Quaker High School in Poughkeepsie, New York (although she apparently told Wolfe she had dropped out of Vassar), yet Wolfe skates on the surface, as is his habit when attempting to draw the other sex.[42]

Hunter S. Thompson, who was writing his book on the biker gang, introduces Kesey to some Hell's Angels members; Kesey smokes weed with them and gets along so well with them that he invites the whole gang out to his commune for a party in an experiment to see if LSD can bring the blessings of peace upon a gang with a violent habits, something that Thompson experienced firsthand when he was nearly beaten to death later by the gang. Wolfe ably evokes the anarchy and zaniness of the encounter with bearded Allen Ginsberg prancing around with small cymbals and doing fey *Hare Krishna* chants, Sandy doing a continuous deadhead dee-jay broadcast atop a redwood tree with speakers scattered throughout the woods where the bark of many trees shines with Day-Glo, and zonked Hell's Angels stumbling about in blissful wonder or hunkered down in narcissistic collapse. While the crosscountry bus ride was an experiment in random sampling, the event with the Hell's Angels marked the beginning of a series of larger happenings that was to reverberate throughout American culture. In Kesey's 2001 obituary by Christopher Lehmann-Haupt, a long-time book reviewer for *The New York Times* and Sandy's Prankster brother, he notes this divide:

> This was the public Ken Kesey, the magnetic leader who built a bridge from beatniks on the road to hippies in Haight-Ashbury; who brewed the cultural mix that fermented everything from psychedelic art to acid-rock groups like the Grateful Dead and Jefferson Airplane to the Trips Festival dance concerts in the

Fillmore auditorium in San Francisco; and who, in the process of his pilgrimage, blew an entire generation's mind.

Yet Mr. Wolfe also narrated the adventures of a more private Ken Kesey, one who in addition to his quests took the inner trips that gave him his best fiction.[43]

This commentary masks a subtle but profound ambivalence on Wolfe's part: on the one hand, Kesey is a maverick cultural hero like the unusual American cultural heroes Wolfe profiled in his first book, but on the other hand, Wolfe disapproves of Kesey's influence on popular culture, especially the popularization of experimental drug use; yet to Wolfe, Kesey is a private hero because Kesey moves from advocating promiscuous LSD experiments to public renunciation of LSD—the graduation ritual to "go beyond acid" which concludes the novelistic arc of the book.

Hunter S. Thompson had warned Kesey that he thought this gathering was not a good idea: "I told Kesey that he would deserve to be shot as a war criminal if he went through with this."[44] Wolfe's summation passage of the Hell's Angel's event derides neither the Hell's Angels nor Kesey's bold experiment, but the insecure ivory-tower mentality of American liberal intellectuals, a point of view Wolfe shared with Kesey, the Pranksters, and also the Beats:

The Hell's Angels party went on for two days and the cops never moved in. Everybody, Angels and Prankster, had a righteous time and no heads were broken. There had been one gang-bang, but the girl was a volunteer. It was her movie. In fact, for the next six or seven weeks, it was one long party with the Angels. The news spread around intellectual-hip circles in the San Francisco-Berkley area like a legend. In these circles, anyway, it once and for all put Kesey and the Pranksters up above the category of just another weirdo intellectual group. They had broken through the worst hangup that intellectuals know— the *real-life* hangup. Intellectuals were always hung up with the feeling that they weren't coming to grips with real life. Real life belonged to all those funky spades and prize fighters and bullfighters and dock workers and grape pickers and wetbacks. *Nostalgie de la boue*. Well, the Hell's Angels were real life. It didn't get any realer than that, and Kesey had pulled it off. People from San Francisco and Berkley started coming by La Honda more than ever. It was practically like an intellectual tourist attraction. Kesey would talk about the Angels.[45]

Note the sardonic, skeptical pun on the ultimate word in the paragraph and Wolfe's seething contempt for this irrational *feeling* among the intellectuals. Also, their jealousy for *real* life that fires their implicitly Marxist leanings: the irony being that Marx's analysis of alienation in the working class more appropriately belongs to academics and that Marxists (implicitly here) merely project a problem that academics have with their own idle lives onto the working classes. In all of his writings Wolfe consistently expresses a patronizing disdain for academicians and their theories, which he perceives as divorced from life, providing a pathological psychological experiment for a self-congratulatory narcissism. The mention of funky spades is directed at academics who advocate writers like the rock-musical Leninist LeRoi Jones, prize fighters a dig at Norman Mailer, bullfighters Ernest Hemingway, dock workers the San Francisco Marxist philosopher and popular culture pundit Eric Hoffer, grape pickers John Steinbeck, and wetbacks Irish-American writers like, I suppose, Jim Tully, Harry Sylvester, Francis Hackett, or Eugene O'Neill (Wolfe admires James T. Farrell). Wolfe's mocking use of French indicates that the life of these intellectuals consists of idiotic lip movement worshiping life in the mud ("Nostalgia for mud"). Wolfe always argues for a salon literature that addresses social realities and if the writer must get out of the salon to do a thorough investigation all the better, but the writer should document and paint in an artistic manner—not wallow, valorize, or pander to them, nor confuse these realities with the ironic intellectual rigors of analysis that the salon demands.

According to Weingarten, the description of a willing gangbang was the one item in Wolfe's book that Kesey strenuously objected to because he thought the event was a gang rape. Also, "He felt that Wolfe was pulling his punches by not naming names and revealing the malefactors."[46] On the one hand, Kesey was there and Wolfe was not; on the other hand, Wolfe probably spent more time researching this particular event, cold-calling up Hunter Thompson and asking for his recollections; Thompson even forwarded some audio tapes he had made of the Hell's Angels.[47] Wolfe's treatment of the "rape" incident approaches sensational lurid journalism. Whatever the ambiguous truth of this matter, and Wolfe may, after all, have it right, Wolfe did have a dramatic interest in portraying the Hell's Angels event as a sensational experiment of Kesey's *Go with the flow* philosophy.

This two-day outrageous party surrounded by a cordon of police ended in no injuries or incidents of violence. Despite Neal Cassady stripping stark naked and taunting the police, the police were unwilling to confront the Angels. Wolfe presents Kesey and eighteen-year-old Mountain Girl as the heroes of this event, defusing the bikers as they were about to bash in someone's teeth; he drops hints it was during this event that an affair began with Kesey and Mountain Girl "in the moonlight ripply bower."[48] The use of bower, one of Edmund Spenser's favorite words in *The Faerie Queen*, has a oddly comic effect in its antique connotations (while its mock-ethereal quality contrasts with the tool shed gangbang) and reminds the reader that Wolfe, like Spenser, is writing a moral epic where surfaces are not quite what they at first appear to be. The characterization of some of the Hell's Angels, especially Buzzard who at one point turns into a giant Buzzard, appear drawn as ogre cartoons descended from Spenserian monsters like Talus.

Chapter Fourteen, "A Miracle in Seven Days," recounts the experiences of Kesey with the Pranksters in tow leading a weeklong spiritual retreat at a Unitarian Conference entitled "Shaking the Foundations." It begins with one of Wolfe's better poems (extending to four pages) employing both short-line stanzas and long-line stanzas with many sophisticated half-rhymes as it breezily provides stream-of-consciousness rap background with spontaneous jam-riffs. These lines indicate that since he has put Allen Ginsberg into the narrative, Wolfe can casually knock off a better narrative poem than Ginsberg, which, in all honesty, is close to the reality. Kesey gives an impromptu and iconoclastic opening sermon by *doing* instead of talking about what he means—in illustrating the irrational Pavlovian emotions behind patriotism Kesey *tramples* on the American flag to the horror of the audience, but with the help of Mountain Girl he is able to calm the horrified spectators who are blinded by their surge of adrenalin. Wolfe presents Kesey as an American patriot who disapproves of imperial war. The straight-laced Unitarians wearing "Intellectual Sport Shirts"[49] have some problems with the colorfully costumed Pranksters who observe no daily schedule at all—not for eating, sleeping, nor scheduled talk sessions. The scandal scent of dope hangs over the conference and the Pranksters play a continual game of whacking the magic bus with strands of kelp, as the conference is seaside. Some Unitarian leaders leave the conference and it nearly falls apart, but Kesey manages to keep it all going with his rap. Some complain that he talks too much, so on the last day he goes around with tape over his mouth. The end result is that those who stick out the conference are so enthused that the church is split into two annual conferences—Young Turks and Old Fogies.

After the conference a female delegate sends Kesey an adulating summary of the conference that contains the refrain: "And the prophet Kesey said. . . . " The Pranksters take turns reading the sacred scroll to Kesey and await his reaction: "We're not on the Christ trip. That's been done, and it doesn't work. You prove your point, and then you have 2,000 years of wars. We know where that trip goes."[50] And so Kesey explicitly rejects the founding of a new religion.

Ironically, despite such deep humility, Kesey takes a megadose of LSD and tops it off with DMT, walking out like Christ into the wilderness to experience and succumb to the temptation of magical power: CONTROL of the weather, exploding a heater through mere telepathic will, walking out before a speeding car, and besotted with a general delusional power over the cosmos itself.

The main theme of *The Electric Kool-Aid Acid Test* remains a moral warning against the use of drugs. From the Puritan perspective the book is about a talented sinner who renounces the source of his inspiration, the excesses he popularized, even the craft of writing bourgeois fiction, while retaining an interest in the production of beyond-acid moral entertainment like The Grateful Dead or theatrical events—and the essays and the small output of fiction he subsequently published contain a deep moral and pacifistic current. Even in his memoir essay on Neal Cassady, "The Day Superman Died,"[51] Kesey implies that Cassady as a public icon has let loose a sinister underworld force amid the counterculture movement that might destroy it. Wolfe highlights the private inner struggles of Kesey in the book to dramatize and explain that the Chief of the movement has renounced the madness that the movement has itself plunged into. So while much of the book has a crazy comic surface that occurs in public, the thrust of the book's novelistic angle remains an interior drama of moral redemption—in the end Kesey is an exemplary hero who acquires Faustlike powers but won't ink the deal with the devil.

There's a curious, mimetic synchronization to the psychological architecture of Wolfe's novel-like documentary on Kesey. Some of the writing in the early chapters appears awkward, a little disorientated in focus, and downright snooty, but as Wolfe provides more of a close-up on Kesey and begins to better understand the man and what he is up to as Kesey's powers of perception and ability expand, Wolfe's empathy for Kesey grows, and Wolfe's own prose begins to soar and grow bolder in its ambition and denser in its allusions to other writers, so that there appears to be a symbiotic megalomania developing in both the narrator Wolfe and his main man. That eerie and magical effect might be seen to some as deriving from the LSD experience itself or perhaps it is merely the writer digging deeper into his subject and growing more confident of his project. Wolfe was reluctant to try the drug, but according to Toby Thompson, he eventually took a 125 milligram trip in Buffalo (a bummer, in the lingo of the Hell's Angels) for the psychedelic experience: "Somehow I was *merging* with this carpet. . . . As I began to calm down, I had the feeling that I had entered into the sheen of this nubby twist carpet—a really wretched carpet, made of Acrilan—and somehow this represented the people of America, in their democratic glory."[52] Two similar descriptions appear in *The Bonfire of the Vanities*: "The carpet was disgusting. Synthetic; the Americans manufactured filthy carpet; Metalon, Streptolon, deep, shaggy, with a feel that made his flesh crawl;" "The dreadful orange carpet blazed away. Right next to the Formica couch he was slouched upon, it had come loose from the floor where it abutted the wall, and the crinkly metallic fibers frayed out."[53] It's a pity that Wolfe didn't step outdoors into the woods—it was perhaps his only chance to discover the Wordsworthian appreciation of nature that Albert Hofmann (the discoverer of LSD) thought was the drug's true value, yet even in Wolfe's first book he clung to an indoor salon aesthetic.

"Cloud," Chapter Fifteen, recounts the story of replacing the La Honda sign welcoming the Hell's Angels with a sign welcoming the Beatles, madly hoping that they might draw the Beatles into their movie. The difference here is that Kesey knew some Hell's Angels bikers and invited them, while he did not know the Beatles from another continent, nor did he invite them. But they get thirty tickets to a Beatles concert, take a large dose of acid, and board the bus. Wolfe gives a long rap of the route they drive and he sounds like Neal Cassady and, no, he's not serving up parody! But the theater is the Cow Palace, the site of a former slaughterhouse that looks like a concentration camp to them and there are 2,000 cops on hand who appear as monstrous exterminators—costumed Pranksters freak out on the super dose of acid Kesey dispensed. Yet even with children in tow, Kesey mobilizes the catatonic Pranksters (who can't even read their tickets) into the concert hall and parks them in their seats. Only Mountain Girl and Zonker like the concert, as Kesey and the other Pranksters fall victim to horrible hallucinations stemming from mass adulation lavished upon the performers which appear to be a monstrous form of fascism to Kesey and some others. Kesey hauls everyone out in mid-concert away from the seething monster. Back at La Honda commune the welcome sign for the Beatles has worked its magic and there are several hundred people there who expect the Beatles to appear for a post-concert party: most of them are teenage girls zonked on acid with "lollipop" eyes. Kesey runs into this little guy Stanley Owsley whom Kesey never heard of, yet Owsley has a bag of the greatest acid ever made. The wiseacre acid king quarrels with Kesey and gets the better of him, but he has this great acid. . . .

Shortly thereafter, Kesey backed a new band called The Grateful Dead and turned them onto Owsley acid: thus we have the birth of acid rock, a form of rock that the Beatles will eventually explore and popularize in several albums (*Revolver, Rubber Soul,* and most significantly in *Sergeant Pepper's Lonely Hearts Club Band*) after *they* belatedly discovered Owsley acid when the top-shelf brand finally wends its way to England; in early 1967 the Beatles dress up in outlandish costumes like the Merry Pranksters, pile into a school bus, and stock it with audio and video equipment to tool around England with hand-held cameras in an effort to make a road movie, but they have so many reels of unfocused film that the project almost dies, but they see this anarchic material as both an artistic and commercial breakthrough: it is shown on British television: *Magical Mystery Tour.* The Beatles belatedly do get into (that is, appropriate or imitate) the Prankster's fantasy movie a couple of years later! Wolfe's delight in recording this irony is so straight, infectious, and Pranksterlike that he seems to have forgotten that he's a satirist. Just as Kesey has tamed the Hell's Angels, so the Yale skeptic has been reborn as a Kesey fan! From now on the double game of irony and journalism has vanished and it's as if the reader has entered into an old-fashioned novel where he roots for the hero protagonist—it's all Kesey, the Pranksters, and Kesey! And like any good novel that is a work of art, the gestalt of the work will be greater than the sum of its characters, facts, or even plot.

The next Prankster happening turns out to be at the Berkeley college campus where Kesey has been invited to speak against the Vietnam War. The event organizers don't appear to be familiar with the Prankster counter-expectation approach to life. Kesey decides to enlist the Hell's Angels as a military escort for the bus, which is repainted the color of blood, dripping war symbols, olive-colored wooden machine guns leering menacingly off the roof railings. The Pranksters carrying wooden or cardboard guns don zany ersatz military uniforms a result of Kesey's wife, Faye, running her sewing machine around the clock. But they are repeatedly stopped and hassled by the police along the way; the cops search and detain them several times, so that they miss the rendezvous with the Angels, inconspicuously pulling onto the campus near dusk. As the penultimate speaker, Kesey was, the organizers imagined, to be the man who helps set the fuse for the 15,000-person march that will battle the Oakland police, but Kesey stands up there at sunset in his Day-Glo outfit and orange hard hat to deliver an anti-rally sermon, punctuating it by playing "Home, home on the range" on his harmonica, the whacky Prankster Day-Glo back-up band playing along out of tune. Kesey tells the incipient rioters not to play the establishment game: Don't riot, just go home, renounce the bad ego trip, and do your own thing, not what the organizers want you to do. The miracle prank works (the march occurs but not the newsworthy riot the organizers hoped for), and Tom Wolfe becomes the scholar St. Luke chronicling a wonderworker and wise man.[54]

Wolfe, healed of paranoia and alienation, will *go with the flow*. Next on the agenda: Introduce acid to the public by conducting random events under the slogan: Can *YOU* Pass the Acid Test? Expecting that people will simply arrive, the Pranksters lack certain social skills in booking and promoting events; they presume people will suddenly arrive to join their movie—they merely have to will it into being! Failing to book a hall, they conduct the first sacrament at Ken Babbs' house and notify the local hip bookstore that afternoon. Some locals do come, but apparently don't imbibe the acid and leave before 3am. Two wings of the party emerge: Allen Ginsberg's and Ken Kesey's. They discuss the Vietnam War: "Ginsberg said all these things, these wars, were the result of misunderstandings . . . if everybody could only sit around in a friendly way and converse, they could get to the root of their misunderstanding and settle it."[55] This simplistic argument carries the day because no one disagrees. Diplomacy remains terribly important in the real world, yet war is far more complicated because it is based upon a psychology of revenge, self-redemption, and peer prestige, but if you are zonked out, it's true that you can often talk out disagreements. Perhaps the solution would be to give LSD to diplomats or generals, but a general on a bum trip might be a bad scene.[56] In any case, the trippers solved the war problem that night without any outsiders, one former soldier (Babbs, a Marine helicopter pilot) present, no government diplomats, or Vietnamese there. So the first experiment was merely a preaching to the converted inner circle and not much of a test.[57]

The second test, when colorful flyers are handed out after a Rolling Stone concert, occurs at another house with The Grateful Dead inventing acid rock before an audience of about 400. Wolfe's description of the event surges in electric sparks while he mischievously tries to make good-humored fun of the black host's futile attempt to convert his hospitality into a traditional beatnik, hat-passing rent party. The house's electrical fuses can't handle the band's amps and keep blowing out. Wolfe affects shock that this guy is worried about paying his rent when he's there to witness the birth of a new musical form in his own house. Most attendants don't appear to know what acid is, but the "contact high" from the band and the strobe lights make it an intimate success, so the Pranksters are now ready for a larger public event.

The third acid test is announced for Stinson Beach, but as they set out they change it to Muir Beach. Only naïve thrill seekers and cops show up at the Stinson Beach blind. Those who've taken their acid will know where to find them and do so at the cabin lodge where The Grateful Dead wail and a strobe light show is calibrated to reproduce some of the surrealistic fragmenting or vivid isolating of caught moments that acid can dramatize, so even if the attendants haven't dropped acid before arriving (most have), the "contact high" and group vibration will happen. The sound system has a lag that will also have an aural effect to simulate LSD. This is the first multimedia public event before the phrase is even coined! About 300 heads show up to enter the telepathic third dimension: "I am you and you are me."[58] Owsley appears in costume and drops acid. The Hell's Angels roar in. Wolfe's prose becomes an ecstatic prose poem. As the linearity of space is shattered by the strobe light, the concept of time disappears with moments of complete blankness, the pudding state, and surges of heightened activity. The Prankster band plays their weird atonal music. Kesey speaks softly over the microphone into the hurricane of night. But Owsley freaks outs on his own acid and begins screaming! He's caught in the French Bastille, 1786, with rats scrabbling at his feet! Kesey has become the demonic Cardinal Louis de Rohan persecuting him! He escapes from the Bastille, jumps into his car and smashes into a tree.

Convinced that Kesey is some kind of demon, Owsley tries to cut off the Prankster supply of LSD, but to no avail. Timothy Leary and Richard Alpert oppose these public tests, concerned that such anarchic events will cause the law to ban LSD, which is still legal at this point. The cops can merely hope their vigilance will net some marijuana busts. Kesey pushes on with a dozen more public acid tests in New Mexico, California, Oregon, and Mexico. Owsley eventually comes around and begins supporting The Grateful Dead and the Beatles with state-of-the-art, high-tech equipment.

Jerry Garcia appropriated the band's name from a dictionary.[59] The theme of The Grateful Dead is one of the oldest archetypal myths: If you help people in this lifetime, when they die, their spirits will intercede later with the gods on your behalf to help you when you confront a future difficulty—in Eastern terms *karma*, but the concept is universal in tribal, global mythology. The Grateful Dead were grateful for the anonymous American musicians who composed eighteenth- and nineteenth-century American folk music, those musical tunes they recycled as acid rock with Robert Hunter's lyrics.[60] In a way, the band's long career *was* those dead spirits personified, helping people discover a healing approach to life, inspiring people to help others overcome their troubles and construct meaningful lives. Their constant road trips around the country were themselves near-sacramental gatherings beyond acid.

Kesey's public experiments with acid launched the psychedelic subculture. The aesthetic effects of acid generated outward in waves: The Grateful Dead, Jefferson Airplane, Mothers of Invention, and the Beatles' acid albums; also Roy Seburn's strobe projections, the revival of Art Nouveau and the popularization of Perceptional Abstraction (as in the work of the Hungarian Victor Vasarely and M. C. Escher) gone gloriously Day-Glo in all those collectible period posters, the rise of the underground comic book with its raucous, humorous cultural critiques, the whole concept of a multimedia experience that took an audience out of linear time to experience parallel time tracts or an otherworldly experience of the ineffable. Wolfe testifies: "There was something wholly new and deliciously weird in The Dead's sound, and practically everything new in rock 'n' roll, rock jazz I have heard it called, came out of it."[61] As an enthusiast of popular culture and the Beatles in particular, Wolfe could appreciate the products of acid culture, even though he disapproved of the culture that inspired and generated such cultural icons.

No doubt there must have been paranoid casualties during these tests that we are not informed of, and not all would have recovered as quickly as Owsley, but at this point Wolfe is *on the bus* and will not brook any criticism of Kesey and the Pranksters because they have made such significant contributions to the flow of American culture, which is probably why he had decided earlier to highlight the case of Stark at Larry McMurtry's house by showing an example of a pathetic casualty then, so as not to mar the rush of his later exalted narrative. The effect upon the reader of a skeptical outsider becoming a true believer mimics the effect of a good novel wherein the reader identifies with the novel's protagonist—in drama when the hero passes beyond the sympathy and pity of the audience and the audience then identifies with the protagonist, something unusual happens in great drama when the viewer thinks that if in that person's shoes I would do no different: Such complete identification can then become transformative, according to Aristotle in the *Poetics*, and we have that mystery of *catharsis*, that occult purgation upon the psyche which is capable of altering our perceptions about life which is the signature of only the greatest dramas like *Oedipus Rex*. When the closet reader witnesses that cathartic effect upon a deeply skeptical chronicler, who has habitual tendencies to satirize others, such testimonial becomes infectious. How can a reader disagree with a man who has a Puritanical attitude toward drugs, who comes from the East coast establishment, chronicles these events as a journalistic outsider, and ends a reluctant believer?

Wolfe positively brims with concise and near-encyclopedic anecdotal detail of many Pranksters and their associates as he chronicles a fulcrum cultural event in the history of this country, giving background as well as the inside scoop of their blossoming creativity. Stewart Brand, the counterculture catalogue compiler (who receives a Turgenevlike encyclopedia entry for biographical background), and San Francisco artist Ramon Sender conceive the great San Francisco Trips Festival of January, 1966: a three-day simulated acid festival "without acid" (Prankster humor) at which The Acid Test would be performed with the Merry Pranksters. Bill Graham would be the impresario for the event and its success of this event would catapult him into the role of Rock impresario. They perform one last pre-test at the Fillmore auditorium where thousands attend the wild event; the cops show up and try to close them down at 2 A.M. by pulling wires because no one can hear their bullhorns, but as quickly as they pull the plugs, they are plugged back in by the Pranksters while Mountain Girl dee-jays on a hidden mike and keeps the party going. The cops give up in frustration when Kesey's lawyers arrive. Like esoteric shamans of the highest order, the Pranksters had conquered the paranoia that LSD could induce in each other and in their group. An acid test was a means of seeing whether they could do the same with a random public sampling (just as the federal government had been doing for nearly a decade on unsuspecting people), preventing novices from freaking out in a variety of raucous settings.

It's a smashing success, but a few days later Kesey, smoking dope with Mountain Girl on the roof of Stuart Brands' Telegraph Hill apartment building, is once again busted for marijuana possession and now faces a mandatory five-year prison term. Wolfe doesn't shy away from addressing the fundamental question which he never states, but only implies through combining and blurring the novelistic techniques of omniscient narrator and first person perception: Why did Kesey let this happen? Is this the paralysis of victimization? Or is it merely pathetic indifference? By letting the ambiguity stand, Wolfe insinuates an ambience of cosmic fate, the *sync* of the reader observing the hero Kesey as if the reader occupies some distant and confused corner of Kesey's mind and is thrust into a mystic riddle under the effects of acid's rainbow gestalt: is this cosmic *karma* (fate based upon past deeds) outside oneself, or is cosmic *karma* generated from within by a self-propelling paranoia?

All these recent great trips in public lead up to a private bummer, but it's a bummer without acid and beyond acid—the time lag of a bum acid trip as if the real world itself swam in the paranoid medium of a bad acid trip where society's creative thinkers and cultural innovators are condemned as common criminals. At this strange climax in the book, we reach a point that is outside of either journalism or the novel: We are caught in the larger cultural ironies that Michel Montaigne, the inventor of the essay, outlined in his essay "On Cannibals" in which the down-home native cannibals eat people raw in local religious riots of hysterical violence that derive from prejudice and blind intolerance. Acid is still legal, but Kesey is persecuted because he has done things that are different and the public custodians of order feel threatened—he has become a savage to be caught, imprisoned, and civilized, like primitive Caliban in Shakespeare's *Tempest.* If marijuana were the real issue, then you'd have to incarcerate half of San Francisco and a quarter of the country's population. Kesey had three-and-a-half grams on him that he had tossed to another building but it was assiduously recovered.

Wolfe's New Journalism—like the multimedia experiments of the Pranksters which synthesize the use of chemicals, atmosphere, and group psychology with visual and aural artistry—synthesizes a repertoire of artistic forms: journalism, the novel with its thematic chapters and short "slide" presentations of collage narrative, the interior psychological nuances of the novel, poetic stanzas that appear like a chorus in a Greek drama, unreeling lists that rival Walt Whitman at his best, purple prose poems that wildly romp across the page, interior monologue, surreal images and events told with conventional narrative, etiological narratives of culture as if this was a primitive epic explaining its tribal origins, Turgenevlike biopic entries on important players, the stage settings of drama with its costumed masks and comic jokes, the probing cultural questions of self and society that the essay usually raises, whether this is done by the narrator (as in "The Unspoken Thing") or the protagonist (Kesey in this chapter). Like the musical innovations of acid rock, this book is a new event in the history of American culture! Who says a journalist can't be an artist? The New Journalism can climb artistic heights beyond all established artistic forms!

And just at the point when wonder for the electrical surge of what Wolfe has done courses through the reader's mind, a crack in the narrative opens: We become aware that Wolfe is not in Kesey's mind, but merely a narrator telling a story—Wolfe is not omniscient and this is not a novel; Wolfe's a journalist who was never *there* and he's just sketching a second-hand picture of the event; he's doing his best to describe the Trips Festival itself in color and strobe with Ken Babbs at the control helm, but it's as if the picture has turned from surreal Technicolor to a fading home print. As Kesey is sidelined at the event, even though he has his silver spacesuit on, he seems more distant as if he's floating off into space . . . and as Kesey's charisma begins to fade from the story, so does Wolfe's charisma, and Wolfe begins to *report* things he's heard—he's reporting Kesey's overly elaborate prank of pseudosuicide with the goof-trip of writing the red herring suicide note, and he's informing you he's left for Mexico, and then recounting rumors of how the Pranksters miss Kesey's charisma. Wolfe is *telling*, not *showing* the reader at this point.

When it comes to the book's title chapter about the monster test on the outskirts of Watts in Los Angeles, with the huge central vat generously laced with LSD, the documentary reel has gone to black-and-white, although that was the concert where Owsley *saw* the sound flowing out of the speakers.[62] A cub reporter who has never had acid before *recounts* the scene for Wolfe; she *tells* us what was going through her head at the time when she showed up for the great happening and how her *first* acid trip affected *her* mind. And she becomes *nostalgic* about the event! The reader is no longer *in* the making of history, but is in the process of going back to get evidence of how it must have been for one person, albeit as a representative of many. The focus is now on the crowd outside of the chosen circle. Without Kesey the account, the "movie," and the special brotherhood has been destroyed. We are back in the humdrum land of reality: journalism and history. We get the bearded academic footnote with long quotations from Hermann Hesse that what has happened to Kesey has been foretold in Hermann Hesse's fictional *Journey to the East*—as if that book, wherein their leader Leo suddenly disappears, functioned as a prophetic Old Testament, a secret riddle for the Pranksters. Wolfe, the scholar and journalist, who was never *there*, has taken *control* of the narrative and his notes are filling up the pages of the book—like any other book you might find in the library and take out to read under a lamp. . . . And, yes, this is decent, workmanlike journalism, but. . . .

Just when the reader has freaked out about this ordinary journalism, Wolfe then comes back into the narrative, and the reader welcomes the return of *his* soothing voice, our acid-trip guide to cultural wonders at the edge who notes that six different kinds of police units are there in bewilderment, but the immediate reason for his returns is to guide the reader through what a freak-out on acid is like: this poor young girl has drunk the Kool-Aid and has collapsed screaming on the floor: "Who *cares*!" And here's a big TEST for the Pranksters: Can they bring her around with total attention, can they guide her into letting the flow of her mind just wander without paranoia, and can they save her from monstrous delusions that well up from inside her frail psyche? And, of course, it's all caught on tape for the archive, filed under freak out. But the drama is live before us—as in a novel. We experience pity in this minor drama. And the Pranksters gather around to heal her. With the miracle healing, this TEST is a success, but it causes a schism in the group because the microphone broadcast of the Who Cares Girl occurs over an open mike and some think it a cruel prank, both for her and others, to endure her freak out experience in public.

The significance of the Great Trips Festival in San Francisco and especially the Kool-Aid Acid Test in Los Angeles is that this Day-Glo LSD genie is now out of the bottle: Young kids by the thousands and by the tens of thousands subsequently experiment with LSD as publicity from these two events expands in leaps and bounds: "Very few realized that it had all emanated from one electric source: Kesey and the Merry Pranksters."[63] LSD was still legal. Eventually, the federal government's response (the CIA) to this would be to release domestically an assortment of deranging drugs like STP and build laboratories in the Caribbean to process hard drugs like cocaine and heroin in order to destroy the new movement.[64]

Life magazine wants to do a spread on the Pranksters. Babbs reluctantly agrees to drive those who want to participate, but he himself will not, and he eventually pranks those who stay for individual shots by stranding them. Pranksters pranking Pranksters? The schism widens. This rift is both journalistic and novelistic because by now our identification with the Pranksters is with Kesey as well as the group.

Meanwhile, down in Mexico, our hero Kesey, who has left his three children and a wife in the United States, finds himself being hunted down by various police units too numerous to mention. We are now back in the novel, but, no, not a novel, a movie—the chapter "The Fugitive" is written like a thriller film-script: the desperate outlaw-would-be-hero on the loose rambling in a philosophical manner, the outlaw haunted by 360 degrees of paranoia, the outlaw dementedly hallucinating like Humphrey Bogart in John Huston's *The Treasure of the Sierra Madre* (1948):

> THEY
> close in to slam you away for five, eight, twenty years . . . driven at last out onto the edge of your professional beliefs. You believed that a man should move off his sure center out onto the outer edges, that the outlaw, even more than the artist, is he who tests the limits of life and that—The Movie : : : : by getting totally into Now and paying total Attention until it all flows together in the *synch* and imagining them all into the Movie, your will will determine the flow and control all jungles great and small.[65]

This will-to-power theme is out of Nietzsche, not the German novelist B. Traven who wrote *The Treasure of the Sierra Madre* while living in Mexico. Wolfe directs both from his own education and from the flow of information in the Archives, and then lets his movie reel snap and flap-flap as he collages his own footage of the Prankster movie that he has been drawn into. Wolfe says that here he felt justified in experimenting with a stream of consciousness as well as point of view because much of "the interior dialogue is taken from Kesey's letters from McMurtry."[66] Wolfe had also interviewed Zonker, Black Maria, and Kesey himself, and Kesey gave him access to tapes he had made during that time.

The next chapter has the Pranksters (including Kesey's wife Faye and their children) turning up in Mexico, appearing to the natives as lurid devils incarnate, yet the novel veers and leaps more like a paranoid prose-poem out of Lautréamont's *Les Chants de Maldoror* (1868), the first surreal poetic prose poem after De Quincey's *Confessions of an Opium Eater* (1821) that profoundly influenced the course of South American writing, and, by the way, we *are* south of the border.

In "The Red Tide" a vampirelike red plankton (shades of Burroughs) swirls in 110-degree heat killing all fish, and in the mucus haze Mountain Girl, eight months pregnant, grows paranoid in the primitive time-warp they all inhabit, but unlike the other Pranksters she begins to learn Spanish as she washes clothes in the salt ocean and Pranksters read the only books they have: The Bible, Burroughs, Nietzsche, and Dostoevsky. Kesey broods on Nietzsche. Mountain Girl decides to marry the sports car driver George Walker (so that the baby will have American citizenship) at city hall and she has Kesey's baby at the local hospital: She is named Sunshine. (Mountain Girl's second marriage in 1981 was to The Grateful Dead's Jerry Garcia with whom she had two daughters.)

The mood of the Pranksters slowly improves—a welcome relief for the reader because it was beginning to look like a nightmare novel that would put the reader's patience to the test. Here Wolfe is at his best with Pranksters as a group and he is able to create a rainbow of camaraderie as Robert Stone shows up to do a piece for *Esquire* magazine on Kesey in exile (never published, but he gives an interesting account of Mexico shenanigans in his memoir *Prime Green*), and Sandy Lehmann-Haupt arrives dust-laden on a motorcycle from New York City to prank them of their Ampex sound machine, and Neal Cassady shows up, forever flipping his four-pound hammer like some Zen doodle. Stone tries without success to persuade Kesey to forget about Nietzsche (good advice!), but to no effect. The chapter collages in Burroughslike cutups and ends with the scene of the electric man Kesey trying dementedly to open up the loop of Nietzsche's Eternal Recurrence and become a Superman as he points to command the lightning, but he collapses, gagging to the sand where Mountain Girl later discovers him. The Prankster clan has been reunited in Mexico for a brief respite of good times, but it is now clear that they need to move beyond acid, beyond the excesses of the drugs in which they have immersed their lives.

The rest of the book provides a journalistic account of Prankster acid tests in Mexico, the comic cat-and-mouse game of cops and outlaws, Kesey's crossing the border (as a happy singing cowboy in the manner of Gene Autry) at Brownsville, Texas, and a lengthy poetic riff, effective with ellipsis, on the Haight-Ashbury scene that culminates in the prank conclusion of The Graduation Test held on Halloween night at which Neal Cassady will hand out diplomas to committed heads. Since this is done just before dawn and the Pranksters run a lengthy, spooky test to dispel those who are not truly committed or confident about this commitment, only about fifty out of thousands of heads hang on for this prank event.[67] Wolfe's moral burnishes clear: You can discover a new awareness through drugs, but you eventually need to bring this new awareness into your life without drugs—life must be lived beyond acid, just as Zoroaster told his followers: "You can't keep taking haoma water."[68] As Zoroaster put aside the mushroom drink and substituted the consecration-incarnation of the Sun God in bread, milk, and wine, so, too, must the Pranksters put aside acid and get back to the task of living their lives in the special awareness that they have gained. Kesey orates:

> For a year we've been in the Garden of Eden. Acid opened the door to it. It was the Garden of Eden and Innocence and a ball. Acid opens that door and you enter and you stay awhile.... We've been going though that door and staying awhile and then going back out through that same door. But until we start going that far... and then going beyond... we're not going to get anywhere, we're not going to experience anything new.... Let's find out where we are. Let's move it around. Let's dance on it.[69]

And they do, the chapter celebration ending with Kesey and Babbs picking up guitars and pranking out a blues duet with an ironic postmortem refrain like actors mocking their own production: "WE BLEW IT!" Wolfe concludes the epic story with a short satyrlike skit as if he's written a dramatic Greek trilogy. This unusual conclusion resonates as a satiric prank broadcast in a time lag that is outside of time—and it is a winsome, even a cute little prankish piece, yet its irony has escaped most readers.

The year-and-a-half-long caper of Kesey and the Pranksters searching for that Garden of Eden within had three principal cultural effects: The revitalization of Western pop music through the creation of acid rock, the creation of unusual dramatic happenings known as the Acid Tests which influenced popular street theater of the period, and the spiritual attention focused upon Eastern wisdom as a prophetic indication of what the future holds—the thrust of Westward, Ho exploration that characterizes the history of America's proclivity to search for a New Jerusalem in open land is now perceived in terms of an Eastern spirituality when the limits of the open land mentality is physically and intellectually reached. Also, it remains hard to admit that if you attend a good production of your local high school band that employs film projectors and/or flashing light patterns that have rhythmic syncopations—this type of multi-media environment was invented and pioneered by the Merry Pranksters. Even the liquid light screen that Windows Media employs when you listen to music was invented by the Pranksters to mimic the synesthetic interaction of sound and color under LSD.

In our culture things often filter down. As a nine-year-old I read an unabridged *Gulliver's Travels* because it was thought to be a children's book; although I could not then understand the satire on science and philosophy in Laputa, I knew that the land of the Yahoos contained a profound and horrifying truth not meant for children. Ironically, Ken Kesey's film script ambitions were fulfilled by many others who appropriated his comic sensibility, from Super Letters to Power Rangers. The amusing *Beetleborg* series of children's films is a good example of this for a preteen audience.

The book's Epilogue to the epic gives a brief, no-nonsense account of Kesey's trial, and his six-month stretch on the work farm—the same length of time the character McMurphy in *One Flew Over the Cuckoo's Nest* served. Was the sentence length by the judge a prank? Neal Cassady dies in the desert from dehydration and overexposure. The Prankster tribe scatters, yet Wolfe had heroically tracked them all down to document their story. The Epilogue reads very much like the death of an era: Owsley was busted the morning of October 7, 1965 on the day that California made LSD illegal and got a three-year prison sentence of which he served one year.[70] October 7 was also the day of the first large San Francisco "Be-In" where The Grateful Dead achieved widespread acclaim and took the torch of leadership from Ken Kesey just weeks before the rigorous Halloween Graduation Test. Kesey is off to prison and eventually emerges to lead a less-public "normal" life beyond acid by putting pen to paper and beginning a new novel.

Wolfe's documentation of Ken Kesey and the Pranksters remains more than the story of a single hero and more than the story of a communal tribe: It remains the inside Ur-story that shook the sensibility of American culture—the country would not quite be the same afterward. Unlike Wolfe's other work, the story itself is not concerned with status as such, but the status of the story itself remains, after all these years, an immense epic in the annals of American culture. And so does the innovative list of Wolfe's approaches to his material from straight journalism to poetry to various novelistic techniques that often operate mimetically whereby events find depiction with the process of their inner psychology. After this book, some American journalists like Hunter S. Thompson, Joan Didion, and Norman Mailer appropriate a new cultural status—the journalist as cultural guru!

CHAPTER 4

FROM REPORTING TO POLITICS

Criticism must then become life-action and pose a threat that goes past the living room and into the kitchen or bedroom, wherever the vital motor is located. I see a coming total journalism in this area which will embarrass you out of every secret you've ever hidden, and if your role is public and cultural, be prepared for the worst because a generation much beater than I was will stop at nothing. . . .

—Seymour Krim, *Shake It for the World, Smartass*

Tom Wolfe's shift to the political right was brazenly trumpeted in June 1970, with an article published in *New York* magazine that attacked the more radical wing of the civil rights movement by denouncing a bail fund-raising party for the Black Panthers. The cover of the magazine was nothing short of sensational: Inside a sky-blue frame three young white women in short dresses wore black gloves with arms upraised in the black power salute, carrying the scandalous inference that young white women were being radicalized *en masse* by having black lovers. In this special issue featuring "Radical Chic," Wolfe attacked those who privately supported the Civil Rights movement with their own funds. He rushed that article and a new one into book form; in the additional article, "Mau-Mauing the Flak Catchers," he sensationalized the government funding of antipoverty programs designed to help lift African Americans out of poverty, describing the anger of unemployed youth and government flunkies (flak catchers) whose job was to receive and ignore complaints. The former article was set in New York, the latter in San Francisco. Collected into slim book format in 1970, the East-West Coast dialectic implied that abusive funding by wealthy Jews and naïve government workers who were routinely intimidated by African-American spokesmen constituted a serious problem throughout the country and that antipoverty programs or liberal supporters of radicals only emboldened violent thugs and criminals, thus undermining the civil fabric of society from coast to coast.

"Radical Chic" begins with a fantasy prank inside Leonard Bernstein's head (although the fantasy dates from 1966), employing Bernstein's own words, as documented by a book called *The Private World of Leonard Bernstein* (a book so fawning that perhaps it deserves ridicule) by his ophthalmologist friend, Dr. Richard Gruen. In a technique Wolfe calls "the downstage narrator,"[1] Wolfe appears to remove his visible presence from the party he attended—as if he were narrating the proceedings from outside the stage proscenium when in reality he's standing unobtrusively at the party taking notes with his ball-point pen. Wolfe derides the photos of Bernstein's family:

> On top of both pianos was a regular flotilla of family photographs in silver frames, the kind of pictures that stand straight up thanks to little velvet-or moiré-covered buttresses in the back, the kind that decorators in New York recommend to give a living room a homelike lived-in touch. 'The million dollar *chatchka* look,' they call it. In a way it was perfect for Radical Chic.[2]

Wolfe cleverly implies that the picture frames used for the family photographs are appropriate for a social *institution* called Radical Chic, a pejorative phrase that characterizes this institution. The swing from family photographs to an ambiguous evil phrase has been established by a mere rhetorical *fiat* identifying the wealthy, who celebrate themselves narcissistically with photos. These elites relieve any guilt of social success by donating money to groups who seek to undermine the class structure of American society. The essay concludes by moving back to into its opening interior monologue, reentering the fear-laden musings of Leonard Bernstein's mind.

Wolfe's theme of status and sloganeering labels most probably was inspired by Wolfe's reading of the leftist Columbia University professor C. Wright Mills (who drove a motorcycle to work); Mills penned several books on the subject of power and status in American culture, as well as editing a volume of Max Weber's essays. The strategy of the burgeoning neoconservative movement was to take the slogan branding that Communism traditionally employed (the bourgeoisie, class struggle, etc.) and turn rhetoric against Marxists by developing impugning tags, casting political liberals in pejorative terms. Alabama governor George Wallace was one of the proficient pioneers of this practice, especially in his popularization of the word "elite," which comes from the Latin word *eligere*, meaning "to elect." Elitism literally means rule by those who are elected by the populace:

> In the 1950s and 1960s, elitism came to the forefront because of the work of sociologist C. Wright Mills, author of *The Power Elite*. But it was the demagoguery of conservative Alabama Governor George Wallace, running for president in 1968, that made elitism a political pejorative. During his 1968 presidential bid,

Wallace attacked the "Washington elite," alleging that they were manipulating the lives of middle-class voters, and failing to understand the interests of "common and everyday people of America." Countless other conservatives soon followed Wallace's lead, and within a decade they made "elitism" a derisive and derogatory term (just as they did with the term "liberal" as well).

In truth, Wallace himself was as elite as they come. As are almost all those who hurl the charge of elitism at others.[3]

Wallace took Mills' concept of the power elite and in a populist although vague manner applied it to the federal government with an "us against them" propagandistic rhetoric, while Wolfe promulgated two propagandistic phrases that ridiculed those who supported the Civil Rights movement: "radical chic" and "funky chic," lampooning liberal leaders of both upper and lower classes. In his spin-off essay "Funky Chic," Wolfe asserts that radical chic *evolved* from the fashionable street trend of funky chic.[4] In "Radical Chic" he mocks ignorance and innocence amid the informality of salon conversation among liberals, while in "Mau-Mauing the Flak Catchers" he praises the out-of-touch efficiency in government bureaucracy, yet Wolfe does not supply any supporting statistical evidence for his implications of featherbedding. Propagandistic perception, based not on facts but on smear phrasing, became the basis for the neoconservative approach to persuading the population at large to vote against their own interests—the coining of contemptuous insults underpinned by explicit or implicit racism was to be their coded calling card.

In appraising the décor of Leonard Bernstein's apartment, Wolfe insinuates that the "Chinese yellow" paint on the walls is ugly (this may be a subtle dig at the etymology of Bernstein's name which means amber, a color very close to yellow). Why is "Chinese yellow" symbolic[5]—as if to imply that the color itself is somehow Communist? Note the superciliously derisive tone in the way Wolfe introduces Leonard Bernstein:

> His success radiates from his eyes and his smile with a charm that illustrates Lord Jersey's adage that "contrary to what the Methodists tell us, money and success are good for the soul." Lenny may be fifty-one, but he is still the *Wunderkind* of American music. Everyone says so. He is not only one of the world's outstanding conductors, but a more than competent composer and pianist as well. He is a man who more than any other has broken down the wall between elite music and popular tastes, with *West Side Story* and his children's concerts on television.[6]

Wolfe dismissively ridicules Bernstein's effort in adapting Shakespeare's *Romeo and Juliet* to a lower-class New York setting in *West Side Story*; no critical analysis accompanies his cavalier dismissal. By comparing Bernstein to an English Lord, Wolfe presents American Lenny as upper-class royalty and the reference to Methodists reminds the reader that Lenny is a Jew, not really part of the Western royal tradition—that he is *faux* royalty, an usurper of sorts, a Faustian figure of the arts who has extraordinary and perhaps hypnotic powers (note the eyes) and who has, probably, sold his soul to the "leaders of the oppressed." The use of the German *wunderkind* concept taunts the reader with the Bernstein family's foreign origin and may remind more literate readers of Thomas Mann's famous short story, "The Infant Prodigy,"[7] where the *wunderkind* turns out to be a clever imposter who amounts to nothing at all. The aside that "Everyone says so" informs the reader that Wolfe will not be a part of this particular "ruling" cultural clique—he will provide an alternative point of view.

Wolfe was never invited to the party—he gate-crashed. He had wandered into the empty office of David Halberstam, saw the fancy invitation on his desk, and phoned in his RSVP acceptance to a phantom invitation.[8] An African American, Don Cox, mispronounces Bernstein's name (Stine not Steen) and this provides an anecdote that reveals the colossal ignorance of the speaker not troubled in the least by this social gaffe at the expense of his host before an audience of educated potential donors. The party begins like an auction manipulated by peer pressure. Lenny donates his next working fee, conducting a performance of *Cavalleria Rusticana* by Pietro Mascagni (a grim story of illicit love and a violent murder of revenge occurring on Easter morning), to the growing pool.

To be fair, Wolfe excoriates both the oppressed and the rich in this meandering article while he deftly captures a sense of social dislocation and cultural misunderstanding between the Black Panthers and their supporters. In that way his satire remains even-handed, yet he offers no solution for social problems other than parading the folly of the rich and the ignorance of the oppressed who may be attracted to excited rhetoric. Wolfe's ridicule tilts toward what is now the so-called "liberal elite" which he labels as "radical chic":

> The black movement itself, of course, had taken on a much more electric and romantic cast. What a relief it was—socially—in New York—when the leadership seemed to shift from middle class to . . . *funky*! From A. Philip Randolph, Dr. Martin Luther King, and James Farmer . . . to Stokely, Rap, Le Roi, and Eldridge! This meant that the tricky business of the fashionable new politics could now be integrated with a tried and true social motif: *nostalgie de la boue*. The upshot was Radical Chic.[9]

Wolfe defines two rules with his "new" label: Radical Chic is based upon sympathy for the oppressed: "One *feels* for them in his solar plexus,"[10] an emotion that Thackeray compulsively mocks among the well-to-do throughout his novel *Vanity Fair*, yet one needs to maintain one's proper social status, which presents a problem with regard to the servants who are indispensible—in terms of both status and practicality. The solution to the problem is, ironically, to indulge in reverse racism: employ only white servants, thus visually denying that the lower classes are exploited—one just banishes them out of sight to the unemployed ghettos and then one can feel sorry for them.[11] Here Wolfe scores a telling point with his customary disdain for the life of unexamined *feeling*.

The origin of the phrase "Radical Chic" was identified by Pamela Walker in a letter to the *New York Times* on June 21, 1987:

> Mr. Krim wrote a critique of The New Yorker for The Village Voice, printed in November 1962. Its main thrust was that this sophisticated magazine was wrapped in a self-protective cocoon immune to the action on the streets. Two weeks later The New Yorker published James Baldwin's "Letter From a Region in My Mind," a white-hot declaration of black militancy unlike anything the magazine had ever printed. To defend himself, Mr. Krim wrote a follow-up article accusing The New Yorker of "stretching its now rubber conscience to include tokens of radical chic and impressiveness on top but not at the bottom where it counts." The follow-up was rejected by The Voice's editor, Dan Wolf.
>
> But the Voice piece and follow-up were printed in a collection of Mr. Krim's essays published by Dial Press in January 1970. In June of that year Tom Wolfe wrote his famous essay about Leonard Bernstein for New York magazine, entitling it "Radical Chic." Later that year Farrar, Straus & Giroux published his collection "Radical Chic and Mau-Mauing the Flak Catchers." PAMELA WALKER New York[12]

Her account is accurate and *Shake It for the World, Smartass* is the title of Seymour Krim's book (the sexually suggestive last word was dropped from the British edition). In appropriating an in-house liberal term of self-criticism for his conservative attack on the left, Wolfe raises an acknowledged, pejorative tag to a lurid and sensational slogan that will become a stadiumlike rallying cry for the neoconservative movement. The term "radical chic" did not originate with Wolfe, as many pundits would have it.[13]

Having seen Krim turn the phrase, it is likely that Wolfe recalled the term Radical Snob from *The Snobs of England, By one of themselves* (written for *Punch* magazine), one of Wolfe's favorite books. William Makepeace Thackeray omnivorously identifies so many various permutations of snobbery that any reader would be offended not to be classified as a snob several times over under various tag headings. Here is the beginning of Thackeray's entry for "Radical Snob":

> Perhaps, after all, there is no better friend to the Conservatism than your outrageous Radical Snob. When a man preaches to you that all noblemen are tyrants, that all clergymen are hypocrites and liars, that all capitalists are scoundrels banded together in an infamous conspiracy to deprive the people of their rights, he creates a wholesome revulsion of feeling in favor of the abused parties, and a sense of their fair play leads the generous heart to take a side with the object of unjust repression.[14]

There's a panoramic humor and wit on display. At his best, Thackeray appears charming and droll when most immersed in sheer frivolity or idle silliness, yet when Thackeray descends to political cant in favor of the imperial Tory Party, he resorts to the kind of snide invective that Wolfe on occasion stoops to: "Some years since, when a certain great orator was Lord Mayor of Dublin, he used to wear a red gown and a cocked hat, the splendour of which delighted him as much as a new curtain-ring in her nose or a string of glass beads round her neck charms Queen Quasheeneaboo."[15] At the time it was illegal and might cost your life to speak Gaelic in public, yet the mayors of Dublin in that century were all colonial English flunkeys, but we shouldn't pay much attention to reality because we are dealing with the predictable xenophobic humor that habitually graced *Punch* magazine. Here the Gaelic language (the alliterative sounds evoked are consistent with the phonetic ridicule Thackeray habitually applied to Anglicized Gaelic names) receives its customary colonial denigration as jungle gibberish, but there is a long history of this kind of thing in English: even in the Anglo-Saxon epic *Beowulf* the Gaelic language (probably Welsh) is demonized as the debased language of Cain, an aspect of the holocaust-minded epic that learned scholars pretend not to have noticed because they are so thrilled by monsters—and can't quite figure out what they represent—or the intricacies of verb conjugations. But let us leave the mead-sodden basement of English scholarship and return to the bright lights of Manhattan where there's a party that everyone could not read enough about.

Thanks to the FBI's efforts to discredit Bernstein through memo leaks to reporters in various newspapers at home and in London, the fund-raising party to raise bail money for the Black Panthers at Leonard Bernstein's had been widely reported in the press, embarrassing Bernstein who gave contradictory explanations for the party and then publically repudiated the Black Panthers.[16] The essay uses Bernstein as a frame that brackets Wolfe's lengthy donnish lecture on one of his hobbyhorse topics, first mentioned in his book on Ken Kesey: *Nostalgie de la boue*. "Nostalgia for mud" is the Romantic feeling that develops among the very rich cultural elite, the kind of thing that made the foreign German queen Marie Antoinette (not mentioned by Wolfe) a pariah at the Versailles court, especially due to her penchant for taking her lovers on picnics and doing it with them (the king was interested only in men) on the lawn (the mud, so to speak). While Wolfe gives a series of anecdotes on this proclivity among the rich to indulge in this delusional fantasy, he never digs into the origin of the problem concerning the nostalgia for mud. As one might expect, Wolfe's anecdotes are amusing and they range from the eighteenth to the twentieth century. There was a crisis in the eighteenth century with an abrupt rise in the population of major European cities and a widening economic gap between the rich and the poor. With the streets of Paris and London (and other cities) awash in garbage, urine, and dung from horses and humans, there was a desire on the part of the rich in these cities to leave for weekends and summer retreats, something still prevailing among the wealthy New Yorkers that Wolfe pokes fun at.

The Romantics idolized nature and those who worked close to the soil, partly because in France there was mass starvation and those who could provide food for others were heroic, even if they were ignorant peasants. But the worship of nature in poetry and prose that so occupied Romantics like Chateaubriand, Wordsworth, and Shelley had earlier antecedent roots going back to the overpopulation of Rome. Properly speaking, the pastoral was an earlier Greek invention rather closely connected to the development of what was later called the novel,[17] but since so much of Greek literature has been lost and what we have appears to center upon the romance of love outside of arranged marriages, it is more practical to look at the late Roman context, which more clearly resembles the problems of eighteenth-century cities.

Rome was a cesspool of squalor, luxury, and decadence—hence a symbol of moral decay. So some poets left Rome and retreated to a villa far from the tiresome round of boasting, drinking, and sexual decadence to celebrate a more moral life of virtue through meditation on the follies of life and the casual beauties of nature. Many poets wrote in this bucolic sunshine, but Virgil was especially successful in this, so much so that he was revered as a later prophet of Christianity. He developed a peculiar and vatic ambiguity in the use of words derived from the effect of sitting under the shadows of leaves—the words themselves were laden with such dense, shadowy meanings and allusions that they were breathtakingly explosive and to this day he still defies translation, despite the numerous attempts that can only capture his basic story line and not the mystery of his poetry. After the fall of Rome, this pastoral genre was maintained by both Italian and French poets. The ambition of the Romantic pastoral was to replace the restricted (only couplets will do!) and artificial diction (only upper-class Salon talk will do!) of the ruling class with a wider emotional spectrum, more varied technique, and more natural diction—the political implication, if not outright statement, favored an egalitarian approach to life because all humans are equal before the forces of Nature, which was perceived as beautiful or transcendent not only in its random patterns but in its awful, barren, and chaotic aspect (mountain tops, deserts, chasms, and caves). Even folk song was held to be art by some of the Romantics—Coleridge idealized the passionate song of an Ethiopian folksinger in "Khubla Khan" as *the* incarnation of high art! In keeping with Wolfe's consistent disdain for the poetry of Wordsworth and the Romantic cult of Nature, he omits any discussion of the *origin* for *nostalgie de la boue* and merely provides several comic illustrations of the rich addicted to indulging their narcissistic follies. Yet these entertaining anecdotes intrude as awkward digressions, much like my own.

Wolfe collages snippets of conversation into a mosaic that becomes a parable about the political left as incompetent, naively ignorant, and guiltily feeble. The purpose of the essays were ultimately threefold: 1) discredit Leonard Bernstein, 2) vilify the Black Panthers as a political organization subject to bouts of anti-Semitism, and 3) perform a backhanded defense of the Vietnam War by associating those opposed to the war with irrelevant idiocy and incompetent reasoning. Behind the scenes the FBI, who had conducted surveillance on Bernstein since the early 1940s, continued to monitor his travel and performances because he was opposed to the Vietnam War and he supported the Civil Rights movement, went beyond intelligence-gathering and "schemed to undermine him with damaging news leaks."[18] These leaks were placed in New York and London newspapers in January of 1970 and stoked the controversy. An alternative explanation for the presence of reporters at Bernstein's party might have been for self-protection from anonymous smears. Because Bernstein knew he was being watched, he may have wanted reporters around to verify that he was doing nothing illegal or treasonous. The reporter Ralph Blumenthal conscientiously later followed up his investigation with further files obtained from the FBI under the Freedom of Information Act.

> Some of the cable traffic shows that when questions later arose about the "informant" for some of the information, F.B.I. officials acknowledged that the source was actually the trash "and is unavailable for recontact." Told of the Government's reliance on trash covers, Mr. Bernstein's longtime agent, Margaret Carson, said, "That's appropriate."
>
> As for possible C.I.A. monitoring, Ms. Carson said: "We kind of assumed it the day Lennie appeared on Nixon's enemy's list. He said to me. 'Between the C.I.A. and the F.B.I., I'm keeping at least a few people busy.'"[19]

The FBI must have been pleased with Wolfe's essay because the general moral of Wolfe's essay is that intellectuals like Bernstein should not meddle in politics because *there* they really are out of their depth—all they do is sow confusion, spout nonsense, and discover embarrassment. Such intellectuals should leave the topic of politics to professionals who understand this country, professionals like Richard Nixon and gutsy journalists like Tom Wolfe and Barbara Walters. While the article accurately documents the angry verve of 1970s trash talk with the public hysteria swirling around the Civil Rights Movement and the Vietnam War, the essay itself stands as a prime example of *that* hysteria and the deeply paranoid response to that hysteria—as well as the sleazy political smearing so endemic to that era of excessive rhetoric which the Civil Rights Movement and the Vietnam War spawned in such abundant and extravagant profusion. Some of the smearing activity extended to faux demonstrations as Bernstein's daughter Jamie later discovered:

> Long after the uproar over the Bernsteins' fund-raising party for the Black Panthers, she recalled, the family learned from F.B.I. files that emerged during a court case that some protesters outside their apartment, who identified themselves as being from the Jewish Defense League, were actually F.B.I. agents.[20]

The publication of "Radical Chic" marks the beginning of a long era in American journalism wherein political ideology became wedded to the celebrity world.

In that same nexus of ideology and the celebrity world Sidney Bernard, the left wing journalist-diarist-about-Manhattan, employed Krim's phrase "Radical Chic" in his essay of that title about "a Mayday extravaganza that *had* to be the New Left's answer to Truman Capote's at the Plaza a few years back" in the gymnasium of St. Peters' Church on West Twentieth Street.[21] This first of May event was eleven weeks after the January 14 party at Leonard Bernstein's, but written before the publication of Wolfe's essay. Bernard's account of Dotson

Rader's party, stylistically in the kind of understated fashion that Wolfe disdains in journalism, pokes fun at the incongruity of celebrity seekers at the chic party and the attempt of strident feminists to derail the counterculture party into the kind ideological harangue that African-American Black Panthers supplied Bernstein's party with and that Wolfe makes fun of in his own "Radical Chic" essay.

One epithet that appears in the mouths of Black Panther advocates at the Bernstein fund-raiser is the insult of "pigs" for "cops." This epithet has its roots in London slang from the early nineteenth century, but it had fallen into disuse. Its revival as an insult goes back to late 1960s Chicago and certain personal friends of Mayor Daley as well as cops with notably porcine features (although the insult appears to have been popular in the Berkeley area also around this time). Among the Chicago police there were several notorious sadists whose particular target was radical students in the Chicago area which was the center of the SDS (their annual convention was held there). That insult was subsequently extended to all cops during the police invasion of a peaceful park demonstration led by Senator Eugene McCarthy. After that notorious police riot, conducted at the specific orders of Mayor Richard Daley, wantonly brutalized many student demonstrators who objected to the anti-war convention delegates of the recently assassinated Robert F. Kennedy being given to the pro-war candidate Hubert Humphrey, the word "pig" entered popular parlance. The repetition of this street epithet in the context of Manhattan high society appears insensitive and alienating, since neither high society nor the middle-class reading audience of the article could possibly understand the corrupt and violent nature of the Chicago police (who were as sadistic as the Berkeley or Paris police) at that point in time. Wolfe effectively employs the word "pigs" as a vulgar stigma, yet curious students of history might want to check out both the rhetoric and period violence on the documentary *The Weather Underground* (2003) or You Tube where one can see even Dan Rather with his headphones inside the Democratic Convention Hall being bullied, pushed, and punched in the stomach by contemptuous security officers.[22]

In a mocking list of radical chic speakers, Wolfe mentions the Irish "Joan of Arc," Bernadette Devlin, a speaker as electrifying as the murdered twenty-one-year-old Black Panther Fred Hampton,[23] who became the youngest woman elected to Parliament in 1969. The author of *Price of My Soul* (1969) was arrested the same month Wolfe's article was published and sentenced to six months in prison for a mere speech, then subsequently assassinated by Loyalist thugs in 1981.[24] Wolfe adds her to his collection of villainous flabber-mouths. Did Wolfe know that at that time Roman Catholics in Northern Ireland did not have the right to a full vote? Satire addressed to the oppressed, no matter what race, ethnicity, or background, is itself a vehicle of repression (blaming the victim, its most common nomenclature) and serves to inspire the bloody bullet of the executioner—yet it has always been the moral duty of artists to upbraid the *upper* classes because that is where the burden of responsibility resides, not among the impoverished. Of course, when the lower classes become self-indulgent in their rhetoric, they may be rebuked in full, as Barbara Walters rebukes the Black Panthers at Lenny's fund-raiser—she's the only liberal able to stand up and vociferously defend common sense (although Otto Preminger does voice some objections) before the crowd of African-American radicals and spineless socialites at Bernstein's event, thus she consequently emerges as the unlikely hero of Wolfe's impressionistic essay.

The minutes of Deputy Director for Central Intelligence Richard Helms's morning staff meeting of December 10, 1970, included in the recently released "Family Jewels" file, contains the following comment:

> DDI noted press accounts of FBI Director J. Edgar Hoover's 19 November statement that the Black Panthers are supported by terrorist organizations. He said that we have examined the FBI's related files and our own data and find no indication of any relationship between the fedayeen and the Black Panthers. He provided the Director with a memorandum on this topic.[25]

The main claim of the Black Panthers was the right to bear arms and defend oneself if attacked illegally, a right guaranteed by the Second Amendment to the Constitution, but in an era that debated the question as to whether African Americans should be allowed to vote, the claim to this right was received was received with hysteria on the part of Nixon's regime and those who supported it. Ultimately, the publicly eloquent Black Panthers were destroyed by the government's COINTELPRO operation that targeted the Black Panthers, SDS Weathermen, and the antiwar movement, yet the government never succeeded in its last two goals. Government propaganda (with the aid of Wolfe, his publisher Clay Felker, and other propagandists) cut off charitable funding of the Panthers—the fundraising at Bernstein's party was for unreasonable bail. While the government's public campaign of assassinating Panther leaders intimidated many, the Weathermen survived longer, posing more of a real threat to the government because its funding sources were never cut off, allowing them to operate underground. The anti-Vietnam War movement succeeded because American soldiers themselves grew ashamed of committing atrocities as they systematically slaughtered millions.

Schooled in Thorstein Veblen and C. Wright Mills (who frequently mentions Yale University in *The Power Elite*), Wolfe well knew the connection between social status and prestige:

> There is another function—today the most important—of prestige and of status conduct. Prestige buttresses power, turning it into authority, and protecting it from social challenge. Prestige lost by way of success, Le Bon has remarked, "disappears in a brief space of time. It can also be worn away, but more slowly, by being subject to discussion . . . From the moment prestige is called in question it ceases to be prestige. The gods and men who have kept their prestige for long have never tolerated discussion. For the crowd to admire, it must be kept at a distance."[26]

Yet Wolfe was after much more than stripping prestige away from Bernstein. Undoubtedly, he was aware of what President John Adams thought on the subject of status, since this passage also appears in Mills' *The Power Elite*:

> ... the rewards ... in this life, are *esteem* and *admiration* of others—the punishments are *neglect* and *contempt*—nor may anyone imagine that these are not as real as the others. The desire of the esteem of others is as real a want of nature as hunger—and the neglect and contempt of the world as severe a pain, as the gout or stone.[27]

In ridiculing Bernstein, Wolfe was aiming at contempt, while covering himself with the detailed notes he had taken at the party to document the event. This was political assassination with a poisoned pen.

Much of the conversation that Wolfe reports at the party consists merely of ranting trash talk, which remains fair game for any mimicking satirist, yet an unsavory atmosphere punctuates Wolfe's satire, so much so that what is potentially amusing might just as likely strike those intellectual readers he so customarily derides as blindly insensitive. Wolfe has great fun at revealing the anti-Israel position of some Black Panthers and after the event Wolfe notes that Bernstein publically denounced the Black Panthers in the *New York Times*. Wolfe's outrageous essay even managed to afflict the lengthy obituary of Bernstein's amazing musical career penned by Donal Henahan in the *New York Times*.[28] Wolfe's essay is, of course, a snidely humorous prank, but it so pushes the limits of the polite envelope that many fairly construe it to be in questionable taste.[29]

Although the essay reads like a frontal attack on Bernstein and the Panthers, I don't think it was Wolfe's original intent to attack Bernstein. Wolfe was really out to attack the Black Panthers who were raising a ruckus at his alma mater where they received support from Yale's President Kingman Brewster, Jr. Wolfe has always been a patriotic alumnus, but like Spiro Agnew, he opposed Brewster. Wolfe accomplished with his pen what the Yale police department could not do: Demean the rhetorical effectiveness of the Black Panthers demanding fair treatment for Panthers arrested in Yale.[30] Wolfe continues to promote the essay, yet his defense of the essay has shifted: He now sees Bernstein's party as the seed prototype of the liberal movement toward "political correctness," a phenomena he continues to view with disdain.[31]

There is much wit and truth to Wolfe's humor in its focus on descriptive detail, especially in his sartorial observations about the upper classes trendily dressing down to look like street savages; American male adolescents continue to be afflicted with the ideal of the pimp-rapper as the icon of high style. The point of Wolfe's lengthy historical digression about why Jews are left-wing serves to pin Leonard Bernstein into Wolfe's glass-cased butterfly collection of absurd follies, just as he attempted rather lamely to ridicule a Jewish liberal writer in the essay "Mauve Gloves & Madmen, Clutter and Vine" in the book of that title. That short story depicts a hapless writer as a composite: Norman Mailer (his politics and the Martha's Vineyard connection), John Updike (his preposterous addiction to turtleneck sweaters, which is a favorite sartorial obsession that Wolfe ridicules in many essays), and Studs Terkel (the Chicago background—his father was a tailor). The title's first part refers to the novelist's imprudent spendthrift bills to a caterer for an unnecessary domestic party while Clutter and Vine refers to a florist's bill for flowers he cannot afford. Since he frivolously lives beyond his means like Ibsen's Nora in *A Doll's House,* surrounding himself with cut flowers, he must churn out popular pulp about paranoia toward the American government inspired by his "tubercular" mind. While "Radical Chic," with its refrain of the repetitive label, does an adept job of ridiculing the Black Panthers who at the time were being hunted down and murdered by the government (Fred Hampton in Chicago is but one example), this vacuous foray into the imagined mind of a nitwit liberal writer falls flatter than a *crepe suzette* cooked on the floor of the Union Square subway station platform during a July heat wave.

Another short story, "The Commercial," finds its setting in the advertising world. An educated black baseball player jumps at the chance to a make television commercial in order to prove that he is more than just an athletic statistic, but the advertising producer wants to create a commercial around exploiting racial prejudice. The story is constructed on two planes, each inside the stream-of-consciousness within each character's head, while there is a third character of whom we get two differing points of view. This is an interesting technique, but the plot remains too much of a corny sit-com skit and the jokes about racism are just not funny. The portrayal of the baseball player's consciousness is not any more believable than the silly plot. A diligent reader will find the odd clever line, but the only successfully sustained writing occurs in the slightly-more-than-a-page epilogue, the satiric style of which resembles any randomly chosen page out of *The Adventures of Gil Blas of Santillane* (1715–35), a picaresque work on folly throughout varied levels of social status, the work being an early precursor example of literary realism.

The *New York Times* review for *Mauve Gloves & Madmen, Clutter and Vine* by Thomas B. Hess, the art critic for Wolfe's home base, *New York* magazine, supplied Wolfe with this snowy Christmas Holiday present by mocking Wolfe's stylistic mannerisms as they relate to the way Celine employed sentence fragments and accusing Wolfe of "whistling Dixie."[32] The influence of Celine may have arrived by way of Wolfe's fellow journalist and friend, Hunter S. Thompson, who became the American Celine of pop culture's underbelly. As a general response to Wolfe's book, this review irritatingly imitates Wolfe's mannered style and notes the shared contempt for intellectuals common to Celine and Wolfe, yet it keeps its focus on the best written piece in the book, "The Truest Sport: Jousting with Sam and Charlie." Wolfe's sociological search for the true-blue American hero that occupies his early books concludes in 1968 with the six-foot-five Yale fighter pilot John Dowd, a former basketball star for Wolfe's alma mater. Dowd was, by anyone's account, a superior fighter pilot (he was the unusual exception to the six-foot-four regulation limit on fighter pilots) who even conceived dangerous strategic runs to voluntarily participate in, receiving the go-ahead from his commanders.[33] Moreover, Dowd was a Navy fighter pilot, a pilot who had to launch his hulking heap of metal from a slingshot and then make his return landing at about 135 knots on a heaving *skillet* in the middle of an ocean![34]

The fighter pilots soaring over North Vietnam are depicted as "jousting" with Sam, the Russian Surface-to-Air Missiles, and Charlie, the Vietcong army. The medieval one-on-one combat metaphor finds currency in the fact that when a SAM attempts to spear a fighter jet it looks like a gray telephone pole, as if it were a lance. The only way a pilot can evade a SAM is by quickly diving to the ground, a tactic that American fighter planes have traditionally excelled at. The SAM will either not be able to make the sharp downward turn, or if it eventually does, it will not be able to make the turn close to the floor, but the pilot must then "joust" with a ground zone layer of artillery antiaircraft fire in his dive, flak so thick pilots would return saying: "It was like trying to fly through a rainstorm without hitting a drop."[35]

In the face of such admirable heroism, Wolfe blames the American press, especially Harrison Salisbury of *The New York Times*, for supporting the propaganda machine of North Vietnam, a propaganda war that Wolfe acknowledges as more expert than the feeble American effort: "They were the champions at this sort of thing."[36] Wolfe then relates the more personal anecdote of the fighter pilot hero Dowd picking up a newspaper in the wardroom of the *Coral Sea* aircraft carrier out in the Gulf of Tonkin and viewing a picture of the Yale University chaplain, William Sloane Coffin, who was at Yale when Dowd was there six years ago, on the front page of a newspaper leading a student antiwar protest. Also appearing was Kingman Brewster, the President of Yale with a "strong face gone flaccid, plump as a piece of chicken Kiev,"[37] the Kiev metaphor clearly signaling that the President of Yale is a chicken engaging in treasonable activity (supporting the Russians—Kiev being at that point in time was still part of the Soviet empire). Here Wolfe and Dowd's alma mater is depicted as colluding with the American enemy, but at no point in the essay is there any explanation of why the Vietnamese people were America's enemies.

According to Wolfe, America, despite such heroism, lost the Vietnam war due to: international pressure for a humane war, a propaganda war in which the American press and especially *The New York Times* gave support to the North Vietnamese propaganda machine, and the treasonous behavior of America's moral leaders, those so-called intellectuals who abandoned their patriotism to support the Russian view of the war and manipulated the greater public into this perspective. All of this is framed indignantly by the personal witness of a great American hero and his out-in-the-field journalist sidekick.[38] The story of betrayal is not only a national one, but all the more moving since (as if it were some heroic and tragic memoir) it is a deeply personal statement of witnessing, a testifying indictment of the political left.

This emotional appeal to flag sentiments remains *abstract feeling*—we never meet Charlie face-to-face in the grand aerial sweep and roar of a jet engine and the presence of two million Vietnamese corpses remains a vague and unaddressed statistic, nor are we offered any probing parallels on how the American

Revolution was seen in England and how English domestic support for the American revolution almost toppled the ruling party of Lord North. We are left with the gripping story of how America betrayed its heroes and this simplistic *crie de cour* becomes the drum tattoo that will provide another Yale alumnus and fighter pilot to attempt a second imperial war with the aid of a monolithic Pentagon propaganda machine which will plant stories, domestically and internationally, around the world with the assistance of a Department of Homeland Security. That Department will spy on every journalist, professional or amateur, and rely on the volunteer patriotism of men like Dowd to die for oil companies in a one-product country. This personal testimony by Dr. Tom Wolfe becomes the gospel guiding light of the noted sports fan George W. Bush.

One aspect of this novelistic essay about Dowd, who came from my own religious diocese of Rockville Center on Long Island, New York, is the metaphor of *sport* which Wolfe sees as a playful imitation of warfare. Wolfe notes that Dowd turned down a professional basketball draft and that when he went into the military he was put on the prestigious Navy basketball team stationed in Hawaii where he could have remained happily for his military service, but he freely chose the higher status of fighter pilot for his military career—the *real* thing where you experienced "the *daily routine* of risking one's hide while operating a hurtling piece of machinery that separated military flying from all other forms of soldiering and sailoring known to history."[39] Wolfe features in this profile just one of the many unknown heroes who populate the military which protects America in the proxy war with the Soviet empire, but the war's critics charged that this proxy war that killed over two million Vietnamese and about 58,000 Americans was a pointless political exercise in bravery turned toward inflicting atrocities on a proud people who wanted to have their own independent country. The reviewer's charge of whistling Dixie calls attention to the journalist as grandstand cheerleader for a violence he cannot possibly understand in any realistic way, yet Wolfe stands in awe of such Romantic fantasies of war that he paints them with the enthusiasm of a Sir Walter Scott, a signature aspiration Mark Twain once decried as the nostalgic ruination of the Southern imagination well before *Gone With the Wind* hit the bookstores and movie screens.[40]

Wolfe had put this piece on Dowd in the collection under the subheading of stories. While the piece begins with journalism and turns to ghosted memoir, the last third of the piece is presented as story, especially the thrilling first-person narration of Dowd's experience of being shot down over North Vietnam and his airlift water rescue near the shoreline. Although the story employs fictional perspective based upon interviews, it recounts a *real* incident, *a real story*, and Wolfe adeptly employs Celine's technique of using extended ellipsis at a climax, as he will do later in *The Right Stuff*. Since this story, as Wolfe calls it, excels at so many levels, it became the embryonic model for Wolfe's *The Right Stuff*. Some of the journalistic writing about Navy fighter pilots between pages 46 and 54 will be recycled as nearly verbatim background in *The Right Stuff*, which has its roots in this memoir story about a Navy fighter pilot from Yale.

Among Wolfe's many books, this collection appears to be the most disappointing book, yet there is one other strong piece in *Mauve Gloves* that merits serious attention: "The Me Decade and the Third Great Awakening," which addresses the problem of emotional insecurity in the identities of Americans, deriving from the announcement that all men are created equal. In brief, Americans have monumental anxieties about class status and what even constitutes class. Because of the prosperity following World War II the middle classes have acquired anxiety status along with a growing selfishness that confuses class values and class boundaries, that is, the middles classes have taken as their ideal the privileges of the aristocracy. Such confusion began to take root in the 1960s under the influence of psychologists like Fritz Perls and his encounter therapy, but a host of other therapies are invoked. By the early 1970s these notions of therapy had invaded two public aspects of American life, the secular and religious realms, through different notions of sex which were no longer directed to the family and communal good. Advertising fueled narcissism and self-satisfaction with the concept of "You have only one life to live,"[41] encouraging sexual selfishness in a consumerist way that led to sexual experimentation, the women's liberation movement, and a Cassanova mentality among men that encouraged them to shuck off their wives. Religion was dying in the 1950s but the religious revival of the 1960s was brought about by LSD, yet Wolfe offers slim evidence for this. He cites his nineteenth-century favorites, Max Weber and Joachim Wach, but offers no statistics or evidence from any contemporary sociologist.

Wolfe claims sexual experience became a religious quest for ecstasy through various forms of therapy whereby individual experimentation led to a monumental self-obsession on the part of both sexes. Some of these excesses included communication therapies and sexual experimentation of various sorts by couples and same-sex people that glorified the orgasm into a mystic religious experience. Wolfe blames all this on the Left, despite the fact that advertising has always remained a stronghold of the Right. As for individual sexual excesses in the seventies, many aspects of American society appear to be at fault and the general cult of Me that Wolfe identifies in his armchair psychoanalysis finds resonance on this topic.

Citing the historian Perry Miller, Wolfe notes that the First Great Awakening of the 1740s helped pave the way for the American Revolution by assaulting both the colonies' religious establishment and by extension British authority; the Second Great Awakening in the mid nineteenth century was a bleak revolution in austerity that allowed Americans to build communities under harsh conditions, yet he omits to mention that Miller identified the 1857 financial depression as the cause of this Awakening which began in the cities.[42] The Third Great Awakening dating from 1970 is the "Let's talk about me" revolution that challenges the "age old belief in serial immortality." De Tocqueville makes a prophetic curtain call to observe that the American sense of equality disrupts "time's pattern." Wolfe sees de Tocqueville's idea of modern man "lost in the solitude of his own heart" as the pessimistic precursor of Marx, Durkheim, Ortega y Gasset, and modern sociologists like David Riesman.[43] In conclusion, the middle class takes the money of the post World War II boom and goes on the holiest roller bender of all: "Me...Me...Me...Me..."[44] The essay ends in murmuring, mocking implication rather than any stated conclusion and invites readers to connect the outline dots that Wolfe has made in order to get the whole picture about America's drift into consumer decadence.

What might at first appear to be a sociological analysis becomes in the end a political prescription more akin to Spartan philosophy as advocated by Plato in *The Republic*: that public morality should be guarded by government propaganda—a far cry from what the liberal framers of the American Constitution recommended. The cure for the middle-class problem of self-indulgence is obviously to reduce its income and even its size, thus restoring time's ancient "pattern" (back before the French Revolution?). A more austere income would force people to be more focused on religion, work, and community, rather than on self, sex, and brooding notions of self-pitying alienation.

Many of Tom Wolfe's core ideas about America and patriotism remain remarkably similar to those of President Richard Nixon's Vice President, Spiro T. Agnew, who blamed first the country's educational system for student protests and then secondly the press for its treasonous support of North Vietnam. Arthur Schlesinger, Jr., the one-time assistant to President John F. Kennedy, penned a lengthy article on Spiro Agnew five weeks after Tom Wolfe's "Radical Chic" essay appeared in *New York* magazine, attacking Agnew for blaming intellectuals (Kingman Brewster, Jr., by name) and college teachers for betraying their country:

> If there is disorder in America today, these men are to blame. "Some of those who call each other 'intellectuals' helped to sow the wind, and America reaped the whirlwind.... If you walked through Harlem, or Berkeley, or Columbia, or Watts at the height of the disorders, you could hear—through the din of the battle between police and rioters—the unmistakable sound of chickens coming home to roost." The Vice President has no patience with the notion that conditions in Harlem, or Berkeley or Columbia, or Watts had much to do with the trouble. "If you want to pinpoint the cause of riots, it would be this permissive climate and the misguided compassion of public opinion. It is not the centuries of racism and deprivation that have built to an explosive crescendo but the fact that law-breaking has become a socially acceptable and occasionally stylish form of dissent."[45]

Note Agnew's employment of the chicken image as well as the concluding jargon. Agnew was known to read with dictionary at elbow in order to bulk up the pyrotechnics of his baroque orations that often exhibited a pressurized autodidactic quality.

Wolfe's earlier essays in his first two books explored life with a zest and curiosity free of politics,[46] but the essays of *Mauve Gloves* take his new journalistic approach into the arena of politics, and while Wolfe is capable of profound or sly implications, the political nuance hangs heavy and diminishes the surprising irreverence of his earlier essays. Once Wolfe's search for the politically correct hero found its apotheosis in Dowd, his prose becomes archer, he becomes more concentrated on identifying fools, and his focus on class status becomes more like the obsessive therapy of an advertising executive on a shrink's couch than a casual humorous sketch done in the open air on a park bench. Wolfe's participation in the vogue of what became labeled as the New Journalism was inventive in a spectacular way. While Wolfe goes to great lengths in explaining how the New Journalism requires more research, work, and creative effort than either the novel or traditional journalism in his articulate and well-wrought preface to his excellent and provocative anthology *The New Journalism* (1973), he makes no effort to remind the reader that these new artistic aims and claims sometimes involve more of the artist's haughty Me . . . Me . . . Me perspective. And much of that perspective is politics.

As for the origin of the term "The New Journalism," Wolfe complains that he doesn't like the tag because of the facile adjective "new," which eventually dates itself as something old. He recalls that the Jewish essayist and antholo-gist Seymour Krim, a left-wing fellow New Journalist who often covered the cutting edge of bohemian art, told him "that he first heard it used in 1965 when he was editor of *Nugget* and Pete Hamill called him and said he wanted to write an article called 'The New Journalism' about people like Jimmy Bres-lin and Gay Talese."[47] Wolfe goes on to cite authors of this new approach to writing: several contributors to *Esquire* and his own Sunday supplement *New York*, adding three other names to the list: Tom Gallagher, Robert Benton, and David Newman. Tom Gallagher was a novelist who pioneered point of view in the documentary novel. The latter two, a notable and successful screenwriting team, had an early success with *Bonnie and Clyde* (1967), which offered graphic realism[48] and cinematic innovation with close-ups combined with varied camera speed, experimenting with point of view—giving the point of view of the outlaws themselves.

The documentary novel had its roots in World War II journalism. *Guadal-canal Diary* (1942) by the journalist Richard Tregaskis provided a vivid partisan narrative of American soldiers amid the gruesome difficulties of war; in today's terms it was an embedded narrative that brims with bias as it recounts the hero-ism of American soldiers. The book and subsequent movie of the book was so successful that this docudrama approach was imitated by many other journalists and writers who penned the legions of books on World War II. The novelist Thomas Gallagher turned this kind of docudrama into a thriller mystery with *Fire at Sea: The Story of the Morro Castle* (1959) about a luxury cruise ship off the New Jersey shore in 1934 that was set ablaze with the resultant loss of 181 lives. The book won the 1960 Mystery Writers Edgar Allan Poe award, but as docudrama it offered an innovation: Point of view from the various lead charac-ters in the incident. The melding of journalism and the novel was inevitable and when it happened there was a ready audience because, as Wolfe points out, it addressed social realities that novelists were shirking. While Gallagher's novel was a modest success, it did not enjoy the enormous success of Truman Capote's *In Cold Blood* (1965).

Both novels employed sensational tabloid themes about crime. In Gallagher's 1959 novel he provided evidence that the radio operator who had reported the 1934 fire actually started the fire himself, so as to put it out, and thus become a hero; the result was the loss of many lives, and Gallagher's hypothesis was subsequently confirmed by other investigators; in Capote's novel the reader gets a portrait of two cold-blooded killers while the narrator's point of view delves deeply into the psychological make-up of the deranged killers from within their own sick minds. Capote's innovation was to take what Gallagher had done in brief by using multiple points of view in his short novels and extending an in-depth psychological perspective from the narrower lens of two points of view throughout the whole fabric of a long novel. Likewise, William Styron then produced a documentary novel with deep psychology from a single point of view in *The Confessions of Nat Turner* (1967). Styron's fairly successful portrayal of an African-American stream-of-consciousness (written with the advice of James Baldwin while he stayed at his house) might have encouraged Wolfe to attempt the portrait of a black baseball player in "The Commercial," just as Capote's two-track point of view may have encouraged Wolfe to attempt a similar technique in that story.

Gallagher, who had previously written three traditional novels, continued to explore the developing phenomenon of the documentary novel, presenting several points of view as he told various tales. *The Doctor's Story* (1967) relates the founding of Columbia University's College of Physicians and Surgeons, employing dialogue gleaned from newspapers and rapidly shifting point of view with a large cast of characters, as it graphically depicts the infamous Manhattan "doctors' riot" of 1788, for which the book was subsequently banned.[49] *The X-Craft Raid* (1971) first appeared serially in *Reader's Digest* during 1969 and 1970; it narrated the extraordinary adventures of several mini-submarine pilots who managed to sink the reputedly impregnable German battleship, the *Tirpitz*, in a Norway fjord during World War II. As a former seaman, Gallagher manages a gripping story of these brave submariners, offering the experiential angle of each pilot. Gallagher's book provided a successful precedent, furnishing Wolfe with a multi-point-of-view military model when he came to write about fighter pilots and astronauts in *The Right Stuff* (1979). Gallagher's submarine book appears to be the documentary novel to which Wolfe alludes.

While Wolfe never identified with the counterculture movement surrounding Kesey or Kesey's crusade to change American popular culture against the backdrop of the Vietnam War, he was fascinated by its religious and sociological aspects, depicting Kesey as a hero for rejecting the role of a messiah. Both Wolfe and Kesey drew: Wolfe sketched cartoons while Kesey drew comic strips. Without the varied currents of the New Journalism at play, it is hard to imagine Norman Mailer's great work of dramatic journalism, *The Armies of the Night* (1968), or many other notable works from that hysterical period. Capote erased his ego in five years of interviews with prison inmates; Mailer groomed his own celebrity ego in the foreground as a protagonist; Hunter S. Thompson chronicled living on the deranged edge of journalism; Wolfe lurked offstage as he whispered strategy and advice to the upper class while he transformed himself into a dignified salon dandy. A significant aspect of Wolfe's transformative advice was the virtue and valor of war that he found among fighter pilots.

CHAPTER 5

HISTORIAN AT EDGE CITY

To survive took everything I knew and had ever experienced in a cockpit, so that maybe one hour less flying time could have been the difference between drilling a hole or landing safely.

—Chuck Yeager, *Yeager: An Autobiography*

At first glance it might seem strange that a man who had chronicled and dramatized the adventures of a group of acidheads and the counterculture life they invented and popularized might take on as his next long project military figures of the establishment culture in *The Right Stuff* (1979), but there are profound links between these two projects: Kesey and the Pranksters were heroic explorers who could not only overcome their own paranoia under LSD but dispel it in others, which is what the public tests were about in a bewildering variety of bizarre settings. They were an elect group beyond the knowledge and experience of leading psychologists and men of religious wisdom. No one knew what they were up to and Wolfe was determined to tell their story.

The constant danger that the Pranksters confronted and skirted was insanity, perhaps even the threat of insanity, living as they did at the locus they had called Edge City. With pilots that edge is even more serious: There was a 23 percent probability that a Navy pilot flying for twenty years would die in an aircraft accident.[1] Wolfe points out that in an Ivy League school like Princeton a fraternity would be a big item in someone's career, but the "fighter jocks," as they called themselves in proud, self-mocking irony, were a "true fraternity." As if straight out of Max Weber, Wolfe describes this pilot fraternity like the "believing Presbyterians of a century before who used to probe their own experience to see if they were truly among *the elect.*"[2] Pilots had to "prove at every foot of the way up that pyramid you were one of the elected and anointed ones who had *the right stuff*, and could move higher and higher and even—ultimately, God willing, one day—that you might be able to join that special few at the very top, that elite who had the capacity to bring tears to men's eyes, the very Brotherhood of the Right Stuff itself."[3] In the final analysis it wasn't speed of reactions, superior eyesight, the ability to multitask, to endure unpredictable danger, or even a knack for cunning that would enable a pilot to survive; these were all requisite skills, but the skill above skills was the one Wolfe labeled the *right stuff*. As with the Pranksters, there was a mystique, if not a mysticism of *performance* that attracted Wolfe to the subject of pilots as heroes.

Wolfe muses on the lack of logic in the minds of pilots, just as he was attracted to the riddling nature of Prankster telepathy and their tendency to speak in ellipses that discover continuity in associational development during group sessions. Navy aviators (they considered those in the Air Force or Army to be mere pilots—the word aviator conferred a greater status) had the extraordinary difficulty of landing on aircraft carriers. The fact that one in four aviators would die meant nothing to them because the figures were averages and "averages applied to those who had ordinary stuff."[4] If you had the right stuff, you "lucked out."

Another parallel story element in an anthropological sense was the presence of fraternal (or tribal) taboo: Among pilots the taboo was to speak about the "unspoken stuff," meaning either the mention or boast of courage or expressing the fear of error, that is, the various possibilities of error in either the mechanics of the machine or techniques of operating the plane were forbidden, unless it was the analysis of why a pilot died, for such analysis put the blame squarely on the pilot's stupid errors or the mechanical crew's ineptitude. Among the elite Pranksters, the great taboo was the subject of a paranoid freak-out because as adepts they were the Supermen beyond the world of mortal paranoia. Just as the telepathic nature of discourse among the Merry Pranksters consisted of *only* a jokingly optimistic *go with the flow* sensibility (the Merry itself indicates as significant taboo), so the constant drinking and talking among pilots consisted of anecdotes about how they overcame difficulties such as engine burnout, flying when hung-over, tailspin, nosedive, or freefall—the continual repetition of such victorious anecdotes on a daily basis over alcohol becomes a life-affirming testimony of optimism that enables pilots to cope psychologically with the near-death experiences they confront almost daily.[5]

Although the humor meter in *The Electric Kool-Aid Acid Test* often fluctuated between sarcasm and opportunistic wit, the humor meter in *The Right Stuff* exudes a winsome charm—it leaves sarcasm behind, exhibiting a relaxed and just plain funny mood in its modestly scaled down-home diction and tone. Some of this change is a mimetic tribute both to Chuck (George) Yeager and the potentially wider audience of the book. Like an anthropologist out to solve a linguistic puzzle, Wolfe explains how the dominance of Yeager, the first man to break the sound barrier (he had two broken ribs at the time), as a pilot goddaddy of the big blue skies led to the popularization of a particular West Virginia accent throughout the test-pilot true Brotherhood fraternity, the accent then dominating control tower lingo, and eventually the down-home drawl of every commercial airline pilot. The cool, matter-of-fact ease and contempt in the face of near-death that exuded from Yeager's drawl in the face of a serious problem—dead controls, broken landing gear, frozen dials, flat tailspin, whatever—dominated a whole profession.[6] While Ken Kesey's mellow, assuring voice and Oregon accent was the calming hypnotic voice guiding the Pranksters during their perilous acid journeys into the interior unknown, it never dominated the hippie subculture, although a case for the immense influence of Neal Cassady's rapid-fire amphetamine rap as being a predominate technique of Beat subculture might be made. The etiological origins of pilot accent remind us that Wolfe once again pens an epic, but he does not indulge in poetry or the prose poem because his main priority is to provide a grand historical sweep of these pilot heroes in action against the backdrop of the menacing Cold War with Russia. The tension of the Cold War space race looms over the book.

Unlike the novelistic identification with Ken Kesey that Wolfe conjured in *The Electric Kool-Aid Acid Test*, the portraits of the Mercury Seven, the first astronauts, emerge as well-drawn sketches that give the flavor of their psychology and character through their words, but never provide that inner psychological identification found in a novel. We can identify with the success of the pilots' and astronauts' projects, but not with the inner drama of their lives; they appear as winged warriors engaged in the alien landscape of space. If there can be said to be any literary model for Wolfe's presentation, one *might* point to the *The Iliad* where we only briefly get inside a few characters' heads (Nestor, Helen, Hector, Achilles, and Priam) amid a large, sprawling cast, but such a comparison would be misguided.

Homer presents war, pillaging, and slavery as the tragic facts of life, and although he admires the valor of men in war, he disapproves of war itself through the grim and gory details of death descriptions and his ultimately ironic perspective on war as a senseless waste of life, something Homer accomplishes by interjecting short obituaries of fallen warriors. Wolfe's presentation of war is more akin to that of Herodotus, the patriotic Greek historian who praised the Greek heroism of Leonidas and the Spartan 300 at Thermopylae and Themistocles' leadership at the sea battle of Salamis, both victories preserving Greek independence from the Persians. While Homer's view of war remains grimly tragic, Wolfe's view is essentially a comic view of history. Wolfe reserves his irony for the ending of the Cold War with Russia: it obliterated the need for the heroic perspective of the dedicated warrior. In the Epilogue of *The Right Stuff* Wolfe registers nostalgia for the vanished heroism of war.[7]

Just as status competition and its attendant boasting amid the toll of casualties is all-important to warriors in *The Iliad*, so fighter pilots struggle up the status ladder amid the loss of fellow pilots to be masters of the sky in Pilot Heaven when, like Yeager, they broke free of gravity. Wolfe's chapter on Yeager with its riveting anecdotes on his legendary prowess charts this heroic backdrop superbly, but the arrival of the astronaut program changed this Homeric ethic completely:

"Astronaut meant 'star voyager,' but in fact the poor devil would be a guinea pig for the study of weightlessness on the body and the central nervous system."[8] To be a passive subject was hardly Homeric—the fighter pilots referred to astronauts as "spam in a can."[9] Wolfe depicts the pilot's heroic status to the ideal of the single combat warrior. Like a medieval knight, the pilot confronts a new ironic barrier: the passive qualities of physical endurance demanded by a kind of "lab rat," the astronaut who becomes the experimental *object* of corporate scientific research. Wolfe's achieves a nostalgic pathos that is elegiac in its limning of a pilot-fighter era characterized by extraordinary heroism, which is required on a *daily* basis. As with Herodotus, Wolfe's primary method of presentation remains the recounting of lively anecdotes based upon interviews.

Wolfe had a larger patriotic agenda. He glanced at the literature produced by Modernism and found that its attitude toward war remained one sided and probably to his mind unpatriotic. In his 1983 Preface for the paperback reprint of *The Right Stuff* Wolfe states:

> Immediately following the First World War a certain fashion set in among writers in Europe and soon spread to their obedient colonial counterparts in the United States. War was looked upon as inherently monstrous, and those who waged it—namely, military officers—were looked upon as brutes and philistines. The tone was set by some brilliant novels; among them, *All Quiet on the Western Front, The Journey to the End of the Night,* and *The Good Soldier Schweik.* The only proper protagonist for a tale of war was an enlisted man, and he was to be presented not as a hero but as Everyman, as much as a victim of war as any civilian. Any officer above the rank of second lieutenant was to be presented as a martinet or a fool, if not an outright villain, no matter whom he fought for. The old-fashioned tale of prowess and heroism was relegated to second-and third-rate forms of literature, ghost-written autobiographies and stories in pulp magazines on the order of *Argosy* and *Bluebook.*

Wolfe had as his agenda the restoration of patriotic heroism. He told the stories of extraordinary men and their struggle to maintain dignity amid the transition from individual sky warriors to willing subjects who became heroes of endurance in the name of the public good. He would do profiles of patriots who *volunteered* their lives in the service of their country and present this as first-rate epic available to a wide public. Ultimately, the restoration of such ideal heroism would become part of the neoconservative argument for a volunteer army.

When sixty-nine jet-pilot fighters were given the high-powered sales pitch at the Pentagon for the Mercury project, fifty-six volunteered to become astronauts. They were not so much interested in the project itself as they were afraid of being *left behind.* In the end they were not manipulated by career considerations or even fear of a rocket blowing up. At this time American efforts to launch rockets and satellites routinely met with humiliating disaster—rockets blowing up on the launch pad or lurching in the wrong direction—with Nikita Khrushchev mockingly calling the small American satellites that were successfully launched "oranges." The assent of the pilots was manipulated solely by considerations of *status* and this glorious status was enthusiastically reified by the American press. Wolfe records the reaction of one pilot's wife, Jane Conrad:

> The thought of Pete riding a NASA rocket did not fill her with horror. On the contrary. Although she never quite put it this way to Pete, she felt that anything would be better, safer, saner than for him to continue flying high-performance jet fighters for the Navy. At the very least, astronaut training would take him away from that. As for rocket flights themselves, how could they possibly be any more dangerous than flying every day at Pax River? What rocket pilot's wife had ever been to more funerals than the wives of Group 20?[10]

One of the virtues of Wolfe's book remains the perspective of how the difficulties and dangers of these pilot warriors impacted their concern for their families and how the families themselves dealt with the tension of living near death, as well as the difficulties of extended absence on their lives.[11] This aspect of the book could very well have been expanded and covered in more depth. One of the many reasons that *Yeager*, Chuck's autobiography written with Leo Janos, endures as such a good read, aside from its thrilling anecdotes and humble humor, is that a considerable portion of the book is in the voice of Glennis Dickhouse, Chuck's wife.

During the Press Conference announcing the Mercury 7 astronauts, John Glenn steals the show with his home-town talk on God, Family, and Country. The press responds by making the seven instant superheroes by acclamation, yet Wolfe's inbred skepticism about the press surfaces with a critical eye:

> It was as if all the press in America, for all its vaunted independence, were a great colonial animal, an animal made up of countless clustered organisms responding to a single nervous system. In the late 1950's (as in the late 1970's) the animal seemed determined in all matters of national importance the *proper emotion*, the *seemly sentiment*, the *fitting moral tone* should be established and should prevail; and all information that muddied the tone and weakened the feeling should simply be thrown down the memory hole.[12]

Wolfe, a long-time insider within the press, registers his habitual contempt for unexamined *feeling* amid this not-so-unexpected patriotic outpouring. While he notes such uncritical mass thinking in press coverage of the late 1950s and 1970s, one might also see this passage as prophetic of the Press Corps' reaction to the Iraq invasion of 2003. According to Weingarten,[13] it was Wolfe's reaction to the media's false presentation of these men that led to his interest in expanding the four articles on the Mercury 7 he had first written for *Rolling Stone* magazine into a book on these seven men—in order to give the real story of these men and thus document a genuine heroism, thus correcting the uncritical media circus that surrounded them. There is probably a good deal of truth in Weingarten's comment, as the previous citation on the media indicates, yet Wolfe himself says:

> I went to work on a book called *The Right Stuff* thinking it would be a story of space exploration. In no time at all, I happened upon something far more fascinating. The astronauts were but part of an invisible, and deadly, competitive pyramid within an inner circle of American military fighter pilots and test pilots, and they were by no means at the apex. I characterized this pyramid as a ziggurat, because it consisted of innumerable and ever more deadly steps a fighter pilot had to climb to reach the top. The competition demanded an uncritical willingness to face danger, to face death, not once but daily, if required, not only in combat but also in the routine performance of his duties—without ever showing fear—in behalf of a noble cause, the protection of his nation.[14]

Wolfe's disagreement with mainstream media is not that these seven men don't deserve the public adulation given to heroic patriots, but that these men were so much *more* remarkable than the public (or he) could ever imagine.

Wolfe then provides a brief historical overview of single combat: From Chinese settings to David and Goliath and to medieval times in order to make the connection between the fates of the gods as manifestations of heavenly will. More highly organized modern armies made such superstitions obsolete, but he observes that the nuclear bomb during the late 1950s restored primitive superstition which was based not upon nature but upon technology. The fate of the entire globe to be in thrall to one of the two great superpowers resides in the ability to launch satellites as proxy proof of one's ability to annihilate the other.[15] And then the next step would be to place single combat warriors into space itself as proof of a country's ability to dominate the heavens and share the fate of the gods: "The men chosen for this historic mission took on the archaic mantles of the single-combat warriors of a long-since-forgotten time."[16] Such armchair anthropological assertions (very common in Herodotus) inject Wolfe's historical account with a primitive epic drama; he then proceeds to roll out Wagnerian kettledrums pounding out the pace of a hectic political crescendo, only to lower the volume with an academic footnote couched as an antique aside: "Thus beat the mighty drum of martial superstition in the mid-twentieth century."[17] Wolfe has a dramatic knack for orchestrating a metaphoric example, here single combat, and turning it into an explosive symbol for the plot of his story. And yet in the previous chapter we feasted on hilarious anecdotes about how these new astronauts were merely to be passive subjects of an experiment. Single combat has been transformed now into a metaphor for heroic passive endurance. Wolfe's proclivity for the exaggerations of epic drama first appeared in the Mexico chapters of *The Electric Kool-Aid Acid Test.*

Wolfe paints a comic pantomime of buffoonlike Washington Senators with nothing to say, all wanting to shake the astronauts' hands and get their pictures taken with the newly anointed heroes *before* their dangerous mission upon which the fate of the country depends.[18] Such comedy is then supplemented with the anecdote of Chuck Yeager being asked about how he feels about not being selected as an astronaut and the dullard reporters are stunned to silence when Chuck declares that he doesn't care at all because there will be no *flying*. In one sentence Yeager dispelled the myth that the Mercury 7 astronauts were chosen because they were the best pilots in America and that they would be exercising their skills as pilots. Yeager actually told the reporters that a monkey would be making the first trip. Wolfe slyly rebukes the Press Corps by noting Yeager's interview appears only in the local paper. While the Senators may know nothing, the press really either knows or has the opportunity (if not duty) to know better, but abdicates its duty to inform the public. Wolfe's grandiose single combat observation with its anthropological resonance is a red herring prank, a straight man in a comic duet.

The pacing of the ironically titled "In Single Combat" chapter follows the pattern of a dramatic public build up, only to be followed by private anecdotal comedy that deflates the public drama. It's an entertaining pacing formula of a dialectic that Wolfe exploits with a practiced bounce throughout the book.

The title of Chapter Six, "On the Balcony," refers to a standing joke that Wolfe developed earlier in Chapter Three to describe the monumental ego of a fighter pilot—that it was like the Pope who appeared from time to time on the balcony and waved to the faithful: that it was this kind of public adulation fighter pilots would like to have as the reward for their dangerous work—an adulation that avoided any close scrutiny of their personal lives. The narrative begins, appropriately enough, with a discussion of the mighty status of the word "astronaut" before giving a portrait of John Glenn that mildly satirizes him as the pious "deacon" who religiously performs daily roadwork before others rise, drives an old car, and is scrupulously faithful to his wife—all the while reminding the reader of how such behavior was not the norm among the crowd of fighter pilots. The main point is that Glenn's piety gains the limelight of the press and will eventually cause competitive consternation among his peers because he appears to be a self-elected deacon among the seven Protestants chosen for the Mercury Project. Wolfe lays down the background for some division in the solidarity of the astronauts. The rest of the chapter satirizes Henry Luce, the publisher of *Life* magazine, the boss of bosses,"[19] as the out-of-touch Pope of Journalism, who came to gaze upon the Mercury astronauts

> as *his boys*. Luce was a great Presbyterian, and the Mercury astronauts looked like seven incarnations of Presbyterianism.... From the Luces and Restons on down, the Press, that ever-seemly Victorian Gent, saw the astronauts as seven slices of the same pie, and it was mom's pie, John Glenn's mom's pie, from the sturdy villages of the American heartland. The Gent thought he was looking at seven John Glenns.[20]

The assonance of Gent and Glenns remains an effective and memorable rhetorical tactic. Wolfe goes on to have great fun ridiculing the special-issue cover of

Life magazine that airbrushed and idealized the Mercury seven wives' appearance:

> *Life* had retouched the faces of all of them practically down to the bone. Every
> suggestion of a wen, a hickie, an electrolysis line, a furze of mustache, a bag, a
> bump, a crack in the lipstick, a rogue cilia of hair, an uneven set of the lips . . . had
> disappeared in the magic of photo retouching. Their pictures all looked like the
> pictures girls can remember from their high-school yearbooks in which so many
> zits, hickies, whiteheads, blackheads, goopheads, goobers, pips, acne trenches,
> boil volcanoes, candy-bar pustules, rash marks, tooth-brace lumps, and other
> blemishes have been scraped off by the photography studio, you looked like you
> had just healed over from plastic surgery. The headline said: SEVEN BRAVE
> WOMEN BEHIND THE ASTRONAUTS."[21]

On the one hand, Wolfe mocks Henry Luce's idealization of passive women
who are only identified by their husband's work, but, on the other hand, his
gifted penchant for lists appears slightly over-the-top runaway, especially in its
gratuitous repetition of hickies, unless one were to split hairs and claim it is not
repetition because it varies from the singular to the plural. In any case, some
women readers may be justifiably uneasy or angry at such a preening peacock
passage of purple lists that ridicules women's cosmetics nearly as effectively as
an eloquent sixteenth-century Puritan divine. But the main point is to ridicule
the 1950s journalism of Henry Luce as preposterous saccharine *shtick*, something
that few today would even attempt to quarrel with. Luce's airbrushed cover is
symbolic of the magazine's superficial and brain-dead content. As with Wolfe's
previous attack on William Shawn and *The New Yorker* (see Chapter Six), Wolfe
displays a gift for reducing intellectual disagreements to a cartoonlike symbolism.
While ridiculing Henry Luce as an out-of-touch Pope, Wolfe invests himself with
Calvin's rhetorical mantle, pouring withering scorn on Luce's idealized idols.

"The Cape" sets forth the geographical and cultural background of Canaveral
peninsula with its drag racing, formidable insects, and midnight drinking. It
deftly probes how John Glenn's righteous piety began to drive a wedge in the
solidarity of the astronauts. "The Thrones," set at Edward Air Force base in
California, examines the slow-developing Mercury Project along with the fierce
competition among pilots with the X15 series of rocket jets. To give a sense
of the historical importance of the project, Wolfe notes an analogy between the
project of Christopher Columbus and the Mercury project—in both cases it was
the invention of recent technology which permitted these exploratory endeavors: In the case of Columbus, "the recent invention of his day, the magnetic
compass,"[22] and the contemporary invention of high-speed computers. That's
a sensible off-the-cuff journalistic analogy, but the magnetic compass for navigation was invented long before Columbus—it dates back to seventh-century
China.[23] Wolfe flies at his best in charting history as he dangles facts and thrilling
anecdotes in his presentation of difficult engineering problems. The "thrones"
on a literal level are seats for both the X15 pilots and the Mercury astronauts
during their g-force gravity training. Wolfe recounts how both the pilots and

astronauts won the day in forcing reluctant engineers to make improvements in their flying vessels. In a symbolic way these practical flyers become the angelic thrones driving innovative research.

"The Vote" refers to the peer vote which was taken to select the first astronaut, but the point of view chosen to describe this event and result takes the first-person point of view of John Glenn, thus giving this chapter a novelistic angle until the subject of how *Life* magazine covered the public announcement of the top three astronauts, then the point of view shifts to the Other Four as they react to the inanity of *Life* magazine's coverage. This may sound jarring, but Wolfe is an expert at shifting gears when he's cruising at top speed. The title may also refer to the unspoken vote of the NASA bureaucracy to pull together and work hard during the pressure of the space race with Russia.

"Righteous Prayer" recounts the story of Al Shepard's ascent atop the Redstone rocket to become the first American in suborbital flight for five minutes. Wolfe portrays Shepard as a schizophrenic: One minute he's Smilin' Al, the next he's the Icy Commander. Wolfe's focus centers upon the comic incongruity of Smilin' Al's lower class sense of humor and the serious enormity of the project he's involved in. Shepard becomes a fictive and nearly diabolic antihero, a veritable prankster who will do anything for a laugh, in contrast to the more dependable and more moral hero of the novelistic angle that the book favors—the virtuous and patriotic John Glenn. Despite Wolfe's satire on Henry Luce's homogenous group presentation of the astronauts, they both agree on their perception of John Glenn as the all-American hero worthy of great admiration. But since we are stuck with the usurper to Glenn's throne for the first American trip into space, Wolfe plays a comic cartoon, retailing Shepard's pranks and jokes. Just before the launch John Glenn had left a small note on the instrument panel, saying: "No Handball Playing in This Area," but removed it after he saw Shepard laugh because he knew the television cameras would see it.[24]

When it comes to the launch itself, Wolfe highlights the danger involved while he deflates any notion of heroism on the part of Shepard by dramatizing the astronaut's need to urinate when the launch is delayed for over four hours:[25] This adolescent humor occupies six bladder-pulsing pages and the urination eventually finds its earthy analogy in the eruption of the volcano Krakatoa. During this time we hear the imaginary, fictive refrain that the chapter's title alludes to: *"Please, dear Lord, don't let me fuck up."*[26] Such blasphemy and self-centered egotism comes across as the opposite of what the reader would expect from the hero, John Glenn, who stands loyally as a spear carrier at Shepard's side, humbly and wittily encouraging Shepard in selfless solidarity when it's clear to everyone that they are really enemies. For the chapter on Glenn's flight the stream-of-consciousness runs as "Please, dear God, don't let me foul up."[27] I don't mean to say that Wolfe is not being representative of each person's personality—he merely takes novelistic liberties in his comic exaggerations.

For the experience of the launch itself Wolfe engages in his own dramatic schizophrenia with an effort to draw a farcical comedy that will denigrate Shepard. At one moment Wolfe satirizes the May 5th launch as a "precreated experience" that appears not to be realistic[28] and hence not heroic because rigorous training has rendered it completely anticlimatic, then he resorts to thrilling the reader with situations that are unexpected,[29] yet in the process he ridicules both the tawdry ineptitude of the space capsule's engineering and Shepard's inability to perform all the tasks assigned to him within a few minutes despite the arduous and repetitive rehearsals. The last paragraph of the chapter recounts Shepard's visual view of the helicopter landing on an aircraft carrier after the pickup at sea: the tone mocks the adulation Shepard is about to receive, for the reader is to realize that the country's mass patriotism has been a Henry Luce con—the feeble capsule accomplished little and everyone blindly cheers not a true patriotic hero but an unrighteous impostor who has just peed all over himself. Wolfe has served Luce his antidote by delivering the real behind-the-scenes portrait of an astronaut without angel wings who was "on . . . the Pope's balcony."[30]

This derisive and clownish portrait of Al Shepard was not shared by fellow astronaut Michael Collins, whom Norman Mailer thought to be the coolest and most eloquent of all the astronauts.[31] Collins thought "Big Al," as he was known, the shrewdest of the astronauts and noted that he was the only one to grow rich, saying of him: "No teddy bear, Al can put down friend or foe alike with searing stare or caustic comment."[32] Yet this does not sound like the Icy Commander tag applied by Wolfe. Much of Al Shepard's subsequent financial success relates to his golf stunt on the moon—hitting the golf ball under weak gravity captivated the imagination of bankers, businessmen, and golf enthusiasts, so that genial Big Al reaped the rewards. Shepard was quoted as saying "The only compliant I have was the flight was not long enough."[33] Due to the poor design of Shepard's capsule and the shortness of his ballistic flight, he could not wax eloquent about what he saw, unlike the handsome Gagarin.[34]

That the Russians were so far advanced should not have been such a surprise to Americans because the Russian scientist Konstantin Tsiolkovski had theoretically solved all the important engineering difficulties of rocket spaceflight, including trajectories and the use of liquid oxygen and liquid hydrogen fuels, back in the 1880s, and his papers were eventually published in 1903, the year that the Wright brothers took off at Kitty Hawk.[35]

Despite the fact that the Russians were well ahead of America in the booster rocket game, both in lift power and rocket reliability, and had successfully launched the first astronaut, Yuri Gagarin, who had made a complete orbit of the earth on April 12, 1961, Americans appeared determined to catch up to the Russians, despite being so far behind:

> Gagarin had flown around the Earth for a total of 24,000 miles versus Shepard's 300. His Vostok spacecraft weighed 10,428 pounds in orbit, against Mercury's 2,100 pounds in suborbit. Gargarin spent about eighty-nine minutes in a state of weightlessness, Shepard five.[36]

President John F. Kennedy saw an opportunity in the space race to put the first man on the moon as a healthy tonic distraction from recent debacles. The announcement to Congress that we were to spend billions to get to the moon first, according to Wolfe, amounted to "delivering a new inaugural address" that provided the beginning of Kennedy's comeback from the Bay of Pigs disaster.[37]

Wolfe provides a short, superficial, panoramic shot about the astronauts' wives meeting Jackie Kennedy as a perk of their new social status, but cuts to a grainy closeup of the guys' (presumably excluding John Glenn) new state of schizophrenia—at one moment at the White House with the media corps popping their pictures for newspaper or magazine covers and then back to Low Rent Cape Canaveral at night with "Drinking & Driving" near dawn in the "Aboriginal Grit" of their primitive and lewd underclass vocabulary.[38] A novelistic scene of a nameless low-rent pilot in a tawdry dinner at the edge of nowhere is conjured in lurid Technicolor.

Gus Grissom had a new capsule with windows and a hand controller, but because Shepard failed to flip one of many switches during the intense g-forces of re-entry, the engineers severely reduced the number of switches, putting as many as possible on automatic. Because the chimpanzee in the previous test flight had made all the switches, Wolfe presented Shepard as a clown by way of imaginative farce, so how does Wolfe respond to Grissom whose flight was, in fact, a fiasco? By sticking to the facts, of course—no need for any novelistic apparatus! "The Unscrewable Pooch" refers to the Mercury capsule. In the chimpanzee test flight the chimp had been bolted into the capsule and had waited for the capsule to be retrieved to a ship where the bolts were then unscrewed. Naturally, this had horrified the pilots and they agitated for an ejection system like they were accustomed to having on a jet fighter. So the engineers made the change and it worked well with Shepard's recovery. Grissom's recovery should have been much easier because he was actually on target for the splashdown, but he spent an extra five minutes fidgeting in the capsule while the helicopter hovered patiently above him; he was either searching for a souvenir hunting knife (his story sounds like an alibi to me) or perhaps removing the condom and woman's girdle that he was saddled with because the wizard engineers had forgotten about Shepard's urination problem until the last moment. The end result of his wiggling in the holster (as Wolfe calls it) was to accidentally set off the ejection door. With the water pouring in, Grissom panicked and swam out without closing the oxygen valve in his space suit. The suit was supposed to act like a super lifebelt and keep him afloat, but water poured into the suit and he began to drown, often pulled under by the rolls of souvenir dimes that he had packed his pockets with. (I presume the plan was to give some out to friends and then use them for a hundred times their value at a bar where they could be framed.) Wolfe's account of the comedy remains all the more amusing because it is strictly factual. He then buttresses his account from Betty Grissom's dissident memoir *Starfall.* Although the scientists lost the capsule with its valuable data, the trip had been declared a success because Gus was still alive and the admission of failure in the political climate was not an option. So the brass had to honor Gus, now suddenly known among other astronauts by the lower status nickname of *Little* Gus,[39] yet management wanted to let him know of their displeasure by humiliating his wife and kids. Betty Grissom, to her credit, refused to take what they wanted to dish out and Wolfe doesn't hesitate to dramatize sympathy for Betty.

The chapter's title refers to the capsule, but it also refers to panic breakdown Grissom displayed in his behavior when he blew the capsule door and his subsequent hysteria on the helicopter ride back. Although treated in public as a god, Little Gus, when he looked into the mirror knew that the letters of his public divinity ran backward—dog, pouch with the loose screws: "Since the pouch proved to be unscrewable, officially, and Gus Grissom's flight was therefore on the record as a success, NASA was suddenly in great shape. John Kennedy was happy."[40] Kennedy desperately wanted a man on the moon before the Russians and any progress was welcome and would ensure further funding.

There is a larger unthinking cultural sentimentality that Wolfe attacks in the Press of the day—not only dimwitted but crassly insensitive. Wolfe, in somewhat novelistic fashion, depicts the panic of Annie Glenn who suffered from a stutter as the Animal mob of the press besieges her house and puts her on the spot with a mike on the morning of January 27, 1962, when John was inserted into the capsule. Outside her house sits Vice President Lyndon Johnson who wants to grab national attention by conducting a personal interview with Annie. He plans to jettison the *Life* magazine reporter in the house and let all news media present in to cover him with the petrified Annie. Neither Johnson nor his aides know that Annie has a stutter and Johnson fumes hotly inside his air-conditioned limo while he insults his staff for not being able to get this woman to cooperate with government business.

In a panic Annie tried to call John. Because the flight was postponed due to fierce cloud cover, John was told to call her back and tell her to cooperate, but he does the opposite, telling her not to let the Vice President inside their house if she doesn't want him there with his media circus. Glenn tells his NASA boss Webb that Webb is *way out of line*.[41] As in a novel, Wolfe puts us inside Webb's head while he examines his options, none of which appeal to him. When he realizes that this would have to go to the President, he gives up, convinced that the President would side with Glenn. While this whole scene is painted with fictional technique, it remains one of the best scenes of the book in terms of realistic comic drama, and it is also pivotal for setting up the book's climax.

For the launch and orbital ride we get a dramatic moment-by-moment narration. This, by far the longest chapter, is the climax the book has been building up to: the first orbital view over Earth. But oddly enough, Wolfe works hard to make this event anticlimatic by emphasizing that Glenn's training has put everything into a ho-hum mode—I've done all this before in training, including pictures of the sights I'm supposed to see and it all looks like the training drills. Wolfe's prose even borders on the drab as it's some dusty bureaucratic file that's not particularly interesting but has historic importance. The reader even *feels* disappointed and out of boredom begins to read more quickly. But we are being emotionally conditioned by the author, setup for the real fireworks climax.

The conventional climax depicts John Glenn as heroic, unfazed by danger, ready to face death. When he lands on the carrier deck sailors outline his wet footsteps with white paint. While Al Shepard was invited to the White House, John F. Kennedy himself greets Glenn when he touches down at the Patrick landing strip. Neither danger nor fame will turn John's head. The real climax is his deportment after becoming a celebrity. Like a potentate of state he addresses a joint session of Congress:

> That was where the tears started.... He said some things that nobody else in the world could have gotten away with, even in 1962. He said: "I still get a lump in my throat when I see the American flag passing by." But he pulled it off! And then he lifted his hand up toward the gallery—this was in the House side of the Capitol—and five hundred pairs of Congressional eyes swung up with his hand to the gallery, and he introduced his mom and dad from New Concord, Ohio, and a few aunts and uncles for good measure, and then his children, and finally, "above all, I want you to meet my wife, Annie... Annie... *the Rock!*" Well, that did it. That turned on the waterworks. Senators and representatives were trying to clap and reach for their handkerchiefs at the same time.[42]

That is the genuine climax. America had found its answer to Yuri Gagarin! John Glenn became the hero who inspired a nation to push forward with the space race. Productivity shot up. Americans were now certain that they could beat the Russians. The chapter title "The Tears" is straight patriotism and not ironic as previous chapter titles—reversal! And now Wolfe's exercise in satire comes to an end with this reversal. As with "The Unspoken Thing" chapter in *The Electric Kool-Aid Acid Test* where Wolfe unburdens himself of his skeptical take on Ken Kesey and begins identifying with him, so, too, Wolfe identifies with John Glenn in this moment of patriotic transcendence.

John F. Kennedy is cast in an intensely patriotic and humble light as he presents John Glenn at the White House to his father, the famous bear Joe Kennedy, who, because of a stroke has one side of his body paralyzed—he's wheelchair bound, he can't speak to Glenn, he replies with tears: "That was what the sight of John Glenn did to Americans at that time. It primed them for the tears. And those tears ran like a river all over America. It was an extraordinary thing, being the sort of mortal who brought tears to other men's eyes."[43] On the one hand, the sentimentality of such patriotism was not connected to reality. Glenn's flight did establish that the United States could briefly put a man in orbit, but America was far behind the Soviets who, just sixteen days after Grissom's flight (six months before Glenn), lofted Gherman Titov for twenty-four hours with seventeen full orbits around the earth, thrice over the United States. The press had labeled, in all solemnity, the Russian lead as the *space gap*, a phrase brimming with ludicrous tautology. On the other hand, Wolfe dramatizes scenes that galvanize the better qualities of Americans, and John Glenn, not politicians, is the divine transforming instrument that unites this country to overtake the Russians in the space race. The heartland hero has defied his superiors, conquered space, Congress, and famously skeptical New York City where the right stuff lives. Just as in the Frank Sinatra song "New York, New York," that's where one makes it—even the Grateful Dead band admits that New York City is where they made it.[44] The

tears shed are joyful, patriotic tears, the real stuff America is made of. During
the New York ticker-tape parade even the cops cry tears:

> They knew it had to do with the presence, the aura, the radiation of *the right stuff,*
> the same vital force of manhood that had made millions vibrate and resonate
> thirty-five years to Lindbergh—except that in this case it was heightened by
> Cold War patriotism, the greatest surge of patriotism since the Second World
> War.... Somehow, extraordinary as it was, it was... right! The way it should
> be! The unutterable aura of the right stuff had been brought into the terrain
> *where things were happening!* Perhaps that was what New York existed for, to
> celebrate those who *had it,* whatever it was, and there was nothing like the right
> stuff, for all responded to it, and all wanted to be near it and to feel the sizzle
> and to blink in the light.
>
> Oh, it was a primitive and profound thing! Only pilots truly had it, but the
> entire world responded, and no one knew its name![45]

The idea that only pilots knew the phrase is an unlikely conjecture and Wolfe's
formulation here sounds like an echo of Ken Kesey saying, "They know *where* it
is, but they don't know *what* it is."[46] The phrase *the right stuff* becomes a patriotic
paean of New York City, the locus of the right stuff, the place where people who
have the right stuff can afford to live, and the place where reporters like Tom
Wolfe, Gay Talese, Jimmy Breslin, and Norman Mailer live. Wolfe's a reporter
extraordinaire who has the *right stuff,* whatever mysterious and independent
ineffability that represents!

"The Operational Stuff" covers John Glenn's friendship with *both* John F.
Kennedy and Lyndon Johnson, the operational sidelining of Deke Slayton due
to possible heart problems, and the orbits of Scott Carpenter and Wally Schirra.
It also ridicules John F. Kennedy's attempt to get a black astronaut into space.
NASA was not happy with Scott Carpenter's performance. He had spent too
much fuel playing around on his first orbit and it was questionable whether he
had enough fuel to get back at all. NASA doubted it. Carpenter's re-entry angle
was nine degrees off and he landed 250 miles off target. When covering the
event Walter Cronkite announced that we might have lost an astronaut after
radio contact was lost for a long time. Carpenter thought he had done a great
job on manual in his descent to avoid certain death. Management thought he
was totally irresponsible, a fighter-pilot whacko. Neither he nor Slayton were
invited down to Houston when NASA moved there. In contrast, Wally Schirra's
performance was cool, more relaxed, and more competent than *any* (even Glenn's)
of the previous flights in his six orbits:

> Schirra named his capsule *Sigma* 7, and there you had it. Scott Carpen-
> ter had named his *Aurora* 7... *Aurora*... the rosy dawn... the dawn of the
> intergalactic age... the unknowns, the mystery of the universe... the mu-
> sic of the spheres... Petrarch on the mountain top... and all that. Whereas
> *Sigma*... *Sigma* was a purely engineering symbol. It stood for the summation,
> the solution of the problem. Unless he had come right out and named the capsule

Operational, he couldn't have chosen a better name. For the purpose of Schirra's flight was to prove that Carpenter's need not have happened. Schirra would make six orbits—twice as many as Carpenter—and yet use half as much fuel and land right on target. Whatever did not have to do with that goal tended to be eliminated from the flight. The flight of *Sigma 7* was designed to be Armageddon . . . the final and decisive rout of the forces of experimental science in the manned space program. And that it was.[47]

In light of Scott's self-indulgent performance, the grandiose name of his capsule appears pompously boasting: the rosy dawn refers to the often repeated Homeric transitional tag from *The Odyssey*; the dawn of the intergalactic age alludes to science fiction writing like that of Arthur C. Clarke or Isaac Asimov; the unknown, the mystery of the universe refers most probably to Eastern thought; the music of the spheres alludes to Pythagorean Theory (sixth century B.C.) and is referred to in Shakespeare's *Twelfth-Night* (III, i, 122), A*nthony and Cleopatra* (V, ii, 85), and *Pericles* (V, i, 231); Petrarch refers to his famous essay "On the Ascent to Mount Ventoux" where he appreciates the beauty of the view as a consumer aesthetic and, in effect, inventing tourism.[48] Wolfe effectively deflates everything down to common diction. Schirra's textbook flight was what NASA had wanted from the astronauts; yet in practice it minimized the human element as well as the scientific, while it proved that many more orbits were feasible. Schirra had landed even nearer to his aircraft carrier than Glenn. Wolfe expertly extracts much humor from describing many of Schirra's witty and hilarious pranks before the successful flight.

"The Club" refers to, on the one hand, the club that the astronauts wives form; on the other hand, it tells the story of how a new crop of upcoming astronauts were brought into the astronaut club; and it also refers to the fact that Gordon Cooper joins the elite club of Glenn and Schirra through his amazing performance. While Glenn experienced some difficulties and his pilot abilities were demanded, Cooper's *Faith 7* experienced the limit of difficulties, the so-called pushing the outer envelope. Cooper's flight was thirty-four hours and twenty-two orbits to Glenn's three orbits, and Cooper performed in the coolest and most relaxed way, but his urine floating about the capsule shorted out all the electronics. With no operating dials at all Cooper had to do everything manually: eyeball his angle of descent (the most critical aspect of re-entry), fire engines at the right time, eject his capsule parachute at the right altitude without any altitude indicators, etc. If there was any doubt that a pilot was needed as a backup for automated systems, then this was the moment of truth, and Cooper performed with ease and astonishing accuracy: "No one could deny it . . . no brethren, old or new, could fail to see it . . . when the evil wind was up, Ol' Gordo had shown the world the pure and righteous stuff."[49] While Glenn's flight furnishes the emotional climax of the book, Cooper provides the resolution of the pilot versus passenger theme—he even splashed down closer to the aircraft carrier than Schirra! A real pilot provides emergency backup. Like Glenn, Cooper addressed both Houses of Congress.

"The High Desert" concludes the subplot of the book, which concerns the development of the X-14, X-15, and X-20 piloted rocket series at Edwards Air Force Base in the California desert that came near to challenging the Houston astronaut project. While this motif wends its way in and out of various chapters, the subject is treated strictly along journalistic lines. For the climax of this subplot, Wolfe presents a novelistic re-creation of Chuck Yeager's attempt to break the Russian altitude record of 113, 890 feet set in 1961 with the E-66A, a delta-winged fighter plane.[50] In a bravura run of six pages punctuated by ellipses, Wolfe narrates from Yeager's point of view his near-death experience after he hits 108,000 feet and the rocket fails. As a read, these pages are the most thrilling ascent of Wolfe's prose in the book. And it is a real thrill. Yeager's re-entry survival remains an astonishing miracle. Yeager's flight ended the X-20 experiment. This is a fitting and stirring conclusion to the heroic spirit of those fighters in a bygone age before the world and its population became dominated by computers. If Glenn was the emotional and patriotic hero, and Cooper the suave perfectionist performer, then Chuck Yeager was the living incarnation of the heroic mystique of the right stuff.

As with *The Electric Kool-Aid Acid Test, The Right Stuff* provides a short, nostalgic epilogue. We are told that the Russians put the first cosmonaut woman, Valery Bykovsky, into space, and that Joe Walker took the X-15 up to 354,200 feet, or sixty-seven miles (seventeen miles into space). Wolfe notes that the Cold War had ended just before the assassination of John F. Kennedy and that Lyndon Johnson was determined to continue Kennedy's dream of putting a man on the moon.

That pilots ever used the phrase the right stuff remains highly dubious, and in his autobiography Yeager (from whom the phrase was purportedly derived) goes out of his way to imply that he never heard the phrase among pilots and that the phrase does not make much sense to him as a pilot:

> Ever since Tom Wolfe's book was published, the question I'm asked most often and which always annoys me is whether I think I've got "the right stuff." I know that golden trout have the right stuff, and I've seen a few gals here and there that I'd bet had it in spades, but those words seem meaningless when used to describe a pilot's attributes. The question annoys me because it implies that a guy who has 'the right stuff' was born that way. I was born with unusually good eyes and coordination. I was mechanically orientated, understood machines easily. My nature was to stay cool in tight spots. Is that 'the right stuff'? All I know is that I worked my tail off to learn to fly, and worked hard at it all the way. And in the end, the one big reason why I was better than average as a pilot was because I flew more than anybody else. If there is such a thing as "the right stuff" in piloting, then it is experience.[51]

Chuck Yeager, whom Wolfe admired so much, was hired as an advisor to the movie *The Right Stuff* (1983) and enjoyed that experience greatly, the visibility of which helped him recharge his fame. It remains unclear where Tom Wolfe heard the phrase "the right stuff," but its populist and mysterioso ambiguity resonates in a culture where inarticulate adults refer to objects and concepts in their life as things and stuff. The book was certainly an attempt by Wolfe to reach a larger audience than with his previous writings. The phrase itself plays an effective dramatic function in the book, especially when employed in the contest concerning individual freedom: Was the astronaut merely the passenger, a lab rat adjunct to computers, or was the astronaut the embodiment of a freedom-loving and patriotic hero? In "The Truest Sport: Jousting with Sam and Charlie," Wolfe had indentified this mystique among Navy fighter pilots as "the ineffable . . . *it.*"[52]

Wolfe's work on fighter pilots and astronauts has stood the test of time and the scrutiny of other journalists. Norman Sims notes that in 1982 when he interviewed longtime *New Yorker* writer John McPhee, he complimented the accuracy of *The Right Stuff.* McPhee said that while he was working on his own book about aircraft, *The Deltoid Pumpkin Seed* (1973), he had spoken with several authorities on the subject who told him that "Wolfe was completely correct in his reporting."[53]

As subject matter for a novelistic approach to journalism, there is an obvious link between the choice of Ken Kesey, John Glenn, and Chuck Yeager as heroes—all were superpatriots. Kesey the outsider tried to take American culture "further" through the legal popularization of LSD on the road, while Glenn the mainstream straight-shooter went into orbit to galvanize American patriotism at a crucial moment in history, and Chuck Yeager was the underappreciated hero who worked far from the limelight. Kesey's experiments stimulate West Coast creativity in the arts, while Glenn's experience becomes a model for successful leadership; Yeager's dedication, tenacity, and skill becomes the model for all gritty operational achievements that make this country great. While Kesey monastically renounces success, Glenn and Wolfe embrace it; Yeager remains indifferent to it, but in an ironic cultural twist, it is Yeager's influence through language, his drawling speech and humor, which has the most lasting impact on the culture of this country. In a similar way, it was not Kesey himself who became the enduring voice of the counterculture—it was his house band, the Grateful Dead, who through three decades wrought changes in the consciousness of many Americans that communes, peace groups, political organization, other bands, experimental art or film groups could not accomplish.[54]

In an oblique way both journalistic novels are companion pieces in charting the extremes of American patriotism during the early sixties. The ex-Marine Ken Babbs once said: "We talked about being astronauts of inner space."[55] One might even see these two novelistic works of journalism as diptychs of early sixties America depicting heroes who in their patriotic confidence had a superior *esprit de corps*—as evidenced in their mutual playful obsession with pranks. Of course, these two strains of grass-roots patriotism collided in the late 1960s with much turmoil and unrest, the fallout from which has left Americans quite divided. But it would be a misperception that the middle-class Pranksters and the military were fundamentally opposed. When both camps united, the Vietnam War ended. The central disagreement in American politics remains how to deal with the desires of the investment class and business managers. Should the military be used to expand the empire and reap related economic benefits that might be passed down to all, or should the business class be encouraged to reinvest in the infrastructure and lifestyle of its workers?

Ken Kesey, Ken Babbs, and Robert Hunter (Grateful Dead lyricist) all worked for the military as LSD research subjects, concluding that *they* not the military psychologists had mastered the proper uses of the drug. Kesey said: "I took these drugs as an *American*."[56] Hence Kesey's obsessive flying of the American flag. The military had been interested in the drug as either a truth drug for use in interrogation or an aerial spray to induce paranoia in enemy troops. Military research on the drug continued for so long because they could not obtain consistent results in their tests. Having mastered the drug, Kesey wanted to make it public as a patriotic act like freedom of the press: hence his version of the public tests. None of the Pranksters came out of the old American left nor did they have any relationship with the Communist Party or any other party in America. They thought Americans could go "further" in liberty, equality, and brotherhood, and much further in creativity, but they had no international agenda. Kesey's antiunion novel, *Sometimes a Great Notion*, could even be construed as an emerging neoconservative strain in American fiction.

Wolfe's obsession with patriotism and the public good attracted him to the subject matter of these two books. Once LSD was made illegal and the assassination of ethnic leaders became commonplace, a great divide opened up: Was this country to concentrate on the extension of liberty to the greatest number or was the growing populace to be kept in check by fear and repression? To many Americans the option of freedom for the masses appeared to sanction self-indulgence, especially with regard to sex, drugs, and racial mingling. The blatantly unselfish model of the military appeared to be the more heroic and patriotic model. These astronauts and pilots patriotically *volunteered* to die for their country. Such volunteering appeared to elicit the greatest heroism, and so Wolfe's book became a public argument for an all-volunteer military that would not be beholden to the interests of lower middleclass citizens, but be at the service of the business class that wished to extend the American way of life across the globe in the name of manifest destiny: Americans as the chosen people of God would bring their good news to the world and part of that good news was the structural models and methods of its business community.

The Right Stuff confirms Wolfe's drift toward neoconservative elitism. On the one hand, Wolfe would accept the freedom-loving innovations of Russian expressionists and adapt the Prankster's approach of multiple techniques to creative journalism, while eventually perceiving the middleclass sensibility of the Pranksters as an anarchic threat to the stability of American society, much as the Bolsheviks perceived the creative innovations of the Brothers Serapion to be a threat to the stability of Russian society. Wolfe saw virtue, stability, and continuity in the American Puritan tradition and he most likely saw nothing but self-indulgence and self-destruction in the path his friend Hunter S. Thompson took. As a journalist, Wolfe can lay claim to the fact that in these two books he documented, explained from within, and dramatized from within the significant cultural forces in the crucial period of the early sixties that formed and influenced this country for the next fifty years. I don't know that any other writer can make that claim. Wolfe had found *The Right Stuff* extremely difficult to write "because there was no central character, no protagonist,"[57] yet he set new standards in journalism for accuracy and dramatic entertainment.

CHAPTER 6

ICONOCLASTIC CULTURE SHREDDING

> Unless there is a revolution on 43rd Street, and it isn't likely, The New
> Yorker as we have known it has had it as a cultural force.
>
> —Seymour Krim

In a 1965 *Herald Tribune* Sunday Supplement *New York*, Wolfe mocks the *New Yorker's* editor William Shawn for his secretiveness and legendary reclusiveness in contrast to the good taste and gregarious habits of Shawn's predecessor, Harold Ross, who was a Westerner from Colorado; the magazine receives a drubbing as being "the most successful suburban woman's magazine in the country."[1] Wolfe ridicules its internal bureaucratic memo system and laments the doily-table mind-set that excluded America's best writers in "Tiny Mummies! The True Story of the Ruler of 43rd Street's Land of the Walking Dead." The rambling but hilarious attack shook up the literary establishment and even garnered a call from the White House. Wolfe primarily ridicules the magazine's suffocating dullness, its incestuous in-family staff, and donnish habits as he sends up the publication for its snobbish pretentions and dedicated mediocrity. An attack on *The New Yorker* was really nothing new—in 1962 Seymour Krim had published one in his magazine *Nugget*, but it had a small circulation among cultural leftists. Wolfe's article was not only larger in scale and sweep, but his salvo roared in a magazine with a large circulation. Wolfe repeats and amplifies many of Krim's charges, even attacking the advertising, while piling on other charges. One choice sentence of Krim's article presages the tone and spirit of Wolfe's more eloquent attack:

> Never had a magazine in this country devoted such theatrical care to the sub-
> tleties of communication, carefulness, tact, finally draining the spirit of its staff

down to the microscopic beauty of a properly placed comma and ultimately paralyzing them in static detail and selfconscious poise, the original ideal of perfection having become in the late 50s and now 60s a perversion instead of a furthering of the journalist's duty to render reality.[2]

Wolfe's sequel the following week, "Lost in the Whichy Thickets: *The New Yorker*" continues the assault with mimetic dialogue that dramatizes William Shawn's stutter and provides a lengthy roll call of great American writers excluded from the *New Yorker*. Wolfe's articles with some corrections and a new postscript find themselves reprinted in *Hooking Up*, yet one of the reasons for legs in the controversy is that "the articles contained so many errors; *New Yorker* historian Ben Yagoda recently wrote that 'almost every time [Wolfe] attempted to state a fact about the workings of the magazine, he got it wrong.' Some seem corrected here, but most do not."[3] Wolfe's second article mentions a recent worthy item, *The New Yorker's* serial publication of Truman Capote's *In Cold Blood* (1965), a documentary novel he acclaims as an exception to the staid claustrophobia of the magazine's usual fare; this ameliorating note mirrors Seymour Krim's comment of recently applauding, as an exception, James Baldwin's "Letter from a Region in My Mind" as a worthy piece.

Wolfe confesses in his second muckraking attack (in style a bit less flashy) his admiration for the hard-edged journalism of Lillian Ross and, in particular, a piece she did about Hemingway stomping the pavement of Gotham: "This story gave a wonderful picture of this big egomaniac garruling around the town and batting everybody on the head with his ego as if it were a pig bladder."[4] The pig bladder allusion derives from the third book of Jonathan Swift's *Gulliver's Travels* where in Laputa the philosophers require assistants to help them remember to micturate and they do this by prodding them with a pig's bladder. (The assistants were called flappers and during the 1920s jazz age some irreverent girls from Wellesley College dubbed themselves flappers, since their fuddy-duddy teachers appeared to have lost contact with their senses and required some elementary prodding.) The reason I call attention to the detail of the pig bladder allusion is that it tells us something important about Wolfe: He is a well-educated and sometimes irreverent critic of high culture. He did not attack *The New Yorker* because it was high culture (which is how many might have misunderstood what he was doing), but because *The New Yorker* had descended into the twilight of frumpy middle-class culture with the false *pretense* of being Old World culture, the same bourgeois flaw that had enraged Krim.

Norman Sims notes that in 1965 most readers took Wolfe's attack on *The New Yorker* as an aspect of the rebellious New Journalism, but that these two pieces were really Wolfe's entry into the field of cultural criticism and as such are more closely related to Wolfe's essays on art and architecture.[5] I would add Wolfe's later *Harper's* essay on the novel, as well as a few essays collected in *Hooking Up*. From the start Wolfe practiced an iconoclastic assault on the received and dominant tastes in literature, painting, architecture, and sculpture; he sought to challenge current trends by championing older, traditional styles in the arts, styles from the late nineteenth century which were also very much admired by Kesey and the Pranksters.

Wolfe's attack on Shawn was personal, something that prefigured his later, more melodramatic, attack on Bernstein, but it also centered upon Shawn as the gatekeeper, the arbiter of taste who would decide what trends in the arts were important—that is, Wolfe despised the mind-set behind what choices were made at the *New Yorker* which to him advocated a pseudorespectability addicted to mediocre formulas.

With *The Painted Word* (1975) Wolfe was to identify a more general yet specific culprit of cultural conformity: A fashionable theory factory in the postmodern critical writings of Harold Rosenberg and Clement Greenberg that advocated flat abstract art in such an exclusive way it appeared as a repressive dogma, stultifying the development of the visual arts throughout the country and confining orthodoxy in painting to New York City. Wolfe quickly glosses over the sudden rejection of representation art just after 1900 by a host of noted painters without discussing the near simultaneous experiment in Russia by Kandinsky or the wide experimentation in the Netherlands by painters like Piet Mondrian. Mondrian slowly moved from representational painting to an abstract geometrical mode that presented representation as a fading ghost before moving toward a stricter and flatter abstract modality. Mondrian was clearly motivated by a quest for beauty in experimentation—as was Kandinsky, although Kandinsky's more collagelike style welded his sense of beauty to a less obvious mystic spirituality rooted in the primitive and obscure northern tribe that inspired his art.

Locating the triumphant transference of flat abstract art to Manhattan after the war, Wolfe identifies two villains: the critics Harold Rosenberg and Clement Greenberg. Both naturally saw that the implosion and devastation of Europe ceded the leadership of European art to America, yet they constructed intricate miniature fads around philosophical theories, which led to a local New York City market that they could dominate and control while the public at large was excluded. So a small priestly class of critics controlled what was orthodox and what was acceptable at a select number of galleries. What was dogmatically excluded was any form of representation. For someone whose hobby it was to sketch humorous cartoons, this appeared irrational. Moreover, what irked Wolfe the most was that such pure abstractionism excluded social commentary, the primary role of the artist in any society. The heroes of Wolfe's narrative are the painters Jasper Johns and Robert Rauschenberg, along with the critic Leo Steinberg who "finished off Abstract Expressionism."[6] Pop art with its quirky admission of realism and unconventional humor made an end run around the high priests of theory who created a special backdoor dispensation for pop art.

Wolfe denies that the category of Op art—he identifies it as "Perceptual Abstraction" and provides a reproduction of Bridget Riley's 1964 painting *Current*, which presents the theme of currents as inherently and paradoxically producing counter-currents, as an example of such art.[7] The work of the English artist Bridget Riley from the early 1960s and the work of the American artist Henry Pearson from the early 1950s were very influential in the development of popular

Day-Glo patterns in the late 1960s, the kind of art that appealed to Kesey and the Merry Pranksters. While Riley's work *did* originate from experiments in pure abstraction, Pearson's work, which appears to have slightly preceded Riley's, originated in Pearson's work for the Navy in topographical maps. Pearson was extraordinarily nearsighted and he worked with wavy lines of minute detail, while Riley's work concentrated on larger visual paradoxes of a conceptual nature. Pearson's late work connects the motif of topographical maps to the earliest prehistorical inscriptions found around the globe, both in the New World and in China, India, and Europe. Pearson's illustrations for *Seamus Heaney: Poems and a Memoir* presents a good example of this style of work as he links patterns inscribed on prehistoric burial chambers in Ireland to the lyrics of the contemporary poet. Pearson's thematic obsession was that all art from the prehistoric to the contemporary becomes the universal expression of humankind's entombment in the earth and the ardent wish to escape and memorialize that entombment.[8]

At all of his gallery openings Pearson served Amontillado sherry in a clear allusion to Edgar Allan Poe's short story, "The Cask of Amontillado," an amusing story about live entombment. At the beginning of his career, Pearson's wavy abstraction of geographical lines alluded to the death of soldiers on the battlefield and as such was a form of antiwar pacifist art because his own work in geographical maps for the Navy led directly to the death of soldiers, since such maps were principally used for artillery purposes or aircraft bombings. On the other hand, Pearson sometimes used nearly invisible tremors in lines as well as larger conceptual patterns to indicate an erotic atmosphere in the manner of a hypersensitive seismographic machine or the meandering qualities of water found in Taoist paintings.[9]

Although Pearson's art belongs to the abstract movement, his sinuous lines convey great emotional resonance and his work contains definite social commentary. Riley's experiments remain more cerebral and don't appear to contain much social commentary, yet they are intellectually engaging and often ironic. For Wolfe to chose the English artist to illustrate his point and ignore the local Manhattan artist (who was a Yale alumnus) indicates a selective disingenuousness that skewers his presentation. The complexity of the problems Wolfe addresses cannot be completely fair in such a brief essay because the sensational and melodramatic manner adopted by Wolfe puts forth the cartoon contest of heroes against villains, yet Wolfe's simplified dialectic does manage to clearly dramatize a fundamental controversy.

Wolfe had some self-righteous ground to stand upon in his rhetorical attack on theory and its taboo on representational art. While Wolfe makes Jasper Johns a hero of the story, as he did with his essay "Bob and Spike" in *The Pump-House Gang*, he might have championed many other artists who were not as commercially successful. For example, an even more conservative realistic landscape painter like the Krakow-born Paul Jordan, a dissident lyrical expressionist, who drank with Jackson Pollock and William de Kooning at the Cedar Tavern. Jordan, whose work may be better known in France because of his work at the United Nations, opposed both Abstract Expression and Pop Art. While his early work

displayed the influence of Marc Chagall, Jordan championed the emotional content of landscapes through the use of harmonic color and sought to continue the
greater European tradition of landscape painting before the arrival of abstraction,
believing that art spoke through images, the point of view that Wolfe advocates
in his essay. Jordan's later work concentrated on landscapes in Venice (Italy),
Arizona, and upstate New York, achieving a personal but nearly invisible style
with a subtle idiosyncratic humor difficult to categorize.[10]

Although Wolfe restricts his discussion of the controversy to New York City,
the debate was at that time international in scope. To go further afield, one might
cite the then current rumpus of the Australian Antipodeans and their defense of
figurative art against abstract art.[11] One contemporary descendent of those Antipodeans whose exquisitely detailed paintings provide a historical and realistic
parallel to the sculpture of Frederick Hart whose work Wolfe enthusiastically
advocates[12] can be found in the work of the contemporary maritime painter
Richard Linton, a painter of historical scenes featuring astonishing microscopic
detail.

The artistic critical community to this day still frowns on the use of realism,
yet Wolfe's attack on the Manhattan critics helped to loosen New York City's
Mandarin orthodoxy, derisively called Cultureburg in the essay. Wolfe's main
point is that theory can never replace the *practice* of art and that the theories of
Abstract Expressionism abuse the right of the artist to use imagination in new
ways, as well as to explore and acquire new techniques. Wolfe's tirade presented
as an exposé is ultimately in defense of artistic freedom and against those "gatekeepers" (critics and museum curators) who attempt to restrict that freedom.
Work on this essay led Wolfe to suspect all aspects of postmodernism supported
by theory. Through his humor and concise writing, Wolfe was enormously successful in bringing this controversy to a wider public and thus encouraging those
artists still working in the figurative and representational styles of painting.

Yet the roots of experimental abstraction in both painting and literature really
go back to just before World War I. Instead of revisiting that period through
painting or literature, Wolfe wrote *From Bauhaus to Our House* (1981), an essay
attacking modernism and postmodernism in architecture. Wolfe thought that
the dominant influence of the Bauhaus school resulted in downtown city centers
of glass and steel boxes that made every American city appear drab and undistin-
guishable. Such unimaginative conformity restricted the creativity of architects
and reflected the conservative homogenization of a corporate culture afraid to be
different or make a statement not dedicated to blandness. Although most book
reviewers saw the essay as more revelatory of Wolfe's reactionary aesthetics,[13]
many saw it as an exercise in the argument of taste rather than a work of research
or reportage; some reviewers vigorously agreed with Wolfe's opinion. Christopher Lehmann-Haupt saw the essay as a popularization of Peter Blake's *Form
Follows Fiasco: Why Modern Architecture Hasn't Worked* (1977), which attacked the
Bauhaus school of Walter Gropius and his postmodern disciples Robert Venturi
and Vincent Scully.[14] Some nostalgia for Victorian architecture finds sympathy, yet Wolfe continues to be disturbed that Americans have not developed

their own distinctive architecture but have merely imported European theories to replicate. The essay concludes by applauding Robert Johnson's design of the Manhattan AT&T building without a flat top. Wolfe was correct in reflecting the considerable frustration and disappointment of numerous architects chained by the unimaginative orthodoxy of conformity. One had only to take a glance at some of the recent architecture pictured on television during the 2008 Summer Olympics in Beijing to see how a city landscape can be transformed into an exciting event outside of the restrictions of Bauhaus dogma.[15] The architecture critic Nicolai Ouroussoff also praised Bejing's new buildings, echoing Wolfe's critique of modernism: "No one wants to return to the deadly homogeneity associated with Modernism's tabula rasa planning strategies. The image of Le Corbusier hovering godlike above Paris ready to wipe aside entire districts and replace them with glass towers remains an emblem of Modernism's attack on the city's historical fabric."[16]

While *The Painted Word* and *Bauhaus* attacked dogmas of postmodernism and modernism, Wolfe published an article on literature, "Stalking the Billion-Footed Beast," that attacked both modernism and postmodernism in literature, but especially what Wolfe identified as a split in the practice of the novel around 1960, whereby the novel abandoned a sociological perspective in favor of more imaginative and creative approaches: "The strange fact of the matter was that young people with serious literary ambitions were no longer interested in the metropolis or any other big, rich slices of contemporary life."[17] Wolfe, sounding a bit like Mark Twain attacking Sir Walter Scott or James Fenimore Cooper for their lack of realism, claimed realism as the "high ground" of the novel and advised writers to return to a more sociological approach to the novel. Wolfe's essay caused quite a hubbub and he went on television and on the college lecture circuit to advocate his thesis. Wolfe is an entertaining debater and he made quite a splash with this essay.

Many people pointed out that the realistic novel had not died and that realism was just one technique that a postmodern novelist might employ. Furthermore, many postmodern American writers have written novels strictly in the realistic vein, and that approach remains often favored by historical novelists like Thomas Gallagher, Thomas Flanagan, and Charles Frazier. After World War II, realism continued to thrive in the novels of John O'Hara, Robert Penn Warren, Mary McCarthy, James Baldwin, Saul Bellow, Nelson Algren, Truman Capote, Chester Himes, John Cheever, William Styron, and Gore Vidal. Accomplished writers like Peter Matthiessen, Anne Tyler, Raymond Carver, Andre Dubus, Louis Auchincloss, Gloria Naylor, Pete Hamill, Amy Tan, Gish Jen, Ward Just, Ha Jin, and Tim Gautreaux, as well as others, continue to explore realism in varied ways. Realism within the confines of the short story has proved particularly enduring, but most Americans traditionally prefer novels to short stories because of a preference for prolixity—they have an intellectual insecurity about density.

What Wolfe argued in his essay on realism was his own personal taste and practice, just as he had in all of his previous essays on culture. In many ways the essay was a defense of his version of realism and sociology as it appeared in *The Bonfire of the Vanities*—just as Wolfe had published an argumentative defense of his techniques employed in *The Electric Kool-Aid Acid Test* in the extended essay that introduces *The New Journalism*, which makes the similar claim that realism itself is the *sine qua non* of literature. Here he argues for the significance, techniques, and popularity of his own approach to the novel. As in all of these essays on culture, Wolfe had a fundamental, excellent point he exaggerated into an Archimedean lever that would thrust the issue into the public stage of debate, thus bringing popular attention to cultural questions, much like the unpredictable Ken Kesey who practiced a different brand of prankster improvisation. Both Wolfe and Kesey were gadflies who enjoyed challenging the parameters of conventional thought. Wolfe learned from Kesey how "not to play their game," how to ask and debate questions outside of any traditional frame and bring that cultural debate to a larger public—to draw that public into your "movie" rather than be the unconscious actor in society's movie—in short, to live outside the shadows of Plato's cave and see life in sunlight.

CHAPTER 7

VANITY RAGS

New York is really a bonfire of vanity.... This is the human comedy.
—Tom Wolfe

Although Wolfe's effort in his few short stories was not promising, it was abundantly clear from his long preface to *The New Journalism* that he knew what to do if he fastened upon the right topic. Instead of spending more time on essays that had begun to repeat themselves with a dose of didacticism, he plunged into the world of Wall Street, the press which he knew well, police, and lawyers with good results: *The Bonfire of the Vanities* (1987) was acclaimed both a best seller and a critical success with few demurrals.

For one thing, there had not been many good novels set in New York City for quite some time. From the Dykman neighborhood on the north end of the upper West Side the Irish immigrant Brian Moore had penned *An Answer from Limbo* (1962) but an entertaining novel about an inspiring young writer was hardly grist for either the best-seller list or the nation at large, nor were popular Mafia novels like Mario Puzo's *The Godfather* (1969) or Jimmy Breslin's *The Gang That Couldn't Shoot Straight* (1970) really novels about the city at large that was covered both high and low by *The New Yorker* and columnists like Jimmy Breslin and Pete Hamill. Ralph Ellison, Chester Himes, James Baldwin, and Ishmael Reed had written on Harlem, while Claude Brown's successful memoir of Harlem, *Manchild in the Promised Land* (1965), recreated the Horatio Alger theme with gritty realism. There were bohemian cult novels like Norman Mailer's *Barbary Shore* (1951), William Burroughs's *Junkie* (1953), and Jack Kerouac's novella *The Subterraneans* (1956). E.L. Doctorow, Jack Finney, and Mark Helprin had written novels successfully utilizing the history of the New York City, while Saul Bellow's *Mr. Sammler's Planet* (1970) remained a peculiar acquired taste for most readers. There was a host of great short story writers writing about New York and many great essays had been written about the city by people like E. B. White, A. J. Leibling, Elia Kazan, Frank O'Connor, Brendan Behan, and Roger Angell. What was lacking was a sweeping contemporary novel that addressed the whole city, both high and low. Wolfe had found the nexus between high and low by linking Wall Street, the press, and politics to the criminal justice system; moreover, he provided the first really amusing satiric book about New York City since Edith Wharton's *The Custom of the Country* (1913). The nation at large had not had a good satiric belly laugh about American follies from a novel since John Kennedy Toole's posthumous *A Confederacy of Dunces* (1980).

Much of the humor in *The Bonfire of the Vanities* revolves around a new kind of character that Wolfe had been trying to invent: the vacillating fool. In the character of Sherman McCoy, Wolfe perfected what he had been groping toward in his portrayal of Leonard Bernstein in "Radical Chic," the anonymous writer in "Mauve Gloves, Clutter & Vine," and the racist advertising producer in "The Commercial." Like all of those portraits, McCoy is a well-to-do, even really wealthy, "Master of the Universe" as he boastingly refers to himself in his monologues of exalted narcissism. When he calls his wife Judy instead of his mistress, he doesn't even have the excuse that he's drunk—there is no excuse. His interior stream-of-consciousness vacillates between a hemorrhaging hyperinsecurity and irascible rage; he has no self-knowledge—not a clue as the cliché goes. He's perfectly willing, as is his whole greedy tribe of unscrupulous profiteers, to ignorantly dismiss psychoanalysis as "weird Jewish shit," just like snooty Russian aristocrats.[1] Unlike the venerable Russian folk tradition of the "holy fool" or the French tradition of the naïve fool (as in Le Sage or Voltaire's *Candide*), or the German tradition of the fool who discovers wisdom in the German picaresque *Simplicius Simplicissimus* (1669), McCoy is just a plain hick when it comes to human relationships, a fool despite his wealthy status. The generational divide between Sherman and his hard-working, honest father serves to clarify and highlight this portrait. As an American fool, McCoy's lineage descends from Babbitt, the character in the book of that title from 1922, and much of the general cast of the book itself might be seen as sharing the general outlook of William Makepeace Thackeray or Henry Fielding.

When Sherman's ignorant but beautiful Southern mistress Maria talks him out of reporting the hit-and-run event, we realize that he is a fool beyond redemption, especially when, after adopting her hometown South Carolina racist point of view, Sherman runs with it—fantasizing like a Walter Mitty character. He dreams of himself as a novelistic hero when his act of throwing the tire originated in paranoid panic, racist fear, and cowardly opportunism. He's a fool completely out of touch with reality and this aspect of his personality receives magnification by the way he treats his wife Judy, his daughter Campbell, and the way in which he revels in the success of his bond trading at Pierce & Pierce. The firm's name displays comic overtones: The greatest work of German literature, the thirteenth-century epic *Parzival*, means "he who pierces through," yet the significance of the name in the epic is ultimately spiritual. The hero of that work is at first sublimely naïve, then dementedly determined to pierce through to heaven with his knightly lance, then finally reborn as a humble Christian who discovers the meaning of the Holy Grail in the brotherhood and communion of all races on earth. Pierce & Pierce (its doubling emphasis is mere inane repetition and perhaps emphasizes its all-white father-to-son continuum) dwells in a one-dimensional earthly level without any portal entrance to the divine and is not about to have communion with humankind.

The amusing scene of Maria asking Sherman if he has ever heard of Marlow and Dr. Faustus slyly opens to the reader the theme of selling one's soul to the devil for wealth, fame, and sex, as in Christopher Marlowe's play *Doctor Faustus* (1604). The description of sexy and wealthy Maria appears like the vision of Helen in Marlowe's play and she becomes McCoy's personal Helen for whom he will suffer in legal battle because it was Maria who had accidentally killed the student on Bruckner Boulevard, a broken boulevard of dreams made notorious to its native citizens though the columns of Ada Louise Huxtable collected in the book *Will They Ever Finish Bruckner Boulevard?* (1970).

Nicholas Lemann was the first to point out the novel's similarity of themes— an illicit love affair and an accidental road killing—with F. Scott Fitzgerald's *The Great Gatsby* (1925), declaring that "Wolfe seems to be using the comparison not just to put himself into a certain league but to make a point about how New York has changed between the twenties and the eighties."[2] Daisy, with Gatsby in the passenger seat, drives Gatsby's car when she hits her husband's mistress Myrtle. Myrtle, unlike Wolfe's student who lingers in a hospital, dies instantly. Unlike Wolfe's long legal drama, events in Fitzgerald's novel are settled without recourse to the law. The narrator of the novel, Nick Carraway, advises the bootlegger Gatsby to flee town for a week, but he stays put. Myrtle's husband, who runs a car repair shop just outside of Manhattan, identifies the distinctive yellow car as Gatsby's, arrives with a gun at Gatsby's Great Neck mansion and shoots Gatsby as he lolls in his swimming pool, then commits suicide. In both cases, the woman has taken the man's driver's seat, but Gatsby indulges Daisy as the driver of his car, while Maria seizes the wheel herself. Gatsby's source of funds comes from illegal bootlegging, while Sherman's source of wealth derives from legal market speculation. Gatsby is murdered while Sherman survives to enter a legal underworld. Wolfe employs the allusion to Fitzgerald's novel, but in ways that counterpoint Fitzgerald's plot and circumstances because New York in the 1980s has changed since the 1920s. For example, back in the 1920s a woman would never have seized her lover's car, but in the 1980s that would be perfectly believable. While Fitzgerald's story is short and straightforwardly tragic, Wolfe's story is prolix and comically baroque. In the 1980s, American society had become habitually litigious, while back in the roaring twenties, people settled scores on their own—who needed lawyers? The counterpointing differences serve to highlight the sociological changes over the past sixty years.

In *Gatsby* the unprincipled *nouveau riche* represented by Gatsby is destroyed while the high socialites, Daisy and Tom, escape the consequences of the accident untouched, even though Daisy is guilty of vehicular manslaughter. Tom has protected Daisy by his silence to the police and by informing the mechanic husband that it was Gatsby's car which hit his wife, but in Wolfe's novel Sherman is too nice a guy, as compared to the cynically scheming Tom. While Sherman is not cynical about his manipulation of people like Tom, he reserves his cynical manipulation for money as a bond trader and speculator. In Wolfe's novel high society men have become somewhat more humane; yet Wolfe presents New York high society as the victim of populist street theater controlled by the left with collusion from a liberal media. While this perception of upper-class society may be squared with Aristotle's *Poetics*, such a view of the privileged elite runs counter to the realistic tradition of the American sociological novel (or even the French) that Wolfe continues to evoke as models, unless one cites the example of Henry James, a novelist whom Wolfe professes to dislike. Wolfe apparently thinks that the civilized republican impulse of educated aristocrats has been overshadowed and displaced by the demographics of ignorant mob prejudice.

The criminals who populate the Bronx courtroom present a veritable catalogue of fools, like the young, pimp-roll strutting Lockwood who thinks it is more important to show off his rebellious defiance of the court to his gang members than agree to a seriously reduced jail sentence—he'd rather waste eight years of his youth in prison than accept a one-year sentence out of which he could possibly reconstruct a happy life. Lockwood will not accept the reduced sentence because it would lower his status in the eyes of the gang. What makes Wolfe's satire effective, however, is its gritty grounding in detail, his close observation of how high society and the courts, especially the judges and lawyers, really operate, instead of some flamboyantly exaggerated staged drama—that is, Wolfe sketches the human drama in its tragic dimensions while his satire caricatures those dimensions.

Wolfe's accurate attention to detail was aided by his friendship with two Bronx district attorneys to whom he dedicated the book. After the book came out, the newly elected Bronx Borough President Fernando Ferrer objected to the characterization of the South Bronx in the novel, particularly the description of the courthouse on the Grand Concourse as a fortress in the chapter entitled "Gibraltar":

> He [Ferrer] said that Mr. Wolfe, "whom I admire and respect," had exercised his own poetic license with sometimes unfortunate effects. For example, he said, "This place is not called 'the fortress.'" Last week, however, at a ceremony naming the building after Mr. Merola, Mr. Gentile said in a speech, "This fortress represents the indomitable spirit of the Bronx and of its namesake, Mario Merola."
>
> Those remarks brought an expression of concern from Burton B. Roberts, himself a former Bronx District Attorney and currently administrative judge of the Bronx Supreme Court, Criminal Branch. Mr. Wolfe dedicated his book to Justice Roberts and one of his former assistant district attorneys, Edward W. Hayes, who finds their respective apotheoses in the novel as Judge Myron Kovitsky and a defense lawyer, Tommy Killian. On the flyleaf of Justice Roberts's copy, Mr. Wolfe has inscribed, 'No words ever written are the equal of the gospel according to Burt.'[3]

Wolfe's portrait of Judge Myron Kovitsky in the courthouse brims with warmth, humor, and courage, while the portrait of Tommy Killian who later becomes McCoy's lawyer displays a more circumspect character with a hard edge—he examines both sides of the equation as well as the bottom line. Eddie Hayes, educated at Columbia Law School, subsequently became the man who handled all the legal aspects of Andy Warhol's estate. Wolfe had met Hayes ten years before beginning the book and Hayes became Wolfe's Virgil, guiding him into the underworld of the Bronx Criminal Justice system.[4]

The more extended case of Herbert 92X who wants to read the Koran aloud at any and all moments hammers home the idea that the court itself may operate as a temporary and somewhat indulgent lunatic asylum. Herbert's pathetic courtroom antics show him to be well beyond being a fool as his defense lawyer acknowledges: "You ever talk to a logical lunatic before? They're much worse than a plain lunatic."[5] The comic scene of lawyers ogling one of the jurors is played to the nines with the intrusion of an authorial aside: "God! If the press ever got hold of that story—but the press never showed up in the courthouse in the Bronx."[6] The observation is effective, and it remains true that local reporters are no longer assigned to cover the boring, routine details of small offenses in local courts. Yet amid all the bizarre jesting, we are aware of the grinding racial tragedy lurking beneath the façade as the "chow" (the criminals) is fed into the maw of justice in the "billion-footed city." For many readers there is the question of racial fairness and stereotyping which threads its way throughout *Bonfire*:

> For William M. Kunstler, however, one of Mr. Davis's lawyers, Mr. Wolfe has captured the essence of criminal justice in the Bronx. "No doubt this is a fortress," said Mr. Kunstler.... He was not especially well disposed to Mr. Wolfe, Mr. Kunstler said. That was not because of his own portrayal as Al Vogel, a manipulative liberal lawyer, he said, but because Mr. Wolfe's *Radical Chic* (1970) destroyed white support for the Black Panthers Mr. Kunstler was defending.
>
> "He's a snide, cynical writer, but a very effective one," Mr. Kunstler said. "From this book, my mother-in-law thinks Wolfe is a total racist. But I thought he was reflecting white society's concepts and fears, which they keep in check here by the criminal law. It's the fear of the black male, and it creates terrible tensions, which all accumulate up here on the hill."[7]

There are stereotypes in the book, both white and black, but stereotypes are the basis of farce. Wolfe was trying to be fair and provide amusing paradoxes, but it remains true that virtues tend to glow in an aura from the shoulders of those in the justice system itself: the cops, detectives, lawyers, and judges, who for Wolfe are the street heroes of American life. It happens that they are all white with the exception of some minor cops in the background. The *Boston Globe* accused Wolfe of being a racist: "a racist, in this case, is a satirist who plays favorites."[8] Yet in fairness, Wolfe was researching his material from the point of view of high society and justice—cops and especially district attorneys—who, in general, are looking to see justice done and must deal daily with many unpleasant cases. Wolfe even lampoons the district attorney Kramer who is more interested in impressing a beautiful juror than in prosecuting the case sensibly and thereby exposes Kramer's unconscious racism with Herbert 92X as his victim. From Wolfe's point of view, realism acknowledges that racism may in fact occur in the justice system, albeit unconsciously. In this instance, Herbert 92X's suspicions of a racist system are confirmed, but not for the reasons he will think. All this remains implied in the cynical circus that the novel evokes and that cynicism should make clearer the reader's perception of Herbert 92X as a victim of Kramer's misplaced zeal.

Although there are white villains, some may argue that they are treated with a generosity not accorded African-American villains in the novel. In his defense, Wolfe blithely quipped:

> He [Wolfe] wanted to write "an honest book of and about the city," he said, as Thackeray did in *Vanity Fair*, Mr. Wolfe's original inspiration. "The subtitle of *Vanity Fair* is 'A Novel Without a Hero,' and there are very few heroic figures in the book," he said. "And I don't see many heroic figures in New York City just now, to tell you God's honest truth."[9]

Vanity Fair provides a faithful picture of Thackeray's period infused with witty social satire, but Thackeray would most surely have found Wolfe's humor coarse and worldly. Thackeray's characteristics in *Vanity Fair* may be summed up as: "Expertise; specificity, realism; the painterly eye for detail; the sense of a world brought into being by a hard, sharp intelligence."[10] While such characteristics stamp Wolfe's style of narration and dialogue, and especially his detailed attention to clothing and what that clothing implies about a character, just as Thackeray did in his novel, Thackeray himself presents a larger moral point of view, which is not the same take on things as Wolfe's pervasive cynicism, yet Wolfe would probably argue that such cynicism reflects the afflictions of New York sociology, especially in matters dealing with race, and that such cynicism was at that time ubiquitous in both the white and black communities.

Toni Morrison identified Wolfe's cynicism as racist because it denies or disables the hope or possibility of racial reconciliation in daily life, and she examples the daily harassment of white cops directed toward black teenagers as a typical strategy emanating from racism. From the perspective of the street, which is not particularly concerned about the accuracy of Wolfe's depiction and more concerned about racial relations, the humorous and ironic effect of Wolfe's cynicism argues a *masked* racism.[11]

The claim or practice of literary realism on the part of an author cannot exempt a novel from political criticism. On the other hand, political criticism almost always accuses a novelist of not writing the particular book that the critic would like to write. The most famous example of such confused political and religious criticism is the reception of Ivan Turgenev's great novel *Fathers and Sons* (1861) wherein Turgenev's newfangled use of realism (picked up from Flaubert) with regard to his atheist character, Bazarov the student nihilist, led to hysterical attacks on him and the work by both the Left and the Right, culminating in an interrogation by the Russian government.[12] In a somewhat similar fashion, people made accusations against Wolfe without thinking through the deep ironic echo chamber that he set up as it relates to race.[13] The vivid qualities of realism sometimes creep under people's skin; the kind of antecedent realism found in Thackeray and *Bonfire* offer acute attention to surface detail of the kind that preceded the more vigorous development of literary realism as a movement with Maupassant, Flaubert, Crane, or Turgenev.

Bonfire's main character, Sherman McCoy, is certainly an antihero, yet Wolfe manages to paint his latent racism, his vacuous pride, and his stupendous self-centered follies as something understandable in his character flaws. Many readers grow more sympathetic to the flawed man in the spotlight than to the plight of the impoverished who have no exit from squalor or violence, yet an author cannot be held responsible for readers' misperceptions or the failure to think things through. The strength and humor of the book reside in pillaring social vanity, whether high or low, and the book works adeptly at depicting the vanity of McCoy's veering stream-of-consciousness as it waffles between preposterous vanity and panicked insecurity. For example, midway in the novel, McCoy handles the police questioning so ineptly, he might as well have given a confession. He enviously eyes the limos on Fifth Avenue blocking the curb from his hired car and then he feels sorry for himself because he can't afford a limo. Since he only makes a million dollars a year, he frets about how much the hired car costs him while the reader realizes he's probably heading for jail!

Back at the offices of Pierce & Pierce, McCoy has a panic attack and he can't focus on the business of trading bonds. With his mind either drawing a blank or wandering into blithering irrelevancies, he mentally notes to himself, "He would be a fool if he told this whole story to Freddy Burton and it turned out to be a false alarm."[14] Although Sherman realizes that in some way he is on the cusp of being a fool, he doesn't apply any self-knowledge to his situation as he thinks to himself: "*I* wasn't driving. *She* was driving. But did that absolve him of responsibility in the eyes of the law?"[15] Of course, it doesn't absolve him from responsibility before the law because he is involved in a cover-up; we realize that Sherman is a thorough fool, which makes the comic scene of reading the newspapers on the toilet all the more amusing.

Not only was the fool Sherman McCoy educated at Yale University, but the same is true of the Episcopal Reverend Fiske and the lawyer Moody (from the firm that McCoy's father had worked at), both of whom are made to look like fools by the Harlem pastor Reverend Bacon who runs circles around them in conversation. They fail to retrieve any the $350,000 for the day-care center that Fiske's board has advanced the money, which Bacon, in an amusing twist of irony, has invested in Pierce & Pierce. Moody makes a fool of himself in the car on the way back downtown with his bluffing comments about a fashionable restaurant with which Fiske is familiar while Fiske mulls over the situation: "Then he snapped out of it. *Fiske... you idiot...* If he [the lawyer] didn't manage to retrieve the $350,000, or most of it, he was going to look like a most righteous fool."[16] The novel receives much of its convincing power by alternating the dramatic pace between heroes and fools, a dialectic that serves to highlight the comic role of the fool, hence the popularity of the novel.

The portrait of the bigoted, anti-American journalist Peter Fallow (apparently a satire on Alexander Cockburn)[17] also portrays him as a fool, yet he is a cunning and cynical fool. With one major sensational tabloid coup that the reader finds to emanate from a brief affair with a "stable runt" of the wealthy, he has managed to land this job in New York City where instead of reporting he remains barren in his production and lives a drunkard's life sneering at Americans while cleverly stinging the foolish Reverend Fiske with a large bill at an English restaurant. As a fool, Fallow is a prankish fool who provides entertainment through his improbable antics.

The City Light, where Fallow works, appears to be a gutter scandal sheet serving up darkness in gory, lurid headlines:

SCALP
GRANDMA,
THEN
ROB HER

The typography down the right side of the front page provides a sample of what Wolfe calls "Pornoviolence" in an essay from *Mauve Gloves* where he cites the success of *The National Enquirer* tabloid formula which engendered a dozen imitators all competing in the arena of violence as a form of pornography to titillate the debased taste of its fast-growing readership. Wolfe remains rightly appalled at this trend, but the essay itself becomes a predictable moral lecture and is consequently not as effective as the moral dramatization here of an opportunistic gutter reporter, a kind of subhuman alcoholic who raises his role of foolishness into serving the realm of the pernicious:

> Had he been feeling better, Fallow would have paid silent tribute to the extraordinary *esthétique de l'abattoir* [esthetic of animal slaughter] that enabled these shameless devils, his employers, his compatriots, his fellow Englishmen, his fellow progeny of Shakespeare and Milton, to come up with things like this day after day.[18]

The vowel "a" here shifts to "e" as fellow is twice repeated: Before the twelfth-century vowel shift that affected all the northern European languages,[19] the word "fellow" would have been pronounced "fallow." Mr. Fallow is no longer a fellow working for the common good and when he spies his haggard, hung-over visage in the mirror, he blithely admires his "*Byronic*" image, which is a self-exaltation of truly ridiculous proportions when one considers Fallows' meager screed output and his talent for cadging drinks and meals. As names in the novels of Fielding or Thackeray, Fallow's name echoes with linguistic irony.

The foreign publisher who had brought this gross "journalism" to the United States appears to be a caricature of a well-known newspaper mogul. To place the owner further in the gutter we find out that he often takes delight in writing the gruesome headlines himself! Peter Fallow had been brought in to humiliate all the upper-class snobs the owner doesn't like. Fallow's office joke of calling his boss The Dead Mouse provides smirking amusement in the office because everyone knows that this foolish prank might eventually end his employment.

Fallow receives a lucky tip from a white friend (the Kunstler figure) of Reverend Bacon's over a free but sparse lunch that serves as a morsel for him to keep his job and set the match to the political farce about to blaze forth. This had been foreshadowed by the episode of the attorney Kramer and the investigation of the Pimp who shot a man in the back three times, killing him because he suspected that he may have stolen a few of his elegant suits. The shocking farce of keeping three witnesses chained to the legs of the detective's desks (for fear that they will flee in a wink) while the unchained "Pimp" who elegantly devours juicy spareribs before a glowing television wets the reader's appetite for the larger farce to come—the political farce that will publicize the tragedy of Henry Lamb, the Reverend Bacon's symbolic sacrificial lamb. What makes the scene of the "Pimp" so amusing is the perception that common sense itself becomes necessarily surreal in the bizarre situations of criminal justice. Such situations of absurdity in the lives of African Americans functioned as the eloquent central theme in the novels of Chester Himes (1909–1984).

When Fallow rings up Mr. Rifkind, Henry Lamb's earnest English teacher who does a kind riff on his student, we are on the stomping ground of two of Wolfe's favorite hobbyhorses—misleading journalism and the woeful educational system in America:

> "Let me ask you this. How does he do on his written work?"
>
> Mr. Rifkind let out a whoop. "*Writ*ten work? There hasn't been any written work at Ruppert High for fifteen years! Maybe twenty! They take multiple choice tests. Reading comprehension, that's the big thing. That's all the Board of Education cares about.... But at Colonel Jacob Ruppert High School, an honor student is somebody who attends class, isn't disruptive, tries to learn, and does all right at reading and arithmetic."
>
> "Well, let's use that standard. By that standard, is Henry Lamb an honor student?"
>
> "By that standard, yes."
>
> "Thank you very much, Mr. Rifkind."[20]

We have the manipulative journalist who, with a little tweak of reality, practices tabloid journalism as he gets to the dark heart of the story: An honor student martyr cut down in the prime of his life from a hit-and-run Mercedes. Perhaps Fallows' subtle manipulation is a minor but unscrupulous use of creatively leading the witness; Wolfe presents the reader with a moral warning about the nature of interviews for tabloids where quotations are customarily lifted out of context. Yet what appears in the newspaper is something a bit different:

> The teacher of Lamb's advanced literature and composition class at Ruppert, Zane J. Rifkind, told *The City Light*: "This is a tragic situation. Henry is among that remarkable fraction of students who are able to overcome the many obstacles that life in the South Bronx places in their paths and concentrate on their studies and their potential and their futures. One can only wonder what he might have achieved in college."[21]

Despite the amusingly exaggerated version of the truth, we as readers know that the real truth, considering Lamb's social disadvantages, is pretty well represented, yet we can heartily despise the cynicism of the reporter.

There is no Colonel Jacob Ruppert High School, but there could just have well been one because high schools are often named after politicians or prominent city figures. Colonel Jacob Ruppert (1867–1939) served in the National Guard, was elected four times to Congress, became a prosperous beer brewer when he inherited the family business, and then became owner and president of the New Yankees from 1914 until his death. Ruppert was responsible for the Yankee acquisition of two Boston pitchers, Carl Mays (the only pitcher ever to kill a batter with a fastball) and Babe Ruth—there is a plaque on the old center field wall dedicated to Ruppert's memory. Between Second and Third Avenue in the Manhattan east nineties, there is a residential building named after the Colonel.[22]

Afterwards at an office bull session, Fallow regales his peers and publisher with lurid racist fantasies about people copulating on the stairwells, playing dice, shooting heroin, three-card monte, smoking crack, and more fornication: "But now lies, graphic lies, bubbled up into his brain at an intoxicating rate."[23] The name of this housing project is the Edgar Allan Poe Towers (Poe lived some of his happiest years in the Bronx) and Fallows' impromptu fantasies resemble some of the alcoholic-induced fantasies of Poe—according to Fallows the Towers resemble some grand sociological inversion of "The Fall of the House of Usher" (a story about incest and murder in which the narrator becomes a duped participant). Here we have a parodist's political reversal: It is not Old World pre-French Revolution upper-class degeneracy that threatens society, but the pre-French Revolution lower classes immersed in drug abuse, gambling, and wanton degeneracy. A reporter at the party evokes parallels with Hogarth's famous eighteenth-century sketches of Gin Lane to leaven the laughter of raucous group racism. This kind of stinging satire emulates Zola's power to shock.

Yet Fallows' cynical ploy to save his job and puff his status at the party has become the nightmare of McCoy and district attorney Kramer. Kramer reacts to this article with disbelief, fear. Deluded McCoy implodes with antic panic (expertly dramatized by Wolfe) in an amusing scene of a transatlantic business conversation bungled by growing guilt. The motives of the *The City Light* publisher are as cynical as Fallows: It appears he ran Lamb's story only because the paper's racist leanings had attracted intense criticism from the black community. Wolfe exposes the thoroughly racist mentality and bigoted self-congratulation behind the headlines, warning readers of such rags that they should be wary of the content, even when it appears to be sincere. It remains ironic that both the reporter and the paper support racial justice out of cynical opportunism.

The depiction of social protest (at the Edgar Allan Poe Towers where Mrs. Lamb lived with her son) as an organized farce manufactured for television derives from Wolfe's disdain for television reporting as an entertainment medium rather than real news, but it remains a coldly snobbish way of dismissing or downplaying racial problems in this case as something either real or serious. Yet the accompanying scene where Sherman watches the television coverage related to the death of Lamb with his daughter Campbell becomes very funny and our cynical pleasure is diverted to the participant in the event. Wolfe's constant cynicism always appears to imply that reality is far more complicated than any neat moral stance can ever be.

Mrs. Lamb is a minor heroic character yet she remains such a bland stereotype that it becomes difficult to identify with the depth of her suffering because her story finds itself so embedded in a political context rather than a deep personal tragedy that would evoke more identification with the reader if she were more complexly drawn or had more space on the stage of the narrative. Yet Wolfe would have understandably shied away from such an approach because, like many male writers, he has great difficulty in portraying the opposite sex with any conviction or nuance. As a writer, his strength is sketching contemporary narcissism and vanity, the subject of the novel, among the very rich in a more direct way than one would find in Thackeray. By the way, the general army of commentators continues to point to the influence of Dickens on Wolfe's use of names in the novel as well as the humor of the plot, which is merely a symptomatic indication that they have not read Thackeray.

The chapter "The Masque of the Red Death," a jewel in style as well as content and certainly an adroitly artistic chapter, sits at the navel of the novel, or it might be better described as the architectural keystone in the arch that the novel arcs, since we are at the apex of both high society and the main plot which will from thenceforth describe the fall of McCoy from that high society perch and scene. It begins as a modern imitation of Thackeray's *Vanity Fair*, but the last quarter of the chapter shifts to parallels in theme and style borrowed from Poe. The smooth Ovidian transformation in style from bemused Tory social satirist to American apocalyptic disdain for the upper classes found in Poe, moving within a contemporary setting, remains a marvelous salon *tour-de-force* and could even stand on its own legs as a short story. McCoy enters the apartment of the Bavardages enviously eyeing Baron Hochswald's wealth and beautiful young wife; he finds momentary small-minded revenge in correcting the Baron's pronunciation. At first McCoy finds himself taken aback by the dazzling décor and immaculate assembly, while Wolfe the narrator indulges in a fireworks display of style and wit, noting the varied types assembled as if it were an operatic pageant. His phrase Lemon tarts and social X-rays appear as coinages that have passed into the language. This is the land of high chic that excludes any notion of Mother.

Wolfe calls attention to the submerged racist and sexist aspects of certain high society gatherings that exclude African Americans—they are permitted to show up publicly in high society only if they pay admission. (That's nothing the self-involved McCoy notices and McCoy even has contempt for his host, the "traveling salesman.") Attention is also called to the alpha male parade of successful men with much younger trophy wives acquired through serial divorce. The detail of age and discrepancies in the age of couples, satiric labels of social function, common French phrases, and the sartorial style of the current season parades a Thackeraylike marionette show, with the end of the paragraph exhibiting the kind of nailing chapter conclusions that Thackeray employed as a pace-shocker to the prolix meandering and gossipy rhythms of his prose. Wolfe hypes it up a bit with his characteristic trill of a poetic list lilting with alliteration and assonance as he adds parenthetical asides from the omniscient narrator, which never intrude upon the first-person narration, as he smoothly switches back-and-forth between first and third person narration with a nearly invisible ease. This entrance passage contains the best aspects of Wolfe's New Journalism as it melds with the literary realism of Thackeray on the Upper East Side of Manhattan, but it arrives more smartly because it is a representational composite fiction of a social class and not a satiric attack on a specific person or social movement.

The throbbing waves of vanity (Sherman claims old family Knickerbocker descent) and anxiety (he overhears a group gossiping about the Lamb story) that afflict McCoy at the party receives excellent tailoring. Inez Bavardage (French, for Chatterer) recounts a colorful anecdote about Sherman's father, the Lion of the law firm Dunning Sponget & Leach (Bill, Swab, and Bleed), and Sherman resigns himself to basking in the glow of his father's reputation (when the reader knows that Sherman will have no reputation to bask in): he "eased the revolver of his Resentment back into his waistband and told his Snobbery to go lie down by the hearth."[24] Amusement for this stream-of-consciousness metaphor depends upon the reader's awareness of Sherman's terror and contempt for dogs, an animal whose general behavior he himself typifies in an unconscious manner.

The dinner itself receives a proper but perfunctory Thackeraylike description and the table talk turns to gossipy homophobia, proceeding with sharp wit. There's a gossip columnist (female) from *The City Light* assigned to cover the party. After dessert the backwoods Appalachian opera singer (who sounds suspiciously like a certain accomplished Welsh tenor) performs his party piece, the laughing sob from the "Vesti la guibba" ("Put on the motley") aria in *Pagliacci* by Leoncavallo. The choice of this opera as a symbolic allusion appears most appropriate since the opera features a play-within-a-play device whereby the actors suddenly assume real-life roles—something that will happen to the featured poet at the party and the message Sherman will derive from the poet's performance. The laughing sob aria that concludes Act One of the two-act opera set in Calabria that is cited voices the tragic fate of the clown: The comedy of entertainment must go on because the public demands amusement and the clown must laugh to provide it despite his own sorrows, even if he is consumed by tears because someone has stolen his girlfriend. Such chiaroscuro literary allusions, characteristic of Poe's Gothic style, provide ambient atmosphere and the Italian setting rings appropriately true because the Poe story finds its setting in Italy and the chapter will have a sad clown (a poet) who must put on performance.[25]

Attention now turns to the guest of honor, Lord Audrey Buffing, an English homosexual poet of seventy who has been on the Nobel Prize short list for some time but has never won the prize. (The Nobel Prize short list consists of a hundred names.) The British Minister of Culture proposes a toast to the poet and this puts him center stage for his party piece. The name Buffing indicates that the poet presents a thoroughly polished surface without any depth. The portrait appears to be a composite of two same-sex poets: the knighted poet and critic Sir Stephen Spender (his lordship without an epic poem), and the dramatic lyricist Thom Gunn (long-time American resident). The poet ingratiates himself with anecdotes about his mid-Atlantic accent (as in Wolfe's first short story, "The Mid-Atlantic Man") then rambles on about his embarrassment at never having written a poem about the United States or even an epic poem as is expected of great poets. Instead of reciting one his own light compositions, he launches forth on a lengthy synoptic recitation of Edgar Allan Poe's "The Masque of the Red Death" which recounts an apocalyptic plague that afflicts the very wealthy who had thought themselves to be immune from the plebian plague because of their wealth. Poe's story, based upon the prologue to Boccaccio's *Decameron*, might be a suitable warning or insult to such a vain gathering of culture vultures, but the reader is aware that it is performed for personal reasons: that the poet obliquely offers a contemporary analogy to the AIDS plague; however, the audience appears to be unfamiliar with one of America's greatest short stories, and oblivious to the AIDS analogy. One senses that the dramatic performance is an act of despairing vanity rather than any kind of original creative performance, and that such a contemporary reading of Poe's story as a prophecy to the modern world presents a literal debasement of Poe's allegory about the temporality of entrenched Aristocratic Society that springs from the trendy and solipsistic literary criticism known as reader-response theory popularized in the 1970s by academic commentators such as Stanley Fish wherein students are encouraged to dispense with any historical understanding of a work and write about it in a confessional vein of exuberant appreciation that uplifts their inner feelings.

Naturally, the party is destroyed, at least in terms of merriment. The reception of the poet's long macabre monologue produces a pall of embarrassing silence:

> They were embarrassed because they felt the need to express their cynical superiority to his solemnity, but they didn't know how to go about it. Dared they snigger? After all, he was Lord Buffing of the Nobel Short List and their hosts' house guest. And they were embarrassed because there was always the possibility that the old man had said something profound and they had failed to get it.[26]

On another level of irony, McCoy himself is tainted with the plague of dishonor and once that dishonor becomes public anyone who knew him will be proclaiming that they never knew him very well at all. Their embarrassment will extend to the whole family: In the book's Epilogue, McCoy's fall from high society finds significant emphasis and his wife Judy will flee with her child to the Midwest. Ironically, McCoy appears to be one of the very few at the party, if not the only one, who understood Buffing's Poe performance to be about AIDS (with the *Pagliacci*-related theme of love leading to murder); he thinks that since the poet is dying, he is long past caring what gossipers might think of him—which runs parallel to McCoy's own feelings about gossip on himself, given his current situation, yet he can't communicate that to his wife who is happily intoxicated by the marvelous social event. In his sullen drunkenness Sherman glumly imagines that Buffing had been dispatched by higher powers as a ghostly medium to warn him of the coming extermination of his home and hearth! McCoy enters *into* the Poe story and becomes a victim of reader-response criticism meant for the teaching of college students—he has been taken to school and received his warning sentence! But like a pathetic fool out to destroy himself or a foolish student resigned to failing a course, he feels that he is doomed to failure and humiliation in a Gothic horror story, so he wallows in silent despair like a foolish adolescent.

In the next chapter, "Tawkin Irish," we are informed of McCoy's legal difficulties when McCoy somewhat belatedly makes his way to see the lawyer Tom Killian, but McCoy is still ensconced like a dunce in his habitual vanity:

> As a Master of the Universe, he took masculine pride in the notion that he could handle all sides of life. But now, like many respectable American males before him, he was discovering that All Sides of Life were colorful mainly when you were in the audience.... How could he let any decision affecting his life be made by this sort of person in this sort of atmosphere? He had called in sick—that lamest, weakest, most sniveling of life's small lies—to Pierce & Pierce; for this slum of the legal world.
>
> Killian motioned toward a chair, a modern chair with a curved chrome frame and Chinese-red upholstery, and Sherman sat down. The back was too low. There was no way to get comfortable.[27]

Sherman can't help superciliously sneering at what he presumes to be a low-life lawyer, yet he is also physically uncomfortable in a modern chair because like nearly every modern chair it is designed for looks not bodily comfort. Likewise, the recessed lighting fixtures in the office are most impractical and based upon the absurd abstraction that the glow from the numerous lights would theoretically recall the intense lighting of Key Biscayne, as if the lawyer at work was to be surrounded by a lolling vacation atmosphere, but due to the dim distracting glare and the impractical heat, the lawyer has only two of the nine bulbs working—this provides the traditional detective *noir* atmosphere by comic default. Faced with the possibility of being sent to a stony cell block, McCoy foolishly squirms in the immediate discomfort of his seat as he discovers that, at the least, he faces felony charges for leaving the scene of an accident and failure to report an accident, but if Lamb who is in a coma should die, he would face a manslaughter charge. The chapter title introduces the Irish-American hero-lawyer Killian. McCoy, who has been in denial, must now face the hard facts of his situation. During his research for the novel, Wolfe acquired admiration for the way Irish cops and lawyers handled the difficulties of their profession, especially their truculent obstinacy when facing serious problems (a product of social conditioning over centuries). The chapter concludes with a brief, cheery advertisement for the virtues of Wolfe's alma mater, Yale University.

"The Favor Bank" explains how the intricate informalities of the legal system work among peers, but not before we get a glimpse of Kramer appearing foolish before his boss Fitzgibbon for the way he spoke to Mrs. Lamb. Once again the reporter Fallow vainly rants on with his imaginary racist anecdotes at the English restaurant to entertain his listeners because he has nothing else to talk about and these imaginary racist anecdotes have now become his comic routine. McCoy's mind turns toward fearful racist disdain in the halls of the Manhattan courthouse where he sees "huddles of dark people, and their voices created a great nervous rumble."[28] Later the imaginary-hero McCoy foolishly wonders if was even safe for a white man "to be in the vicinity of a building that daily, hourly, brought together so many defendants in criminal cases."[29]

The Favor Bank, a shorthand metaphor, is the common currency of lawyers (and sometimes judges) that explains how the legal system works to build community and trust within that community. Lawyers do each other courtesy favors, which usually consist of information exchange. When you have enough favors in the bank with someone you may call in a contract, which is a binding agreement that is usually about what procedures will be followed during the course of a case. The phrase "the favor bank" from Wolfe's novel has now passed into academic sociological discourse.[30]

Witness Roland finally comes forward to make a deal. In exchange for the dropping of drug dealing charges, he will give evidence, but he gives a version of the event that exculpates him and Lamb from the attempted shakedown for money to buy take-out food. He incorrectly identifies Sherman ("Shuhman" in Maria's Southern accent) as the driver when Lamb was hit by the Mercedes, most probably because Sherman had thrown the tire at him. This is bad news for Sherman; his lawyer Killian arranges for him to turn himself in rather than be arrested at work or home. The plot here moves with lean dialogue and sparse setting at a swift pace as in a page-turning thriller.

The arrest itself doesn't work as smoothly as advertised. The longest chapter in the novel, "Styrofoam Peanuts," as the title indicates, will depict a surreal, artificial, and absurd scenario. Styrofoam is, of course, reprocessed garbage made into packaging. This conjures up the image of arresting criminals and processing them through procedures of humiliation, leading to the possibility of making something minimally useful to society once they are booked, put into the criminal justice system, tried, and either released or convicted, and then released as minimally recycled human beings. The Styrofoam first appears as accidental debris in the car of the two cops who come to arrest and transport Sherman to Bronx Central Booking at the courthouse. From their shape these particular Styrofoam bits appear in peanut shape, presumably brown as Styrofoam is made in brown, white, yellow, or even pink.

The peanut theme relates to the circus metaphor surrounding the media frenzy greeting Sherman outside the courthouse back door; it moves to the cell holding pens, and finally the courthouse itself. It's a surreal trail of peanuts, like some postmodern mobile art happening, for the three different kinds of circus crowds: the media, the clowns in the holding pen, and the howling circus mob blindly out for blood in the courthouse.

On the way to the station McCoy spies Yankee Stadium which appears to him as an iconic anchor with memories to hold onto, except that we find out that these memories are tawdry and trivial. With the big white image of the House that Ruth Built looming before him on the Cross Bronx Expressway, McCoy's mind suddenly leaps ahead in panic to his destination—the single word "Congo."[31] We are reminded that in McCoy's mind he is entering "the heart of darkness." First of all, this exposes McCoy's unconscious racist fears. Secondly, the symbolism of the great white dome building in Joseph Conrad's novella *The Heart of Darkness* refers to the Belgian government's capitol in Brussels, which Conrad calls a whited sepulcher—a symbol of imperialism, inanity, and greed. The sophisticated reader is asked to make the connection here—we might recall that the subject of Yankee ownership was previously brought up in the novel as Wolfe bestowed heroic homage on Colonel Ruppert, the eccentric and humorous owner who turned the Yankees into a super dynasty. One may draw one's own conclusion about subsequent ownership.

The metaphor of the Heart of Darkness is developed throughout the chapter. In Conrad's novella there were three things at the heart of this darkness which was ruled by mindless hysteria: the slave trade, the ivory trade, and the tribal and imperial wars that exploited these trades. Amid this farcical "heart of darkness" Wolfe's chapter features three scenes, as in a three-ringed circus: the media frenzy surrounding McCoy's arrival where he is grossly insulted and abused by the press; the scene in the holding pen where amid cockroaches and mice (the mice routine is good slapstick), we have a zany intermission clown show to entertain us, and the impassioned, ignorant mob yelling inside the courthouse, trying to make the bail hearing a circus.

The first scene with the press brims with drama: "The mob seemed to shake itself, like a huge filthy sprawling dog."[32] In *The Right Stuff* Wolfe had compared the press to a beast that attempted to prey upon John Glenn's wife. Here the dog metaphor discovers resonance because McCoy seems to be headed to the bowels of Hell where the booking receiver is ironically named Angel, but the dog image conjures up the classical guardian of the underworld, Cerebus, the three-headed dog—one head being the salivating press, another the maw of the holding pen, another the teeth of justice in the courtroom. Throughout these scenes Sherman appears as a hapless circus clown with his wet pants falling down as he shuffles about in his unlaced squishy shoes.

The Heart of Darkness metaphor appears slightly over-the-top and perhaps frivolously opportunistic, since Conrad's masterpiece deals with predatory tribal holocaust.[33] On the other hand, we are in the realm of underworld farce that identifies lesser systematic evils: The nasty, gnawing hunger of the tabloid press, the viciousness of common street criminals, and the debased abuse of the courtroom by an idle mob for purposes of sporting entertainment. The latter two items in this instance are inspired, goaded, and abetted by the first evil, the press— the moral misuse of which has been an obsessive theme in Wolfe's work. We witness the press working in various ways to undermine the civic fabric of our society by sensationalizing matters of race, celebrity, and political opportunism— here represented by two politicians, District Attorney Abe Weiss and Reverend Bacon—one white, the other black, thus giving a balanced symbolism of how matters involving racial sensitivity and outrage may be exploited by politicians of any racial background. Bacon, Weiss, and the prosecutor Kramer are not evil, but their ambition and narcissism govern their careers more excessively than the common good would advise. On the other hand, heroes like Martin, Goldberg, Killian, and the bench judges resist such pressures, shun the circus spotlight, and have a sensible contempt for those who put themselves into the public spotlight. A portrait of the criminal justice system as a flawed but fundamentally good system emerges.

The exhausted McCoy, who is not the *real* McCoy because his mistress is actually the guilty party, concludes the chapter with a meditation on suicide in the manner of Hemmingway with his shotgun. After having played a role not unlike a Pagliacci clown, the reader begins to pity the foolish and vain McCoy because he is now the humiliated victim—not that he's completely innocent, but the forces of zealous and vain self-interest are now arrayed against him in an evil alliance: If you see a man slipping down the social status ladder, kick him!

The press appears in a lurid light. While *The City Light* has the shallow Fallow, the *Daily News* has the principled and gutsy Flannagan who appears to be a heroic tribute to the columnist Jimmy Breslin. For the most part, the newspaper business receives a satirical flogging, especially in the scene where reporters nearly torture McCoy's six-year-old daughter, but there remains a vestige of hope in the business and the process. What Wolfe denounces is a herd mentality and its accompanying conformity: *The City Light* attacks and smears, a real estate broker spies an opportunity to convert friendship into cash, and the building's board president wants to evict Sherman. For McCoy, the latter event provides a revelatory and salutary rebirth—his contemplation of suicide evaporates with the gratuitous insults; he resolves to fight for himself as Killian cheers him on.

At the heart of darkness in the criminal system there is no demonic Kurtz-like figure—there is much ambiguity, but there is a villain: McCoy's mistress, the femme fatale Maria. When people lie, for whatever personal reasons, they subvert the basis of the judicial system and undermine the fabric of civic life. The judicial system can often sift and expose lies, but in situations when it is one person's word against another person, then such sifting becomes difficult. When two people (Roland and Maria) construct lies to protect themselves from their own crimes, the judicial system is undermined. So the civic lie, not some demented personality like Conrad's Kurtz, sits at the heart of darkness in Wolfe's novel. The slightly corrupt lawyer Kramer behaves more like a fool than villain.

While themes of personal and social justice raise the novel into the realms of art, the humorous cartoon of a white primal scream against a black mob during the climatic courthouse riot leaves the reader with the impression that both the court and society itself constitute a madhouse wherein the sane might become victims of the insane as in Kafka. Sherman momentarily drops into the maw of insanity, yet this reversal from a realistic perspective strains the credibility of the narrative; it screams off the page like one of Wolfe's manically exaggerated cartoons collected in *In Our Time* (1980).

Wolfe sometimes engages in thematic repetition that is occasionally effective, yet at times appears overwrought. For example, the plague theme from the Poe story appears again in the farcical restaurant scene depicting the procession of Mr. Ruskin's corpse amid the diner's tables:

> The diners could not believe what they were seeing. Ruskin's stricken face and white gut were now being paraded by their very tables ... the grim remains of the joys of the flesh. It was as if some plague, which they all thought had been eradicated at last, had sprung back up in their midst, more virulent than ever.[34]

Likewise, the Pagliacci theme finds a brief evocation: "He put tears into his voice that would have embarrassed the worst hambone Pagliacci."[35] Such repetition serves to enhance Wolfe's themes in an amusing and effective manner. But Wolfe also employs repetition in a propagandistic manner that lectures rather than entertains: "he was learning for himself the truth of the saying 'A liberal is a conservative who has been arrested.'"[36] And in another passage: "(Yes, it is true. A liberal is a conservative who has been arrested.)"[37] The repetitive insertion of such a political polemic both deflates the comedic atmosphere and advances the author's point of view in an obtrusive and alienating manner. Such an editorial tactic belongs to the essay rather than the novel. There occur moments in the novel when the novel appears divided by a journalistic desire to answer problems with political statements rather than to dramatically paint those problems with an artistic palette, a flaw that also occurs in the late nineteenth-century novels of Benjamin Disraeli who, like Dos Passos in his *U.S.A.* (1939) trilogy, depicts a two-tier divided economic world in *Sybil: or, The Two Nations* (1845). The major difference between the world of Dos Passos and Disraeli is that the contemporary world of Wolfe's novel contains an advanced judicial system: The lower tier where the disadvantaged dwell has recourse to that legal system, which though not perfect, remains a significant social improvement.

Wolfe's novel derives much of its power from the cynical twists that animate his sinuous plot. The weakest link in the plot occurs in the *deus ex machina* appearance of the landlord's tape—here the author's manipulative and overly clever satire walks a tightrope made of string not wire; yet the reader *might* accept such a device because the unethical reputation of New York landlords remains as much fact as legend. Perhaps this element of the plot was inspired by the famous Nixon tapes of Watergate.

As social farce, the novel deals in stereotypes and we cannot expect characters to be drawn in depth. That said, the best drawn characters appear to be Judge Kovitsky, the hero of the novel who is too much off-stage for the role of hero in any novel; Killian with his hard work, rough solicitude, and practical tact is drawn well yet the reader never sees his private life; Reverend Bacon with his suave and self-confident aplomb also never admits us to his home; Maria, a stock comic character, who achieves continuity and amusement by her cunning consistency; Judy, Sherman's wife, especially in the delicately nuanced undertone of her disappointment in both Sherman and the unpleasant turn of events when she speaks to him on the telephone from their summer house.

The well-written Epilogue remedies the hysterical note of the concluding chapter in its emphasis on the judicial system as process in search of justice, despite the flawed personalities involved. Cynicism is directed toward the role of the press, a subtheme of the novel. Although Peter Fallow receives the Pulitzer Prize for a story that had been handed to him by the lawyer Vogel, the reader knows that the piece of journalism penned by one Overton Holmes, Jr. exhibits the research and fairness that the reporting of Fallow lacked, and, moreover, it is better written than any of Fallow's pieces. The problematic nature of McCoy's guilt or innocence has once again been raised in a more serious manner by the news of the student Lamb's death.

While such extended satire, influenced in technique by Thackeray, has realistic elements in the description of clothing and setting, such signatures are not the basis for literary realism in itself, yet signal characteristics of prerealist anticipation. Wolfe will administer a more authentic realism in his next novel when he will look to France for literary models to inspire a new direction in his writing.

CHAPTER 8

CULTURAL DRIFT

I was literally made, shaped, whetted and given a world with a purpose by
the American realistic novel of the mid to late 1930s.
—Seymour Krim, *Shake It for the World, Smartass*

With two successful bestsellers, *The Right Stuff* and *Bonfire of the Vanities*, under
his belt, Wolfe turned his attention to writing a more ambitious novel. Rather
than relying on mere comedy, he would attempt to plunge into deeper themes
as a novelist. Having used New York City and Wall Street as the background
of his first novel, he would turn toward Atlanta and the building industry,
profiling an important business as Emile Zola did in *Au Bonheur des Dames*
(*The Ladies' Paradise*, 1883), a novel on the invention of the large department
store, which became such an economic force and sociological marvel late in
the nineteenth century. Moreover, he would investigate the sociology of male
machismo within Southern culture, testing how it operates on different levels—
from the sports field to the bank board room. Two central aspects of American
male fixation would provide focus: money and sex. That aspect would frame and
give context to the theme of decline through bankruptcy and loss of virility in
the main character, something that runs parallel to the historical sweep of the
Old Confederate South giving way to the New Atlanta of ambition, lust, political
correctness, and highways of the future throbbing with rap music.

The theme of sex is hinted at in the prologue: Sixty-year-old Charlie Croker,
a builder tycoon with a physique like a backwoods bullfrog, quail hunts with
his twenty-eight-year-old trophy wife in tow who ambles behind with an
eighteen-year-old heiress, Elizabeth Armholster. She's the daughter of an old
money chemical empire, about to entangle herself in a date-rape scandal with a
Moorehouse College (the prestigious college Martin Luther King graduated

from) star fullback named Fareek "the Cannon" Fanon, an ignorant lout from the slums.[1]

The third chapter, "Saddlebags," refers to the monstrous half-moons of sweat on a debtor's shirt that a bank's vicious psychological "artiste" brings out upon his victims when he gives them a military style dressing-down for defaulting on debt. We see the lavish lifestyle of Crocker under the lens of a portfolio scrutiny that exposes his spendthrift self-indulgences. The bank wants his self-indulgent toys sold in order to make their investment in him more redeemable. In a well-done but unexpected reversal during this one-on-one contest of insulting bulls, Croker upsets his rival and walks away limping from an old football wound incurred from his glory days as a football star. Wolfe employs a grinding literary realism in the description of settings and character that is full of energy, vitality, and swift word-play.

Deflated and angry, Croker with his economic assistant, The Wiz, departs in his luxurious jet to his plantation where he hears word of a large rattler; he takes off to confront it. The battle with a large rattlesnake has a couple of important iconic predecessors in American literature: its memorable and symbolic use by Willa Cather in *My Antonia* and by Zora Neale Hurston in "Sweat." Hurston's short story is a stunning masterpiece, but the former is the relevant item here. In Cather's wonderful South Dakota novel, the young Jim Burden who is about ten or eleven goes poking around prairie dog holes for birds' eggs with Antonia, four years older than he. Antonia screams and begins to "jabber" in Czech: Behind Jim is a huge twenty-four-year-old rattler coiled to strike. Jim lunges at the snake's neck with his spade, repeatedly hitting it until it is dead, though still writhing. Up until this point Antonia had treated Jim like a child, but her attitude now changes:

> That snake hung on our corral fence for several days, some of the neighbors came to see it and agreed that it was the biggest rattler ever killed in those parts. This was enough for Antonia. She liked me better from that time on, and she never took a supercilious air with me again. I had killed a big snake—I was now a big fellow.[2]

Clearly symbolic of Jim's passage into puberty, this feat enables Jim to fall in love with Antonia, the unconsummated love of his long life, as she now begins to treat him as a grown man (but only as a brother to whom she opens her heart). In Wolfe's novel we have the situation of a sixty-year-old man reaffirming his sexual potency and gambling courage by snatching a rattler by the neck, showing it off at arms length to an admiring audience of field hands, expertly bagging it, and placing it in his Snake House aquarium—it is the largest snake ever seen in living memory on the 29,000-acre plantation. As a result of Croker's macho performance, he "felt almost whole again."[3]

This skillful echoing of Cather's symbolism from a reverse chronological perspective enhances the symbolism because it injects an ironic poignancy into the older Croker's struggle to retain his vitality in the presence of his young wife, while he tries to re-invent the psychology of his ego under crushing economic duress. For a picture moment, Croker appears to have his old charismatic power back. He arrives at a definite decision when moments before he was depicted as dithering in impotent indecision, but the echo of Cather raises in the mind of a reader the question: Is Croker really up to it or is he deluding himself? Later, Wolfe returns to this theme more explicitly:

> Literary references, which he never got, annoyed Charlie, and he gave his wife a wary once-over. She was wearing her little salmon-colored silk robe and not much else, judging by how much of her he could see. For a moment he was afraid she had come in to coax him into bed to have a go at it—something that had not occurred over the past several weeks.
>
> He was afraid. That was the word. Since he believed that his performance as a developer, as an entrepreneur, as a plunger, as a creative person, was bound up with his sexual vitality, then he also believed that if he ever lost that, he would lose his...power...in business and everything else. And now he was afraid that the pressure had rendered him exactly that: impotent. He could sense it; he could feel it; somehow he *knew* it. But he didn't want to have to take that test and find out for sure. Not tonight.[4]

The joke here is that Wolfe thinks his readers will not get *his* literary references. The perception of sex as a form of sympathetic magic romps through the novel in its symbolic function within the consciousness of men, while women appear to be attuned to the conspicuous display of money in public settings where they can either attract other men or sympathetically criticize men between themselves, later demeaning their mates for lack of social grace.

Cather's use of the rattlesnake motif announces Burden's ascension into adulthood as it demarcates Burden's descent into the quandary of unfulfilled passion. From an ironic perspective, Croker's display of his virility in snatching the snake announces his climacteric impotence because after this event he appears to cease having sex with his young wife. All his life Croker has been the embodiment of snakelike cunning—that cunning will now fail him as his ego begins to disintegrate under looming insolvency. In both novels the rattlesnake motif resonates as a portal to a new world: Cather's world is one of optimistic romance where sexual attraction leads to sublimation of the sex drive which finds fulfillment in poetic memories and generous deeds that benefit others; contrarily, Wolfe depicts a postmodern world of narcissistic sexuality that attempts to find fulfillment in an evangelical passion that benefits nobody. Wolfe calls attention to a change in the sociological realities: Cather's secular world remains inspired by core small town virtues instilled during youth; Wolfe's contemporary America finds its roots in small town opportunism and financial cynicism. This cynicism evolves into a larger social cancer of social corruption that blights the landscape, bankrupting what was once called the soul. Wolfe records the sociological change to question what has become of the values that once made America great.

Wolfe's historical tour of Atlanta finds its literary precedent in Balzac's tour of Angoulême at the beginning of *Lost Illusions*. Balzac describes the town as

geographically divided between a declining aristocracy in the upper town and an
emerging commercial class in the lower town; aristocratic dominance discovers
itself challenged by ignorant but wealthier families.[5] Both Balzac's divide as well
as Wolfe's is economic, geographical, and social, but the geographical and social
aspects now present a reversal: Atlanta's aristocrats are the men of commerce
who occupy the hilly heights and views, whereas in the time of Balzac the
men of commerce occupied the lowlands. Balzac's novel records how some men
emerging from the commercial class are not all ignorant while Wolfe will record
how the men of commerce pretend not to be ignorant yet live in ignorance as they
search for merely physical acquisitions. Wolfe records the new social divide as a
product of American racial history. Mayor Wes Jordan gives his childhood friend
Richard White a political and historical tour. Both have escaped the black ghetto
of their childhood which was poor but not as despairingly decadent as it is now.
Much attention is paid to the city's demographics: 70 percent black population,
30 percent white; the racially divided neighborhoods eloquently speak their
history through their respective landmarks with the CNN tower, in the words of
the mayor, hovering above as "the biggest thing to hit Atlanta since the railroad
and the airplane and the Gulf War was the luckiest break the business interests
ever got."[6] Yet more importantly, Croker's tower looms as a narcissistic and
symbolic phallic monument.

If Atlanta is the New Rome with its mostly unoccupied Croker Tower of
Desolation (much like the half-empty World Trade Center Towers in New
York City before 9/11) and the CNN Tower a contemporary Tower of Babel
for the masses, and the stadium star Fareek "the Cannon" Fanon an American
gladiator, the theme of sinking cultural decline becomes evident when a mansion
is described as Venetian baroque—all this before we see the incredible desolation
of the city's degraded crack slums.

The lengthy exposition of the Atlanta tour describes much of the geog-
raphy and sociology of Atlanta, accompanied with digressions verging on
homophobia—and an explanatory lecture on how ghetto and jail fashions of
sartorial embellishment exhibit a continuity with domestic ghetto life. All of this
segues back into the plot with the mayor's announcement that he will back the
athlete Fareek who emerged from the crucible of a crack neighborhood; he hopes
to do this with the assistance of the cracker Charlie Croker, a former Georgia
football star, whose quail-decorated mansion they had just viewed. The tour
of Atlanta is blatantly didactic but enjoyable and enlivened by Mayor Jordan's
disdain for Western figurative art made more pleasing by his great love for
Western music—Mahler and Stravinsky, in particular, where the late Romantic
urge for the primitive crosses over into the beginnings of modernism, African
sculpture being the inspiration for European modernism in sculpture and in
painting (Picasso being the best example). The beige mayor, an enthusiast of
Yoruba sculpture, faces re-election against a blacker huckster candidate backed
by Inman Armholster who believes he has found his puppet. The stage is set for
the sex scandal to be a political football.

Croker has a minor tiff with his young wife Serena in the wee hours of the morning when Croker suffers a bout of insomnia during which he sets off the house alarm. In a minor symbolic gesture, Croker puts his booted feet on the bed's silk sheets. Such an insensitive move would offend nine out of ten wives. Although I'm not sure Wolfe is referencing the moment when the drunken poet Paul Verlaine plopped his muddy boots on the conjugal pillow one night after drinking with Rimbaud, thus punctuating the inevitable disintegration of Verlaine's marriage to Malthilde, any reader knows that such incidental derangements lead to something greater.[7] Croker looms as an antihero with an ego the size of a football stadium and we watch in fascination for the eventual demolition explosion, nagged by the question what is it that really makes a man in full: His courage, pride, testosterone, reputation, his determination to succeed, the way he treats other people? None of this matters: The novel assumes the burden of imagining a bizarre type of religious revival in a city where "ministers were the political leaders, like the party district leaders or ward chairmen in other cities."[8]

Conrad Hensley, a tenor to Crocker's bass, the spawn of Haight-Ashbury hippies who devoted their lives to drugs, group sex, and the neglect of their son, arrives onstage as the novel's hero. Conrad's father had adopted Ken Kesey's motto *"Go with the flow,"* managing to pursue a lifetime of near-idleness. In a novel that purports to be realistic, this absurd caricature of Conrad's parents as ignorant and selfish slobs (how they pay the rent is not clear) who produce a naïve religious seeker of truth strikes an off-key note—a cartoon emanating from Wolfe's political and cultural bias. The scenes of Conrad working at Croker Global Foods in the freezer unit are convincingly presented, but when Conrad saves a fellow worker's life, he is fired by the insensitive bureaucrats who execute Croker's mass lay-offs. Unemployed, he goes to an employment agency where he scores 100 percent on computer skills; when asked about his typing skills Conrad confidently admits to being able to type eighty-five words a minute learned from two semesters of community college courses, but he can't even manage twenty words a minute (thirty being passing) because his hands have grown so large from working in the freezer unit during the past two years (an anatomical unlikelihood). Presumably, this little skit was added for comic relief to set up Conrad for the loss of his car, but such minor incongruous details work against the atmosphere that a realistic novel requires.

When out of self-righteous anger Conrad refuses a plea bargain with the court, he dooms himself to a jail stretch. The gritty realism of the jail's hysteric atmosphere receives a thorough coat of paint. Through Conrad's deranged debasement the reader experiences a vicarious entry into the underworld heart of darkness adumbrated by Conrad's first name.

The first third of the novel sets the background, as one would expect from any novel. In style and content this background is realistic and the expository writing remains stimulating, but as the plot develops it swerves toward satiric statements about culture and politics, sometimes even including parenthetical editorial asides—the intrusion of the author in such an obvious way is not consistent with *how* a realistic novel works, whether one talks about Maupassant, Flaubert, Crane, Bierce, or Zola. Wolfe even resorts to outright ridicule rather than letting readers draw conclusions. The nomenclature of characters in the novel bears the burden of allegorical content (as in Thackeray or Dickens), which was something discarded by most realists because such a tactic reveals the intrusive prejudice of the author. Wolfe's writing sometimes remains closer to the didactic essay than a realistic novel where the reader must come to conclusions through inference—for example, "The egotism of the male of the species is such that he is embarrassed to let another male get an eyeful of his infirmities, no matter who it is."[9] The realistic novel remains closer to both journalism and the prose poem than other forms of novel writing.

Wolfe had declared a new approach to the novel, convincingly announced in "The Billion-Footed Beast" and "The New Journalism," but problems of continuity in style persist as Wolfe appears unable to shed the skin of his essayistic writing. Instead of identifying this problem, reviewers jumped to condemn, ridicule, or hurl derisory abuse at the excesses and absurdities of Wolfe's novel; the few passages that most reviewers cited with approbation were confined to the first quarter of the novel, yet that could be a mark of laziness.

It is ironic that Wolfe, who so disdained academic theories of painting or architecture and even critical modes of literary discourse, adopts a theory of the novel that he tries to execute, but his own cultural and political obsessions intrude, and he cannot get himself enough off-stage as a narrator to let the practice of his theory work its own course. I'm sympathetic to Wolfe's view of the novel—its sociological responsibility and the historical vitality of realism, but a good theory can never substitute for the real thing. The proof is in the execution of the novel, not in some ideal novel one would like to write. It's worth recalling that rigorous realism remains difficult to write—even most of Flaubert's novels were dismal failures, although there's nary a false note in Tolstoy who worked as effectively in realism as any writer, eventually even transforming realism into spiritualism; nor a false note in Chekhov who turned realism into modernism in his late short stories and plays.

Perhaps it's better not to think of Wolfe's theories about the novel in connection with *A Man in Full*, just as one would ignore Zola's theories on the naturalistic novel when considering *Germinal* (1885), one of Zola's masterpieces of great raw emotional power that contradict his cold, mechanical theories. If we take Wolfe's novel as a postmodern performance that admits the essayistic bromide, descriptive techniques adapted from realism, comic sketches, editorial asides as in an eighteenth-century novel, an inclination to indulge in symbolism as if he were a symbolist, a propensity for Thackeraylike satire, and the use of the bifurcated plot so endemic to the modern novels that Wolfe vociferously belittles, we may arrive at a clearer assessment.

The template popularity of the bifurcated plot in the modern novel derives from James Joyce's *Ulysses* (1922). A bifurcated plot has two distinct main characters whose lives are separately drawn, then brought together. Their intersection brings together different sociological, intellectual, and emotional threads. In

Ulysses this is Bloom (the upper-middle-class merchant with an unfaithful wife) and Stephen (a lower-middle-class university student in search of sexual experience). Bloom is a not particularly observant Jew and Stephen an ex-Catholic atheist. While Stephen engages in a brilliant search for truth, his thinking runs the gamut of Western thought. Bloom is a practical man who has a problem— he hates his wife's lover, a music hall singer. At the end of the novel both are brought together, Bloom inviting the young insomniac talker back to his house for breakfast; in an effort to displace his loathed rival, Bloom makes the pitch that Stephen could solve his sexual angst by having an affair with his earthy, libidinous wife. Stephen politely declines; the last chapter features an extended monologue on sex and the blunt insensitivity of men by Bloom's wife, Molly.[10]

Joyce's *roman á clef* novel is a *tour-de-force* exploration of ideas that finds itself in the end swamped by the comedy of earthy emotion. But its real subject is the music of language itself and each chapter employs a distinct musical format that plays language like an instrument or orchestra with regard to the chapter's theme. The structure of the seemingly rambling work finds parallel guidance from the events in Homer's *Odyssey* (c. 710 B.C.). It was Homer who first invented the bifurcated plot, dividing the action between Odysseus and his son Telemachos, and uniting them for the climatic final battle. As in either Homer or Joyce, Croker and Hensley enjoy separate narratives before being brought together by circumstances.[11] The name Joyce does appear in Wolfe's novel, albeit as the first name of a minor female character, Joyce Newman, who is the catalyst for the dramatic museum dinner climax. This kind of submerged nod is quite common in Wolfe's novels.

In Wolfe's novel, Croker, who comes from the lower class, rises to the brink of the upper class, but (as Aristotle recommends in his *Poetics*) has a tragic fall. Hensley fails to survive his economic plight in the lower class and ends in jail where he discovers by accident the philosophy of Stoicism. Both of these characters are alienated at least as much as the main characters in Joyce's *Ulysses* and such alienation will serve to bind them together later.

Wolfe proceeds on mark when in gritty dialogue he dramatizes the vicious and obscene insults men routinely practice, both in prison and in the corporate world; also when he narrates stream-of-consciousness male sexual daydreams inside a character's head. Yet once these points are made reiteration displays diminishing value, while women readers might find this theme adolescently tiresome. The triad of the three male characters exhibits the following functions: Charlie Croker, the macho antihero; Conrad Hensely, the quester-hero who exudes innocent charm; Roger White, the sensible man of moderation who referees and stands in the wings as an observer of the follies. Women characters receive little development with the possible exception of Croker's first wife. The scene where two divorced women talk after an exercise class (satirized through its use of rap music) discovers a sympathetic realism that eventually plays a significant role in the novel's plot, yet the portrayal of women characters skims the surface while they function as male trophies or sex objects—a worthy point of realism but the occlusion of half the population from a novel that purports sociological sweep provides a severe limitation.

While the world of commerce finds itself portrayed as an opportunistic jungle, the world of traditional Christianity finds itself dismissed as largely irrelevant, except as a hypocritical opiate. The real target of the novel is Atlanta's bourgeois pretentions to sophistication in its newfound desire to compete with New York, Los Angeles, and San Francisco. Wolfe also targets sexual deviation in the world of art and literature. Part of the problem is that realism works indirectly, while Wolfe sometimes allows his satiric impulses to dictate the perspective on subjects; such editorial meddling dispels the illusion that realism attempts to project.

In "The Breeding Barn," significantly the longest chapter in the novel and a chapter that can stand on its own as a short story, a claque of big-bellied old men whose virility remains questionable slouch comfortably around Croker's plantation dinner table mocking the AIDS epidemic:

> Billy and the judge redoubled their laughter, which pleased Charlie, who was afraid that up until then he had fallen behind in the rounds of wisecracks. Oh, this was the real thing! This was vintage manly humor deep in the huntin'n'shootin' atmosphere of Turpmtine! This was the sort of good times among men that the Gun House and this Gun Room had been built for! "Let's Rap for Clap!" "Let's Riff for Syph!" "Let's go hug a dyin' bugger!" Jesus, Billy was one funny old sonofabitch! This was letting it all hang out down here below the gnat line!"[12]

Among those mocking the AIDS epidemic are a minister and a judge. The second half of the chapter presents a graphic description of a track stallion named First Draw who had won the Breeder's Cup mating with a mare with Croker's crowd of guests looking on open-mouthed:

> His teeth sunk, instead, into the leather mantle that had been placed over her neck and withers for that very reason. Otherwise, in his uncontrollable sexual fury, he would have chewed her raw. All the while, his haunches, his thighs, his buttocks, the seat of the stupendous power that had propelled him, the great First Draw, this great poem in motion, this embodiment of power and coordination, to glorious victories on the track—this magnificent engine was reduced to a single jerky, spastic, conclusive, compulsive motion: rut rut rut rut rut rut rut rut rut rut rut.[13]

The eleven ruts here become symbolic of the relentless compulsion of the male sex drive. The spectacle so unnerves his guests that Croker himself becomes unraveled and he transforms himself into a complete fool by calling one of the guests (whose business patronage Croker is trying to court) Hebe instead of Herb, thus offending Herb's touchy, liberal sensibility:

> Herb Richman continued to smile, but his eyes were about 33 degrees Fahrenheit. Then he made a grunting noise deep in his chest, approximating a chuckle . . . or a punch in the solar plexus.

> Charlie didn't dare look at Marsha Richman or Serena or Wally or anyone
> else who might have heard. A wave swept through his central nervous system
> and told him he had just blown seven floors of the Croker Concourse tower and
> $10 million a year in income.[14]

Serena had previously nagged Croker about the unseemly nature of the AIDS jokes and reproved him for laughing at the way his son Wally had contributed to the jokes ("nuke 'em"). Embarrassed and a bit confused because he didn't think Wally had done anything wrong except support the judge and minister, Croker accepts Serena's warning that Herb wouldn't approve of such jokes because he's both Jewish and liberal. This makes Croker self-conscious about Herb being both liberal and a Jew, so his social gaffe probably would not have happened if he had continued to regard Herb as just another normal guy—Croker's fear of not being politically correct in his speech has triggered his fumble. The legendary football player (and confident builder) famed for causing others to fumble while he scored on their mistakes now stands as the foolish fumbler. The reader experiences a slight tinge of pity for Croker because we are aware that he is not anti-Semitic—he doesn't know anything about Jews and he accepts Herb as a sharp businessman no different from himself, but the idea of special treatment befuddles his mind.

The chapter has two juxtaposed scenes: One dramatizes the vulgarity of Old Southern culture as it defensively mocks the homosexual decadence of New Southern Culture; the other panel reiterates the vulgarity of Old Southern Culture and presents Croker's inability to integrate into the New Southern culture of diversified ethnicity. Wolfe presents this diversified ethnicity itself as something decadent—a political correctness so laxly permissive it argues against the behavior of the natural drive to perpetuate one's genetic heritage. From Wolfe's point of view political correctness remains a form of self-destruction nearly as toxic as Old Southern vulgarity and prejudice.

Despite the outrageously vicious jokes and the animal vulgarity of the horse metaphor, a sophisticated subtlety lurks below Wolfe's raging surface. The theme of horses and male machismo was famously exploited by William Faulkner (the favorite author of Wolfe's mentor Fishwick)[15] in the "The Spotted Horses," a story integrated into Faulkner's great novel *The Hamlet* (1931). In that novel Ben Quick flaunts his exploitative bravura and trickster acumen by fleecing a whole crowd of farmers as he auctions off wild horses trained to return home.[16] The literary allusion to Faulkner, as with Cather, works by contrast and referential irony. Croker's verbal incompetence stands out against Quick's impromptu eloquence. In Faulkner's story there are many horses while the focus on one horse in Wolfe's story is symbolically effective. While the unknown roustabout Quick, thought by others to be a talentless outsider, plays the notoriously successful trickster, Croker, who has a legendary reputation for being a smooth operator, becomes the trickster who tricks himself by attempting to be sensitive to the current trend of political correctness governing discourse. Like the Cather rattlesnake episode, it presents an ironic updating of a literary theme showcasing how the culture, manner, mores, and sensibility of Americans have changed. The subtextual implications embedded in the story illustrate how liberal discourse from the educational system, popularized by the media, has changed the way Americans think and speak. Caught in the tide of this cultural tide from Old South to New South, Croker is a frog out of water.

Yet Croker's outsider perspective will remain the only sane perspective in the central chapter of the novel, "The Aha! Phenomenon" where multiple plot lines intersect in a series of quick-moving conversational slides whose montage builds a thrilling thrust amid upper-class social banality. Wolfe had previously defined "The Aha! Phenomenon" in an essay as "that moment of blazing revelation all scientists dream of having."[17] Amid these intersecting plot lines the reader expects to discover a revelation related to the use of Conrad's name. Any reader of *Bonfire* might recall the use of the whited sepulcher allusion to Conrad and find it once more:

> The museum, built in 1983, was pure white and modern in the Corbusier mode. It stretched on for the length of a football field in a parade of white geometric shapes, from cubes to cylinders and everything in between and back again, all of it adorned with white pipe railings. *Le tout Atlanta* was there, for this was the opening of the notorious but glorious Wilson Lapeth opening.[18]

The mayor of Atlanta had previously said of the museum that it "looked like an insecticide refinery."[19] Across the street sits the stony neo-Gothic First Presbyterian church with its tasteful Victorian architecture, yet here squats the implication that this ugly Corbusierlike museum is the new secular church that has gathered the wealth of Atlanta under its roof. Wolfe had originally intended this novel to be on the theme of the excesses of modern art in an international context, taking *The Painted Word* to a global level.[20] Dominating the museum inside, as if it were a Renaissance painting of the Crucifixion, hangs an erotic painting of chain gang prisoners with two prisoners about to engage in anal sex. Instead of Christianity's asceticism we are treated to the worship of phallic hedonism. The painting is called *Arrangement in Red Clay, 1923.* Croker pretends to read the title and utters aloud: "Two cocksuckers down in a ditch. 1923." A friend of his grunts a guffaw, but his wife Serena says with an "exterminating hiss," *"Don't be stupid!"* and the scene concludes: "The great Charlie Croker was being treated like a child who has done something infantile in church."[21] From Wolfe's perspective, academic political correctness reduces upper-class intellect and sensibility to a devotional worship of the prison *itself* in a new secular church. We witness a ritual of sybaritic gentility that adores homosexual triumphalism in a romantic vein that has no connection with the reality of prison life—prison life through rose-colored glasses.

Because Wolfe declares this novel to be influenced by Zola,[22] it's appropriate to point out that Wolfe works in counterpoint (as with the allusions to Cather and Faulkner) to Zola's 1886 novel *Le chef d'oevre* (*The Masterpiece*) which profiles the talented painter Claude who fails to complete a huge canvas that was to be his great masterpiece. The artist satirized by Zola was based upon his childhood

friend from Aix-en-Provence, the landscape painter Paul Cezanne, who revolutionized perspective in painting and with whom Zola had had a falling out.
Cezanne avoided rendering the human body. This projected epic painting was
to depict society at large, portraying men and women at their varied labors, a
hymn to work, the foundation of society. While Zola's character fails to complete
his masterpiece because of his vagrant and hedonistic lifestyle, Lapeth has com-
pleted his sociological portrait of society as a prison with the tumescent phallus
and bare buttock as the foundation of societal relations. Zola perceives work,
whether physical or artistic, as the basis of society; he critiques his painter's lack
of discipline and his libertine alcoholism, which destroys his masterpiece. Wilson
Lapeth's paintings appear to be a satire on Michel Foucault's book *Discipline and
Punish* (1977), but John Leonard saw it as a satire on Robert Mapplethorpe's
photos, describing the passage as "a nasty sendup."[23]

The gospel preached by the featured speaker presents the texts of Michel
Foucault[24] as a gloss on the paintings of Lapeth, as if Foucault were a modern
St. Paul. (Foucault became a libertine masochist outraged by social sadism.) Wolfe
satirizes Foucault's perception of society as a prison,[25] ridiculing Foucault's
idea of the Benthamite panopticon, a pervasive system of government spying
on all citizens; yet ten years after Wolfe's novel virtually all journalists and
writers in America have had their private work and household emails logged
into government computers, although one may presume that those writers and
journalists who publicly support the imperial war in Iraq (like Wolfe) are exempt
from this new omnivorous encyclopedia of private thought. While this may be
politically disingenuous, Wolfe presents Lapeth's work as a secret homosexual
panopticon evoking a sociological norm the public is not familiar with, and *that* is
what purportedly makes him a great artist who records the private hedonism of
a suppressed population, prisoners being heroes in the contemporary pantheon
of the new secular church, which inverts the cultural and religious norms of
preceding eras. So both the urban ghetto and the new church of art harmonize
in the cultural perception that prison represents the ideal all American strive to
imitate. Political correctness turns the world upside down—in terms of fashion,
morals, and intellectual ideals, with the end result that everybody high and low
becomes transformed into deluded fools.

The cultural event at the Atlanta museum resembles (in its provinciality) the
climactic cultural soirée of Louise de Bargeton in the "Two Poet's" section of
Balzac's *Lost Illusions*.[26] Both episodes satirize the ignorance of the attendees
but Balzac's Lucien appears as young, naïve, and unknown, while Croker is old,
cynical, known to all present. The French texts at the events have changed with
time: André Chenier's poems recited in Balzac's novel are great poems, while
Lucien's own poetry is minor, yet competent and promising; Wolfe provides the
contemporary text of Foucault as a decadent example of how far the glories
of French literature have fallen in the past two centuries: The sublime to the
ridiculous.

Croker's considered reaction to the spectacle as he steadies himself on a railing
consists of observing a "confused cackling gabble swelled up from the atrium

floor. The fools! Reminded him of a flock of turkeys."[27] Croker's commentary presents a fool speaking wisdom, as in the older tradition of the medieval fool: The vulgarity of the Old South speaking truth to the New South gospel that now acquiesces to the international gospel of political correctness and confused conformity.

The proprieties of political conformity in discourse preoccupy other characters in the novel: Croker's first wife Martha and Croker's melodramatic adversary Peepgass. But such scruples are especially dramatized in the consciousness of a colored lawyer by the name of Roger White II whose nickname is Roger Too White. His overzealous scrutiny of his own speech stems from his innate sense of fairness, ambition, and insecurity because of his ghetto roots. While he is an attractive character who wins the sympathy of the reader, he occupies in the larger picture, an example of how political correctness presents a mode of hypocritical politeness that masks the racial hostility lurking beneath the surface of all civilized discourse in Atlanta, discourse that facilitates the money that makes the "Atlanta way" palatable to all races. At a press conference White's pride in his education gets the better of him and he shows off by quoting Wolfe's favorite philosopher, Nietzsche. White mentally scourges himself for showing off: "You vain, overreaching fool! You... Roger Too White!"[28] Such internal conflict within White enhances his credibility as a character.

To diffuse a scandal the Atlanta way, Roger and football coach McNutter have a meeting with another lawyer, Croker, and Fanon. If anything can possibly go wrong with their preplanned script, it does, and the atmosphere needs only a match to set McNutter's house ablaze, but McNutter's young wife Serena takes a page out of Homer's *Odyssey* to set things right when trouble appears to be getting out of hand. Fanon and Croker begin to trade ranking insults in code while their body language foreshadows a fistfight. The annoyed Croker declares football mere charades for war—kids' play, practice for the fighting, he did in Vietnam—implying he could take Fanon in a physical fight if that's what Fanon wants. Just at that moment, blond Serena appears like a magical apparition on the scene:

> "Mr. Croker? One Scotch-and-soda!"
> At the sound of the woman's voice, Roger opened his eyes. Coming through the doorway was Val McNutter. She had her strange leering smile across her face as if this were the happiest bunch of Buck's pals who had been in the house in a long time and they were all panting for the arrival of Venus in the flesh. She carried the tall glass of Scotch-and-soda as if it were a gift from the goddess.
> One belligerent, Crocker, was suddenly neutralized, as if a switch had been flipped. The other belligerent, Fareek, was speechless, all eyes.
> "Thank you," said Croker in an oddly faint voice as he took the glass, "thank you very much."
> Then Val McNutter pivoted on her high-heeled pumps, and this and that and them and those went hither, thither, whither, crevice, crevasse,.
> "Anything I can get for any of you *other* gentlemen?" Such an insinuating leer!

"No," said Roger, almost meekly, "no thanks."

"No thanks, Val," said Buck McNutter in the voice of a whipped male.

Fareek, drinking in this vision as if preparing for a trip across a terrible desert, just shook his head.

The goddess stood motionless for a moment, turned to leave, then turned back with the most suggestive grin yet, and said, "If you change your mind, just... let me know."

Say what you want about her, thought Roger, but Madame McNutter's wiggle in her walk had just defused a bad situation.[29]

This scene works as amusing entertainment, yet it imitates a well-known passage from Book Four of *The Odyssey* when Helen enters the room and gooses the wine Menelaos and visiting warriors drink:

Now Helen tried to improve their conversation by drugging the wine with an herb that banishes all sorrow. Whoever drinks such a mixture will not shed a tear all day, not even if a father or mother drops dead before their eyes, or sees a brother hewn to bloody pieces before their eyes. The daughter of Zeus had such an array of herbs, good medicines well-known to Egyptian doctors who learned the art of healing from wise Paiëon, art not known elsewhere, like this sweet drug of such potent power and marvelous strength, which had been given to Helen by Polydamna of Egypt, wife of Thon, a woman who grew all kinds of plants, some for spicing up bland food, some for poison.[30]

Helen manages to shift the morbid drift of conversation to higher ground. Wolfe once more employs another literary template referent to make another point, ironically: Coach McNutter asserts that the mores of the times have changed and that young women now fling themselves on football stars, begging them to have sex, and that such behavior is unlike anything in past history. In counterpoint, Wolfe knowingly winks at the literary reader to illustrate the French proverb: The more things change, the more they stay the same. In *Bonfire* Wolfe invoked Marlowe's Helen, while in *A Man in Full* another incarnation of the Helen of Homer (who was half-goddess, Zeus being her father) appears as the savvy, seductive hostess, but this invocation also reminds us that the sexy Elizabeth Armholster is herself very much like Homer's Helen of *The Iliad* in her seduction of Fanon—just as the young Helen seduced young Paris, Elizabeth impulsively seduced Fanon. The cabal of football and legal warriors assemble at coach McNutter's house in order to prevent a *nouvaux* Trojan race war from burning Atlanta down in the name of the new-age Helen.

After White calls the mayor to tell him that Croker has phoned his consent to participate in the deal, White puffs his chest like a bullfrog, but by the end of the next chapter, he rebukes himself for dragging his wife to the Atlanta symphony when he realizes she detests these events because as the only African Americans at the symphony they are stared at, and he belatedly realizes that this discomforts his wife, making him "feel like a blind fool."[31] Yet White is not the only one doing the warrior fool dance—nearly every character in the novel hops to that tune. White receives the reader's respect for two reasons: He has a conscience concerned about others and he knows how and when and why he dances, while others merely stumble in the dark. Wolfe's interior monologue vacillations in the mind of White give him more depth than most characters in the novel, as contentious debates and perceptions in his mind undergo intellectual and emotional vacillations that endow his character with more probing humanity than others. White possesses ambition, a desire for respectability, and an internal diffidence that makes him exciting, yet Wolfe's compulsion to satirize even this character sometimes materializes.

The only character in the novel free from satire is the West Coast hero Conrad whose unlikely escape from an Oakland prison and subsequent adventures in the picaresque mode provide him with a job as a male nurse to Charlie Croker on the other end of the continent. Although a hero in the novel, Conrad's moral character remains too one-dimensional to be thoroughly engaging or even believable. For the elementary aspects of Stoicism, Conrad becomes the naïve instructor of Croker. Like Stephen Daedalus in Joyce's *Ulysses*, he meets the failing Croker who shares with Joyce's Bloom a crisis in moral acumen. Conrad, now working under the pseudonym of Connie, instructs Croker on Stoicism. Quotations from an anthology on the Stoics fill up a number of pages as the novel bogs down in retailing information rather than developing the drama of the plot. That an innocent man in prison would be attracted to Stoicism operates as good realism because people in prison are desperate for some kind of consolation,[32] but that a wily character like Croker would be attracted to Stoicism is hardly realistic—characters like Croker most often try to attempt one last big scam to escape their financial problems and usually end up gripping the cold steel of jail bars.

Amid anecdotes about the Stoics, it comes as no surprise that the character of Ulysses finds mention. Ulysses (Odysseus) finds citation as a model of self-reliance when he builds a ship after being shipwrecked on the island of Ogygia, which Croker refers to as the ubiquitous "wherever."[33] Part of the humor of this passage relies on the old joke that Croker and Conrad conceive Ulysses a character from history rather than fiction. Furthermore, at this point in *The Odyssey*, Ulysses (the Latin pronunciation of Odysseus) had become the sex slave of the goddess Kalypso. Ironically, Croker's wife is the sex slave of an impotent man on the verge of bankruptcy as he recovers from a *leg* operation, since his knee functions like an Achilles' heel in the novel.

Wolfe manages to inveigle into his text an apology for employing the name of Joseph Conrad and giving his character Conrad the working-class job of having worked in Croker's Global Foods freezer unit:

> It was about quarter of ten when Charlie said, "Connie—by the way, I'm gonna have to keep on calling you Connie. 'Conrad' just don't fit. I couldna had nobody named Conrad working in one of those damn freezer units. I'm sorry."[34]

Such indirect address to the sophisticated reader on the part of Wolfe supplies a minor comic moment as it comes from the mouth of an illiterate character, but this kind of witty out-of-frame reference is a self-conscious signature joke characteristic of the postmodern novel that Wolfe so vociferously decries. The name Conrad has appeared in all his novels and even goes back to the mention of Jane Conrad in *The Right Stuff.* In an interview Wolfe declared that the name Conrad Hensley was a name picked from his distant Shenandoah past, but this may have been a curve ball by the former pitcher.[35] Given Wolfe's neoconservative leanings and his interest in Southern fighter pilots, it is possible that the name Hensley as hero is a tribute to hard-working Jim Hensley, the Budweiser distributor, whose daughter Cindy became the second wife of a former fighter pilot, Senator John McCain. Like the stoic Admiral Stockdale, McCain had been captive in what Wolfe would have considered the "heart of darkness"— North Vietnam.

The education of Croker has its parallel in the education of Elmer Gantry in the novel of that name. Elmer gives himself up "trustingly to scholarship" but he does not know what scholarship is and his education continues to flounder in a feeble autodidactic context. Elmer continues to be as naïve in his reading of ecclesiastical history as his reading of literature. He reads Robert Browning with great difficulty "and there was so much stuff about Italy and all those Wop countries."[36] With this amusing reference to Browning's famous feminist poem, "My Last Duchess," Sinclair Lewis evokes both irony and satire as Elmer continues to be an oblivious sexist in his pursuit of evangelical seduction. In contrast, Conrad's autodidactic understanding operates free of such prejudice and behavior while it contains a grain of genuine wisdom. Conrad works from an anthology published by the University of California which has some academic guidance; Elmer works from a text alone. For the autodidact the opportunities for successful education have improved because libraries and texts have improved, not only in availability, but in the academic apparatus of the texts themselves.

On the level of literary realism, the concluding chapter, "The Manager" fails to convey credibility, exhibiting similar problems with realism that afflicted the ending of *Bonfire.* On the level of social satire, the conclusion functions effectively. Croker's snap-finger conversion to Stoicism is not believable as realism any more than his honest and bizarre performance before a press microphone erases years of selfishness, racism, neglect of his children, exploitation of others, or a lifetime in pursuit of opportunistic narcissism.[37] In this climactic chapter he lives up to his eponym, croaking in public like a puffed-up frog announcing his new-found honesty as he expires in an autumnal landscape of navel-gazing preachers.

Unlike the rampant political cynicism of *Bonfire, A Man in Full* offers a more bemused account of politics while offering hope in the political system and the ability of Americans to solve their problems. The epilogue to the book provides an honest dialogue between the mayor and his old friend Roger White. Although there are some cynical political observations in this discussion, readers can have no doubt that the newly incumbent mayor is a good man working for the common good. The conniving political culture of "the Atlanta way" has given the city some temporary sanity; the villain Peepgass has become a trophy husband by marrying the former Martha Croker; the gold-digger Serena disappears with the baby the callous Croker doesn't care for; the bank gets the shaft of debt and endless lawsuits; White gets a raise and his stodgy Old South law firm has made the successful transition to the New Atlanta of prosperity, thanks to his success, and he may be in line to be the next mayor. Charlie Croker, the novel's antihero, has been sidelined from construction and politics as a born-again Zeus revivalist who has fallen to the travelling tent "healing" circuit. While this is an amusing dig at the Southern evangelical tradition of personal witness testimony, it fails as convincing realism. Connie-Conrad returns home and luckily finds a generous judge to give him a two-year probation sentence, so that he's reunited with his family, yet none of his problems in life are solved, except that he has found happiness in his new religion that has no church because it is a dead philosophy and not a religion at all. Wolfe implies that Stoicism would have been a better alternative to Christianity because in theory and practice it provides an inherently more honest and less hypocritical model for behavior. Wolfe's Epilogue reads more like an amusing re-invention of eighteenth- or early nineteenth-century picaresque satire.

Wolfe's novel was attacked at length in print by Norman Mailer and John Updike in *The New York Times Book Review* and *The New Yorker*, respectively. John Irving also made a rather vicious and incoherent attack on Canadian television. A thorough, balanced, and on the whole impartial account of this literary feud was covered by Anthony Arthur. In a letter to Arthur, Wolfe amusingly asserts that "I have never, ever, thought anything I've written as satire, in fiction or non-fiction." Arthur wryly comments, "Perhaps Wolfe is joking here." I'll leave it at that; Arthur observes that Wolfe's "métier is a rather cool, even chilly hyper-realism, a frequently grotesque mixture of satire and comedy that, while sometimes brilliant, appeals more to the mind than the heart."[38] In defense of Wolfe's first two novels, one might justly reply that an antihero must appeal more to the mind than the heart, yet the charge that Wolfe's characters often lack emotional depth carries resonance. Conrad Hensley, the working class hero of *A Man in Full*, lacks any complications in his portrait; while readers may pity Conrad, they are not moved to the kind of heartfelt transcendent, much less transformative, identification recommended by Aristotle.

In Wolfe's rather lengthy argument defending *A Man in Full* against novel-writing reviewers, "My Three Stooges," the only non-previously-published piece in *Hooking Up*, Wolfe's self-justification comes across as angry contempt combined with a vaunting boastfulness that he is the only rational being in a madhouse. He resorts to showmanlike invective that displays more temper than reasoned argument, but becomes calmer toward the end when he paints a larger context. He cogently identifies three problems with the contemporary American novel: French theorists opposed to realism have successfully sold their ideas on experimentation and abstraction to Americans; most young people today look to the movies rather than the novel for art or entertainment; novel writing itself has been imprisoned in workshop classrooms where the grooming of narcissistic prose rather than any writing connected to life emerges. Wolfe thinks the American novel is dying of anorexia in a bulimic culture.[39] Such astringent cultural criticisms take on an apocalyptic tone that projects self-serving dramatic exaggeration. Yet the length of a novel is no indication of its achievement—Wolfe himself frequently alludes to Joseph Conrad's *The Heart of Darkness*, not any of his longer novels.

Wolfe is, I think, correct about the subversive and dominating influence of French theory in the American academy which expanded the vocabulary of academic discourse to fill the void created by the collapse of Marxist discourse; it also encouraged various avenues of academic folly that defied common sense. The French are perhaps less opposed to realism itself than they are addicted to abstract theories about how things work, a cultural defect that preceded the French Revolution. Abstractions are more suited to the French language itself, while the English language remains grounded in a Baconian practicality that makes realism perhaps more effective in English than in French. Many American novelists try to link principles of French academic theory to the Madison Avenue advertising practicality of penning glitzy workshop gimmicks. Perhaps this stems from the kind of cultural insecurity endemic to Americans—a favorite theme of Henry James, especially eloquent in his novel *Portrait of a Lady* (1881).

Wolfe's advice to novelists to conduct research rather than read tomes in their study remains good advice. Although the state of the American novel is hardly approaching famine, it remains true that the contemporary Chinese novel, where both realists and fabulists flourish in novels both large and small, offers a far more exciting scene—a scene both experimental and rooted in the realities of life more than the American novel. Perhaps the larger cultural problem in America is that Americans as a people have embraced the adolescent sensibility of narcissism as an accepted norm: Wolfe's Charlie Croker is a paragon of such self-indulgent ignorance.

A Man in Full is neither the travesty of Wolfe's detractors, nor the masterpiece Wolfe claims. It constitutes a superb novel with lively social themes and well-done set-pieces, yet many characters continue to suffer from the weak portrayal typical of social satire; the novel's varied didactic threads blend a bit awkwardly yet amusingly with its satiric sketches. Wolfe's dialogue and representations of local accents are, as usual, amazingly accurate. *A Man in Full* displays a growth in Wolfe's ability to move toward more depth in themes and to provide a more realistic assessment of American cultural behavior. The particular crisis in banking and building that Wolfe identifies is, if anything, all the more current a decade after his novel when the crisis has become national, rather than a matter confined to the urban New South.

Wolfe plays with other literary texts in a knowledgeable and innovative manner that offers both contemporary social commentary as well as oblique commentary on the characters in his own text. Such double-layered legerdemain is hardly the domain of popular writing, and those critics who excoriate Wolfe for popular pandering may fairly be accused of not being sophisticated enough to understand what Wolfe accomplishes; consequently, hysterical damnation of him remains completely vacuous, except as exhibitions of competitive jealousy when such critics are novelists. Wolfe has achieved a notable work, but this novel is not the great American novel, merely an excellent one, perhaps on a par with

Lewis' *Main Street* to which it bears a resemblance in its critical focus on the local culture wherein both authors grew up.

The central quandary of Wolfe's novel is that it employs journalistic research as in a realistic novel, but it uses what realism it unearths for comedic purposes, and consequently it is not a novel of Zolaesque realism, despite Wolfe's assertion to the contrary.[40] The realistic novel evolved from the realistic short stories of Maupassant and breathes the air of inescapable necessity that Aristotle delineates in his *Poetics*, an atmosphere and structure much like Sophocles' great tragedy, *Oedipus Rex.* The great realistic novels of Flaubert, Zola, Tolstoy, Crane, Melville, Norris, Dreiser, Steinbeck, Lewis, and others have their shocking impact because they are inescapably tragic: Society has brought about the defeat of the individual, family, or social sector. In Zola's novels of realistic naturalism, there is an element of inevitable determinism, yet in his best novels this determinism plods in muted tones to the climax—for example, in Zola's 1874 *La Conquêt de Plassans* (*A Priest in the House*) where the ambient determinism finds its muted motor moving toward a pathological apocalypse in its amusing satire on Roman Catholicism; its greater 1875 sequel *La Faute de l'Abbé Mouret* (*The Abbé Mouret's Sin*) provides more poetry and incisive psychology, but remains brutal in its observations. Even when Zola determined to be optimistic in *The Ladies' Paradise*, he resorts to irony; in bitterly tragic novels like *Germinal* (1885) and *La Terre* (*The Earth,* 1887), short poetic codas provide slight uplift. When Flaubert attempted a novel of realistic comedy about bourgeois idiocy in *Bouvard et Pécuchet* (1881), he failed because of its oblique and repetitive humor, just as Melville's attempt at realistic comedy foundered in obscure sensibility in *The Confidence Man.*

Perhaps the only realist who transcended the tragic-genre aspect of realism was Mark Twain, especially in *The Adventures of Huckleberry Finn* which employs the picaresque, yet its varied humor remains more wry than rollicking. Tolstoy's *The Death of Ivan Illych* (invoked at one point in *A Man in Full* by the scheming Peepgass in order to ironically display his ignorance and utter lack of spirituality) provides a positive spiritual ending of repentance, but the road to that transformation wallows in such narcissistic tragedy that Tolstoy's novella can hardly be called comic in any sense of the word.[41] Realism remains an intractably tragic modality and Wolfe's attempt to lighten it with his particular brand of comic satire creates lively reading, yet a close scrutiny reveals some minor artistic inconsistencies, inconsistencies that are often accepted trademarks of the big postmodern novel. Such minor criticism does nothing to mar the great achievement of Wolfe's sociological "realism" in *A Man in Full*, which rivals the work of Farrell, Steinbeck, or Lewis in its devotion to period detail and psychology.

Ambush at Fort Bragg, included in *Hooking Up*, but previously published in serial form in *Rolling Stone* and then in audio form with the actor Ed Norton, is a novella spin-off from Wolfe's research on *A Man in Full.*[42] In technique it is more grindingly calculating in its use of realistic dialogue, but its portrayal of a murderer and his gay-bashing friends as more dedicated patriots than dullard television reporters who are opportunistic hypocrites belabors a lame political invective against an imagined unscrupulous liberal media. This sordid piece is itself an illustration of the pitfalls in blending satire and realism. Zola often gets away with this in symbolism that drives to a climax, but he never descends to awkward blatant editorializing like the "corporate predator in chief."[43] The story is so manipulative and over-the-top that it loses credibility while it opens itself to the charge of prejudiced hypocrisy. (The theme of overly pre-scripted media runs counter to Wolfe's use of the television media in *A Man in Full.*) Much righteous dander is invoked about the liberal press illegally spying on people—such absurd accusations are laughable after the government spying programs that preceded 9/11 by six months. As an attack on political correctness, it might very well convince many readers that political correctness is a much-desired virtue. The despicable behavior of a few American soldiers and conservative reporters in the Iraq war has, in an unintended way, validated this piece as "a bit of mean-spirited realism."[44]

This attack on fools in the media fits into the theme of fools and heroes found in *Hooking Up. The New Yorker* pieces (a slightly revised reprint) attacking William Shawn as a fool persevere in amusement, Wolfe's self-defensive essay "My Three Stooges" shrills more stridently, although it scores several significant arguments. "In the Land of the Rococo Marxists" attacks the foolishness of trendy academics, while "Sorry, But Your Soul Just Died" examines foolishness in the sciences. Four essays consider the subject of heroes: "Two Young Men Who Went West," "Digibabble, Fairy Dust, and the Human Anthill," "The Invisible Artist," and "The Great Relearning." In the latter two, the sculptor Frederick Hart and writer Aleksandr Solzhenitsyn receive acclamation. In the former delightful journalistic excursion, the dissenting Congregationalist connection between pioneer Josiah Grinnell and engineer Bob Noyce, who invented the integrated circuit (better known to lay people as the microchip), are linked together in a cultural continuum. "Digibabble," perhaps the most interesting and eloquent essay in the book, divides into two parts: The first part profiles two men whom society regarded as romantic outsiders and fools, Teilhard de Chardin and Marshall McLuhan, who by the time of their death became regarded as hermetic, heroic geniuses; the second panel profiles Edward O. Wilson, the inventor of sociobiology, who began his career as a genius making significant and heroic contributions to science, only to evolve into a modest celebrity who announced a theory that claimed to explain all life as a deterministic mechanism. This balanced meditation on the delicate border between genius and foolishness strikes me as Wolfe at his best, cheerfully strolling across a high wire at the edge of thought-provoking paradox, evoking the frontiers of consciousness where perils and achievements breathe their frailty.

Whether charting cultural drift in engineering or science, the effects of LSD on the culture, the transition from jet pilot to astronaut, the ethical temper of Wall Street and the racial pulse of New York, or the building and banking sectors of Atlanta (and by implication America at large), Wolfe's talent for such flexible themes continues to enlighten and entertain, but when he descends to political argument his acheivement appears diminished. When Emile Zola presented his first book, *La Fortune des Rougon* (*The Fortunes of the Rougons*, 1871), the first of twenty novels describing the natural and social history of a family, to his revered master of realism, Flaubert reproved Zola for expressing an opinion in the novel's Preface: "A thing that, in my personal poetics, a novelist does not have the right to do."[45] With his next project, *I Am Charlotte Simmons*, Wolfe will attempt another form of postmodern literary realism: A contemporary *bildungsroman* wherein he dramatizes cultural change and social humiliation in America's educational system.

CHAPTER 9

THE IVORY TOWER IN RUINS?

Don't interfere—we have enemies who are both treacherous and extremely
clever.

—Balzac, *Lost Illusions*

The academic genre novel displays a prolific pedigree: Mary McCarthy's *Groves of Academe* (1951), Randall Jarrell's *Pictures from an Institution* (1954), Kingsley Amis' *Lucky Jim* (1954), Vladimir Nabokov's *Pnin* (1957), Philip Roth's novella *Goodbye Columbus* (1959) and his novel *The Human Stain* (2000), Bernard Malamud's *A New Life* (1961), John Barth's *Giles-Goat Boy* (1966), Eric Segal's *Love Story* (1970), Amanda Cross' *Poetic Justice* (1970), David Lodge's transatlantic trilogy *Changing Places* (1975), *Small Changes* (1984), and *Nice Work* (1988), Don DeLillo's *White Noise* (1985), Ishmael Reed's *Japanese by Spring* (1993), Michael Chabon's *Wonder Boys* (1994), Jane Smiley's *Moo* (1995), Richard Powers' *Galatea 2.2* (1995), John L'Heureux's *The Handmaid of Desire* (1996), Donna Tartt's *The Secret History* (1996), Jon Hassler's *Rookery Boys* (1996), John Orozco's *Delano* (1999), Tom Perrotta's *Joe College* (2000), Jack Kerouac's overlooked *Orpheus Emerged* (2000), Francine Prose's witty *Blue Angel* (2000), and Joyce Carol Oates' bitterly ironic novella *Beasts* (2002). These are just some recent highlights of the more than six hundred novels in this genre.[1] The point of view usually adopted by these novels is that of a professor, but several include a student's irreverent point of view. For most writers it's a fun topic in a mischievous genre, and inevitably, a satiric one. While not always great literature, such novels offer amusing reads. Within this genre Wolfe attempts a masterpiece on the level of Flaubert's *Madame Bovary* (1857) and its greater Russian imitation, Tolstoy's *Anna Karenina* (1877).

That ambition finds its announcement in the very title of the book, *I Am Charlotte Simmons*, a reference to Gustave Flaubert's famous quip, "*Madame Bovary, c'est moi*" (Madame Bovary, that's me, after myself"), which is generally considered an autobiographical confession of romantic frustration.[2] As for the actual phrase, *C'est moi*, it is reputed to be second-hand reportage from conversation or a perhaps a sentence from a lost letter. Yet there exits the possibility that Flaubert's most famous critical confession might be apocryphal, even though, for many, it rings true.

The reviews of Wolfe's novel landed in right field, left field, a home run, a foul ball, and a strike-out—all over the park. Many reviewers appeared unnerved about the depiction of sexuality in the novel, yet oblivious to the erotic sexuality that lay behind the creation of Flaubert's novel. In a similar way, Russians were outraged when Flaubert's friend Turgenev brought this diffident combination of romanticism and realism to Russia in *Fathers and Sons* wherein he added a sociological generation gap (based upon curriculum changes at the University) to the fissure between older romantics and younger realists. Wolfe's novel stresses changes in the educational system since he went to college: Changes in curriculum, attitudes, manners, and sexual mores, but especially how these relate to his favorite obsession—status. Wolfe's essay "Hooking Up" may be seen as a thematic warm-up for the novel, since Wolfe links contemporary language with the changing sociology of sex:

> In the nineteenth century, entire shelves used to be filled with novels whose stories turned on the need for women, such as Anna Karenina or Madame Bovary, to remain chaste or to maintain a façade of chastity. In the year 2000, a Tolstoy or a Flaubert wouldn't have stood a chance in the United States. From age thirteen, American girls were under pressure to maintain a façade of sexual experience and sophistication. Among girls, "virgin" was a term of contempt.[3]

Wolfe discusses "hooking up" in high school, the commonplace acceptance of oral sex on the part of teenage girls to please boys, and how women are encouraged to imitate the predatory mores of men through impulsive and even anonymous "scoring" in a celebrity-fixated culture, creating a competitive striving among women for sexual activity as status trophies.

That theme opens the Prologue of Wolfe's novel when the Dupont college student Hoyt jokes that the woman he slept with last night informed him that she has been re-virginated in reply to his buddy's accusation that she's a slut. Humor, language, clothing, associations, and habits underpin the sociology of status-seeking on a college campus as the central leitmotifs of the novel. The Prologue is preceded by a lengthy quotation from a fictional reference book, *The Dictionary of Nobel Laureates*, 3rd edition, the kind of prank that one might come across in the work of Jorge Luis Borges or perhaps a book to be found on the shelf in his short story, "The Library of Babel." The shocking Prologue features a graphic scene of sex and violence, a secret scandal that will become central to the plot. The reader becomes a hidden camera witnessing the sexually predatory state governor, a promiscuous female student, and two campus villains—the extroverted Hoyt and the reserved Vance—who by their wits and fists manage to manhandle a burly bodyguard.

Charlotte Simmons, like Flaubert's Emma who is a farmer's daughter, comes from a humble background, Sparta,[4] in the North Carolina hills; both characters have a youthful ambition, gleaned from reading novels, to accomplish something with their lives as if they thought their lives to be novels, yet neither possesses a clear idea of what it is that they want to accomplish. Bright and naively romantic, they set forth to find out who they are. In both cases they are ultimately devastated to discover that reality is more brutal and banal than they had imagined. The major differences between Flaubert's novel and Wolfe's novel are threefold: Flaubert's prose displays a subtle and elegant lyricism that remains passionate although curiously detached, while Wolfe's satiric, well-conceived scenarios grind away with hysterical realism in a hyperkinetic tenor with hilarious touches to its register. Emma remains more passionate than intelligent, while Charlotte exhibits more intelligence than passion; the scope of Flaubert's novel presents the full panorama of life until death, while Wolfe's novel remains limited to the formative year of college life, the freshman year. Flaubert admired Chateaubriand's prose-poem novels as his lyric antecedents, while Wolfe saw the problematic treatment of Flaubert's Emma as a type to be seeded on fertile campus ground in America.

Dupont College was thought by most reviewers to resemble either Duke University attended by Wolfe's daughter Alexandra or Stanford University where Ken Kesey and his friends became butterflies, yet it is a composite. Over the years Wolfe had spoken frequently on the college reading circuit; he spent some time wearing a blue blazer at the University of Michigan at Ann Arbor, Stanford, Chapel Hill, and the University of Florida in Gainesville for his research in order to give a composite portrait of a college in the novel.[5]

The pathetic scene of Charlotte's arrival at famed Dupont College with her hovering parents ("helicopter parents" in current slang) evokes a tragic poignancy as it presents Charlotte's self-conscious anxiety about being embarrassed by her lowly origins, a background that we know she's bound to escape one way or another. When abandoned to the lonely mercy of a testosterone-fueled student on alcohol in a dorm, waking her up at 1 A.M. in the dark, the ghost of Joseph Conrad appears:

> a tremendous crash down the hall, followed by a boy yelling: "Well, you sure fucked that *dawg*!" Raucous laughs. The rap music pounded on. The boy's curly head turned to look, then turned back. "Barbarians," he said. "Exterminate the brutes. Look—uhhhh, needn't stand on ceremony —"
>
> With a burst of anger Charlotte pushed herself upward in bed with both arms. "I *told* you! I'm trying to *sleep*!"
>
> "Okay!" said the boy, pulling his head back and holding his palms out in front of his chest in a gesture of mock defensiveness. "Whoa! Skooz!" He walked backward with a mock stagger. "I wasn't even here! That wasn't me!" He disappeared down the hall, going, "Oohoooo . . . oohoooo . . ."[6]

In *The Heart of Darkness*, a text often read by freshmen in college, the sentence "Exterminate the brutes" issues in sullen utterance by the monstrous and demented Kurtz who projects his personality-cult ersatz tribe in holocaustlike warfare. Kurtz's helter-skelter warfare to amass ivory and gold lacks any sense of morals or even semblance of methodology. The drunken student knows the text and speaks with a wink, showing off this allusion as he superciliously puts down other students, but the irony lingers that he himself operates unconsciously as a Kurtzlike would-be sexual conqueror without any morals or sense of order in his mad quest for random and anonymous sex in the dark, proffered as he had declared earlier as a "courtesy" to the newcomer. The animal mating call of "Oohoooo" depicts him as the sort of howling monkey one might hear in the midnight jungles of Belize. As with Wolfe's literary allusions in his previous two novels, the literary reference illuminates by way of oblique irony.

Charlotte's roommate, Beverly, in her situation at college bears some reverse parallels to Mark Twain's character Sally Sellers from *The American Claimant* (1892),[7] a sequel to *The Gilded Age* (1874). While attending a snobbish college, Sally is humble, democratic, and practical, but through a quirk of fate she suddenly becomes Lady Gwendolyn (later repudiating the title). Beverly from Boston revels retroactively in the status of her aristocratic prep school background while her family indulges her with gobs of money. Both characters function as satiric foils. Sally designs and makes her own clothes, while Beverly has a conspicuous talent for cadging the clothes of her peers. The counterpoint of significant change between the two relates to how manners and mores in American colleges have changed over the past century: Sally is charming, chaste, and observantly witty while Beverly is a crass alcoholic, boastingly promiscuous, and so snootily narcissistic that the reader wants her packed off to rehab as soon as possible.

As with *A Man in Full*, Wolfe employs the bifurcated plot (Charlotte with the basketball player Jojo), but with an amusing twist: The Odysseus-Bloom figure of fatherly wisdom, flat-top Jojo, limns a spoiled fool twirling his ball. Such inversion of expectations highlights the novel's theme of American culture turned upside down, as students have developed, with the approval of college administrators, a Maoistlike culture of youth that subverts the process of education. The irrelevant and ignored professors become reduced to helpless babysitters who retreat to the library to compose their obscure prose symphonies of arcane jargon while the drunken orgy of self-indulgence literally rages across campus. This satiric caricature exposes the anti-intellectual roots of American society within the ivory tower itself.

Charlotte and Jojo meet in a class on the French Novel, From Flaubert to Houellebecq,[8] which Charlotte has enrolled because of her reading abilities in French. She's shocked when the French teacher reads the opening of the novel in English, since she has worked so hard at reading the novel in French. It turns out that the class is geared toward students, mostly jocks, who need some faux language credits in order to fulfill the language requirement. After class, the teacher tells Charlotte she's in the wrong course and should transfer to another course, contemptuously referring to the class as his "community service." But the class lesson on how Flaubert employs the first chapter to imprint on the mind of the reader the impression of Charles Bovary's character as that of an "idiot" (in Charlotte's word) functions also as a lesson on how to read Wolfe's Prologue, which leaves us with the indelible impression of Hoyt as a malicious opportunist.

As a star basketball player with professional hoop hopes, Jojo is painted with more complexity than one might expect, since he's intelligent, diffidently interested in doing well, yet too weak in character not to play the cool fool before his peers. But his central character flaw stands out clearly: He is a spoiled product of a corrupt bribery system that showers athletes with cars and money, resulting in a kind of slave class programmed by privileged narcissism. The name Jojo alludes to the Beatles' satiric song "Get Back" where the character is described as a loner. For Jojo the question is: Can he overcome his narcissism, connect with another, and escape the slave mentality of being a jock and get back to his real self?

The poignancy of Charlotte's first few traumatic days and the intelligence and angst of her sharp observations as they combine with her emotional insecurity allow the reader to identify with her more than any other of Wolfe's characters. Especially effective is a two-track stream of consciousness when she writes a letter home to her parents and when she speaks on the telephone to Laurie, a high-school friend at another college. The unwritten anger she represses before her beloved parents contains transcendent pathos (as well as delicious ironies), while the honest but fearful confessions she makes to Laurie leave her psychologically exposed more than the reader would wish—this is transformative. We cannot help but identify with Charlotte because she represents at this point the better self of our lost youth caught in a box. Just like Flaubert, Wolfe has painted a major tragic heroine who is both realistic as well as a type. And such delicacy remains true of even minor characters like Adam the newspaper reporter, not one of the privileged seeds at the college; yet Adam's Turgenevlike bio slide and interior stream-of-consciousness ably captures his ambitions, resentment, and his overall decency as a person. The basketball coach, Buster Roth, despite his bluster, eventually emerges as a more complex and decent person than most of the hubristic faculty.

Wolfe's focus on the fragility of the freshman ego in the first month of school illustrates a profound truth: This first month of social "boot camp" is the decisive pitched battle where innocence, self-reliance, and self-respect are trampled by the peer herd and one's previous identity undergoes erasure in the sex-crazed brainwash of loneliness. By the end of the sixth chapter, our star Charlotte Simmons has "all but forgotten the Force: I am Charlotte Simmons."[9] Her high-school friend Laurie at another college has already capitulated to peer pressure—an example of a willing victim plunged into self-indulgence by her new freedom and its conformist cultural ambiance as illustrated by the popularity of the rapper Dr. Dis who seduces students with his raunchy cynicism. By confining his inclination for comic satire to dwell among the minor characters, Wolfe creates a tragic heroine who soars above the pranksters and fools.

The episode of Charlotte being sexiled (exiled from her dorm room while her roommate Beverly has sex) and reading the women's magazine article about how to sexually please a man provides amusement and an all-too-realistic depiction of such women's magazines. The politics of the school newspaper, the *Daily Wave*, and the satire on its purported independence offers no exaggeration, while the basketball coach's rant about the superior virtues of basketball as compared to philosophy transforms realism into effective comic satire. While Wolfe habitually pushes the limit of satiric believability in his novels, his measure here is considerately savvier and consequently more effectively realistic while retaining a wicked humor.

Charlotte's confused emotions of embarrassment display too much paint as the pacing of the narrative slows down for emphasis. Her self-scrutiny while talking to her new friends about just how much of a fool she had made of herself over Hoyt's "heartless sexual prank"[10] after she realizes he had attempted a clock-timing seven-minute seduction as a show-off before his frat brothers allows Charlotte to navigate more of the double-tracking consciousness that was so effective in her letter to her parents. Such blatant surface irony lacks the subtlety of Flaubert, yet presents a more appropriate and consistent stitching to Wolfe's style of writing.

Dispensing ginger ale and beer in identical plastic cups is traditional practice at fraternity parties throughout the country. While the elaborate secret underground room may be rare, it is effective at introducing a Poe-like Gothic atmosphere of awe that Charlotte breezily discounts. The beer-soaked stench of the carpet and furniture rings true. Although there are no masks outside of excessive make-up on the girls, there is an apocalyptic ambiance of desperation to the frat party in the frenzied attempts at sexual seduction through grind dancing, the on-line anxiety of making it to the bathroom before vomiting, and in the leaking girl who passes out unconscious in the underground den. Wolfe expertly evokes suspense at the party—in Charlotte's conflict between suspicious unease and curious wonder—as to whether Charlotte will succumb to Hoyt's seduction, which may evoke comparison to some scenes in Richardson's eighteenth century novel *Clarissa*, yet Wolfe wisely avoids any melodrama. The degrading anarchy of the frat party is a portrait of students in a cultural hell of their own construction that might bring to mind the paintings of Hieronymus Bosh. More even than the pursuit of any sexual pleasure, the supreme goal relates to status considerations—bragging rights on the part of men and the swapping of gossip between women, as everyone appears to take mental notes on who is with whom.

It does not take Charlotte long to size up the situation accurately in terms of status:

> The boys sang their choral response of manly laughs, bellows, and yahoos. To Charlotte, this bawling had become the anthem of the victors, namely those girls who were attractive, experienced, and deft enough to achieve success at Dupont, which, as far as she could tell, was measured in boys.[11]

While Wolfe excessively highlights Charlotte's naïveté, this may not be inept portraiture, as some reviewers have claimed, but a display of Wolfe's compulsive inclination to satirize.

The journalist and novelist Mark Bowden, one of the few reviewers to get a sensible bead on the novel, puts the situation this way:

> Into this rampant promiscuity wanders beautiful, innocent, idealistic, painfully traditional Charlotte Simmons, a *Candide*-like scholarship student from the deep-backwoods town of Sparta, North Carolina, in search of the "life of the mind." Some of the novel's critics have complained that a *naif* such as Charlotte in this day and age is implausible, but Charlotte is a construction, a device, one in a long and celebrated series of satirical vehicles in English literature, all the way back to Henry Fielding's *Joseph Andrews*. On the surface she is fragile, but underneath she is a warrior, a "Spartan." [12]

While the journalistic elements of the novel in its careful scene-painting present close-to-the-bone journalistic realism, the fluctuating conflict in the mind of Charlotte satirizes both the extreme Puritan end of the spectrum as well as the inevitable temptation to self-indulgent hedonism. Although partly a throwback to the picaresque novel, Charlotte has considerable depth, especially in her stream-of-consciousness second thoughts, while retaining her mildly satiric double shadow.

Bowden's reference to Fielding delivers resonance at the beginning of "The H word," with its direct address to the reader. Such direct addresses in Fielding's novel *Tom Jones* (1749) begin each of the eighteen Books that comprise the novel. In these addresses to the reader Fielding either announces or comments on a theme or character, or gives a parablelike parallel to the situation at hand. In announcing his theme of humiliation, Wolfe quotes George Orwell's comment that seventy-five percent of ordinary life consists of humiliation. Various forms of humiliation among students—sexual, athletic, conversational—find dramatic exploration in the next several chapters.

In Chapter Fourteen, "Millennial Mutants," the name of a student club searching for the matrix that will be the key to membership in a new aristocratic meritocracy, a dramatic crisis occupies Charlotte's mind. After attending a lecture on Charles Darwin (and the question of whether we are self-conscious rocks or our own willed movers) in which she impresses her Nobel Prize professor with her response to his question, she speaks to the professor after class, and the professor is clearly impressed by this earnest freshman who has actually read Darwin's *Origin of the Species*. Professor Starling (who correctly notes that Darwin was not an atheist) doesn't know her name and requests it. She gives it to him and blithely strolls across campus: "Sailing! Sailing! Gloriously drunk on cosmological theories and approbation," [13] thinking she is not like other students for she is *Charlotte Simmons*. In the background tolls the campus Ridenour Carillon (no such item but the French etymology of laughing finds invocation) to the traditional wedding processional tune while the omniscient narrator jokes that Charlotte was unaware of Rudyard Kipling's lyrics to it, a somersault reference to Kipling's 1897 poem "Recessional,"[14] a religious reminder of empire's transience and a warning against foolish, boastful words—a theme that will surface later in the chapter.

Charlotte has had her Cartesian illumination. René Descartes had rebutted the dominant Pyrrhonist philosophy of skepticism.[15] Descartes had sat huddled in winter by a clanking wood stove while he smoked his pipe, dismissing all previous philosophy as he decided to begin philosophy anew with the one proposition that we must take on faith the observation "I think, therefore I am." Likewise, Charlotte asserts her self-confident commitment to wed the intellectual life on campus—in an early fall stroll with the open air carrying the wedding tune to the only student truly committed to live outside of the culturally dominant deterministic flow amid the rampant nihilistic conformity that circulates like a virus on the campus: "Yes! She had found the life of the mind and was . . . *living* it!"[16] An effective scene, it creates the suspense of whether this sudden "wedding" to the intellectual life will endure.

Two informal fraternities confront each other in less than civilized debate: The Millennial Mutants, who work on the campus *Daily Wave* newspaper, find themselves confronted by a group of muscled lacrosse players. Amid the exchange of bitter and shocking insults, Charlotte stands aside silently as an awed bystander after Adam has invited her over for conversation. Adam and their leader Greg are humiliated by the giant lacrosse player, but the petite feminist Camille Deng provokes some personal insults; she wins the obscene ranking match with the super weapon of political correctness. This low verbal dueling serves as an effective contrast to Charlotte's intellectual epiphany. The chapter concludes with an ironic touch: Virginal Adam, the most gifted intellectual among this group of overachievers (hence mutants in comic book fashion), is shyly attracted toward Charlotte, yet he turns to her, smiles, and winks, only to utter typical banality at Charlotte: "Hey, babe."[17]

While one track of the plot follows football with its seventy-thousand-seat stadium bowl and its attendant tailgate party in the parking lot, another track bounces along the wooden court with its fourteen thousand seats. This simultaneous dialectic of football versus basketball as vicarious political drama appeared as a minor theme in *A Man in Full* as a metaphor in the mayoral race where the victorious football-backing Jordan wins re-election over the basketball polemics of challenger Fleet. Charlotte's presence is the catalyst for a brawl at the parking lot—Hoyt takes an awful bloody beating; the senior Jojo, in a grim psychological battle on the court and bruising backboards, undergoes a humiliating drubbing and is pulled from the game for a freshman replacement.

In the comic chapter "The Sublime," Charlotte has Adam escort her to the Saint Ray fraternity so that she can guiltily proffer her thank-you to Hoyt for saving her from being mauled at the tailgate part. Hoyt appears battered and bandaged in such a grotesque manner that he resembles a Frankenstein-like creature. The chapter expertly evokes both danger and awkwardness on the part of both characters distrustful of each other: Charlotte guiltily confused and

Hoyt wary of losing his prey. After Hoyt valiantly drives her back to her dorm, Charlotte kisses the disfigured monster on the lips: The Romantic conception of the Sublime embraces the ugly and awkward as beautiful when treated with empathetic inspiration. As Charlotte re-enters her dorm, she realizes she has been behaving like the "little conscious rock," behaving with a falsely rationalized free will in following conventional routines expected of girls on campus as male trophies. The unlikely but revivifying image of a Sargent painting floods her wandering cortex—this imaginary surge of realistic inspiration serves as a tonic to restore her real identity: "In all of Dupont college, only *she* was Charlotte Simmons."[18] While amusing and witty, the use of a color reproduction from a realistic painting as a magic talisman for profound psychological healing also reveals the author as a field reporter shaman bent on conjuring up his own tribal god: The ghost of Emile Zola dedicated to a deterministic realism that whimsically wings its metaphors as little conscious rocks.

Zola appears in the next chapter, "The Lifeguard," with reference to his 1890 novel *La Bête humaine* (*The Human Beast*) as the book is rather arbitrarily worked into a conversation with Professor Starling who has summoned Charlotte to discuss her paper on Darwin. Charlotte appears unaware that there are only three possibilities for a professor to summon a student to discuss a paper: Either to get the student to confess to plagiarism or forgery; to compliment the student on the paper; or to recruit the student into the professor's field of study. Charlotte insecurely takes each question as an accusation of failure in this amusing Inquisition. Professor Starling then recruits her into neuroscience lab. Having been roped into such drudgery, Charlotte is naively enthusiastic and flies "like a swallow over the campus," as if she were an incarnation of Athena "with amazing speed and exhilarating swoops and dives, in Heaven, but with no destination."[19] Professor Starling functions a model lifeguard, trying to keep an eye on Charlotte.

Charlotte plunges into a trendy bar with phony identification where all the girls smile with perfect teeth thanks to the goddess Orthodontia (as if the bar was a temple where the physically perfect display themselves) while they gaze into the boys' eyes "as if never in their lives had they heard such mesmerizing wit or wisdom."[20] Hoyt, whom Mimi refers to as Charlotte's Saint Ray lifeguard, appears. Charlotte presumes he walks toward her table, but he swerves to a table occupied by a Britney Spears type with whom he dances the raunchy grind, escorting the swooning blonde out of the bar. Charlotte feels wounded—Hoyt is exposed a negligent lifeguard, while the old bird Professor Starling occupies the sterling role of the true lifeguard in the chapter. The reference to Zola's *Human Beast* functions to underscore the portrayal of the overcrowded bar as a bestial place of lust, noise, and stench: A breathing bestial animal, the antithesis of the intellectual life, much as the train engine in Zola's novel achieves realization as a major allegorical character incarnating implacable sexual drive. To those familiar with the grim and shockingly powerful novel or even the great 1938 movie starring rugged Jean Gabin, the theme of sexual jealousy leads to an inevitable murder—alarm bells sound and serve to ratchet up the emotional betrayal engulfing Charlotte in the dark cage of the high-decibel zoo, another "heart of darkness."

But the appearance of sexual jealousy doesn't rear its head until several chapters later (Chapter Twenty-Three) during the off-campus Saint Ray Frat Formal in Washington, D.C. where Charlotte has accompanied Hoyt as his date. On her first alcohol high, she sees Hoyt's frat brother Julian dancing in his boxer underwear for her benefit and this evokes the jealousy of his date in an amusing reversal of high dog, low dog, competition. While Vladimir Nabokov is often praised by academics for his sardonic satire on Freud in *Lolita* (as well as his sarcastically seedy descriptions of American motels), Wolfe elegantly mocks the pretentious décor of a luxury hotel bathroom with comic variations on cheese motifs:

> The bathroom was a cramped space done in sad pale tones of—what?—stale cheese. The bathtub and the toilet were the color of stale mozzarella. The shower curtain looked like rubbery stale mozzarella. The counter where the basin was ran the width of the wide plate-glass mirror. That counter was a thick piece of plastic with fake bluish veins in it. It was supposed to look like marble. Instead, it looked like Roquefort—and then the cheese conceit began to make her bilious, so she abandoned it.[21]

While at first glance this witty cheese riff in Charlotte's mind appears to be an amusing set piece, its symbolic resonance carries into the following chapter where repeated observations on the extensive cleavage on sundry girls at the formal dinner become an extension of this cheese motif. When Charlotte descends from the hotel room, she proudly displays her own cleavage. Charlotte, who had ridiculed the vileness of the bathroom décor, will later that night be spewing vomit in that very bathroom, witlessly drunk as she grovels on all fours across the bathroom floor. The status reversal motif in the "Model on a Runway" chapter doesn't belong to the life of the mind, yet its pinching irony runs off the page with droll humor.

Ever since Charlotte's ecstatic *kairos* experience at Professor Starling's lecture, she has been descending into the collegiate life of status competition: Participating in satiric ranking with the Millennial Mutants, agreeing to testify for Jojo at his trial for handing in a paper written by Adam, necking and petting with both Adam and Hoyt. After Charlotte's great "revelation," her only concern has been the life of emotions. The *kairos* experience itself has been a red herring, a false revelation. While Wolfe found this mystical term to be somewhat illuminating when it came to describing Ken Kesey's drug experiences, Wolfe the Enlightenment rationalist employs this mystical term in a satiric manner here when applied to Charlotte. For one thing, this *crossing* concerns the thinking of two men, the agnostic Professor Starling and the atheist neuroscientist Delgado who puts the "*soul* in quotation marks," "proving" it with a bizarre testosterone experiment that puts his life in jeopardy. Ironically, Charlotte perceives Delgado as "the man who revolutionized the way the human animal sees herself."[22] The point of view remains exclusively male in Delgado's performance proof. Wolfe depicts Charlotte "high on ideas—no, high on the excitement of discovery, of seeing the future from the peaks of Darién. O Dupont!"[23]

When John Keats wrote that famous sonnet about the peaks of Darién, he committed a notorious gaff with the conquistador Cortez, not Balboa, standing on those Darién peaks as the first European to view the Pacific Ocean. Although the omniscient narrator cheerfully mocks Charlotte's mystic "revelation," such false starts or "intellectual revelations" are commonplace mirages among those freshman and sophomore students who ardently attempt to mount intellectual peaks with spontaneous enthusiasm. In the chapter entitled "Get What?" Charlotte falsely gets *it* at her "revelation"; JoJo slowly begins to get *it* as he begins to hit the books, while Hoyt continues *not* to get the intellectual life at all. Charlotte has slowly slid down the conformist slope to be juiced with vodka *before* the formal dinner of the frat party as her status-protector Hoyt Thorpe massages the muscles of her bare back.

Wolfe presents the seduction of Charlotte by Hoyt from her point of view, drunkenly "rationalizing" that she will halt Hoyt at the next stroke of the hand or next removal of clothing. This "conscious little rock" hurtles through both the dinner and seduction high on self-sustaining images of her status ascent in the eyes of others; the inevitable dénouement arrives with her deflowering which Hoyt refers to as "dusting her off." The deflowering itself is presented as a quasi-public ritual that echoes the seduction scene in *Elmer Gantry* (1927) where Sharon capitulates to Elmer before an altar that she associates in her mind with the goddess of fertility.[24] The counterpoint here is that the hotel is perceived by Charlotte as a temple of superior status and her capitulation to Hoyt during the bacchanal consists of her rationalizing her loss of virginity in the ritual of acquiring enhanced status. Amid the excess of the orgiastic revels, Charlotte's seduction appears as self-rationalizing abasement, unlike the orgiastic evangelism in *Elmer Gantry*. The seduction ritual proceeds in the name of functional sterility and not sensual fertility, as Hoyt produces a condom that appears snatched out of thin air like a magical, talismanic fetish object. As the high priest of this ritual, Hoyt remains more embarrassed and disappointed in his ritual obligation and he completely abandons Charlotte as soon as the ritual is concluded; he then verbally boasts before an invited audience of friends whom he lets into the room while Charlotte lies naked on the bed, passing her off as a joke to his "religious" peers. Charlotte realizes this and freaks out:

> She curled herself up into a ball. She took a self-destructive, self-hating pleasure in wrapping her body about such a filthy, sordid memorial, a shrine not only to a little fool's illusion that men fell in love. Men didn't *fall* in love, which would be surrender. They *made* love—*made* being an active, transitive verb that rhymed with *raid*, the marauder out for blood, *laid* the raider who got laid, *daid* as a bug I got my killing ov'ere'at the Hyatt Ambassador *Ho*-tel in Washington, D.C.[25]

Charlotte performs a self-hating and self-mocking wigger rap in her own rural Appalachian dialect as she introduces the theme of lost illusions that will occupy much of the later chapters. Indeed, *Lost Illusions* (1837–43) by Honoré de Balzac appears by name in the very next chapter, "How Was It?" which begins with the words, "Like a fool" as Charlotte's meandering mind drifts toward home:

> What grand lie could she dream up to explain away Charlotte Simmons's dusty, scuffling, bungling hangdog retreat from the other side of the mountain, where great things had awaited . . . Charlotte Simmons's return to Sparta and the three stoplights . . . Up her brain stem bubbled Lucien de Rubempre's ignominious return to Angoulême from Paris on the outside baggage rack of a carriage, hidden beneath a heap of suitcases, carpetbags, and boxes in *Lost Illusions* . . . [26]

To readers familiar with Balzac's trilogy this return conjures a particular poignancy: After some modest success in Paris the talented poet and journalist Lucien returns home in defeat, having driven his family into destitution from financing his education and career. Will Charlotte do the same to her beloved and humble parents? Balzac describes both literary and journalistic circles as corrupt and venal, just like the fraternities and sorority circles on campus that depend upon extravagant dues and perpetuate a world of status seeking and status climbing. In the sequel to *Lost Illusions* (*The Splendor and Misery of Courtesans*, 1839–47) Lucien falls in love with a courtesan who commits suicide because of a bestial client and when it is discovered that she, unknown to herself, is a wealthy heiress, Lucien, falsely accused of murder, hangs himself in his jail cell. The evocation of Balzac here serves to heighten the excitement of the literary reader, except that we already know that Wolfe consistently employs literary allusion as counterpoint, so the grim ironies of Balzac's despairing and wrenching realism are not likely to dust our Charlotte's shoulders.

Yet as readers we do have to wonder how many high-school students have managed to plow through Balzac's tragic trilogy and its gruesome sequel. And if Charlotte had read those novels, why should she be so surprised by the turn of events? This hardly sounds like realism on the part of Wolfe at all. But we are not in the nineteenth century and this is a typical if whimsical freedom permitted by postmodern novelists when they play with time and literature as they uplift the status of their literary credentials, something that postmodern novelists in this competitive arena of literature have a propensity to perform as a kind of steroid supplement. While such a practice is legal, the question remains: Is such literary obsession, affectation, or casual allusion effective? I think, yes, but it raises a question about Wolfe's amusing literary counterpoints: Who is the audience for these? Certainly not the best-seller list that Wolfe would like to soar up on; certainly not university libraries who in the main boycotted the purchase of this novel, even though they bought his other books; certainly not college students— above all, they resent being told that Wolfe is cleverly playing counterpoint to the straight narrative; certainly not parents who send their children off to college as one might send a child off to war, fearful of knowing any of the messy and gruesome details or the likely pitfalls.

A short interlude occurs in the plot: The gossip of Charlotte's adventure rages across campus as she clams up in misery amid her self-inflicted hell of humiliation. She dreads running into anybody, overhears some unflattering remarks about her adventure, and ducks returning home at Thanksgiving, but Christmas with the family and friends cannot be avoided. The next chapter presents a long intermission from the events at the college, featuring Charlotte in Hell visiting the shades of the home town people she once knew, the longest chapter in the novel, "In the Dead of the Night," which refers to Charlotte's dark night of the soul with snow drifting in the night, giving the lie to the once-familiar landscape. Charlotte's two younger brothers ask her to talk about some of the star black basketball players whom she doesn't know. Some things have changed back in small southern towns since Norman Jewison's 1967 film *In the Heat of the Night* and Charlotte herself has endured immense changes at her college boot camp. Just these few months have made Charlotte a different person who can no longer be honest with her family.

It becomes hard to explain to Mother that college students don't date, hard to lie to her best friend Laurie who had admitted to Charlotte that she had lost her virginity, hard to keep a straight face amid the multitude of lies, but we now realize that Charlotte the girl who could not lie to her peers at school because she did not know how to tell lies, has returned home and is now acquiring the subterfuge mask and skill of the liar: the home Christmas visit becomes another boot camp experience that steels her resolve to be an individual cut off from her roots. This chapter drags with a Sinclair Lewis-like dramatization of small town ennui. There is one thing that has not changed about small southern towns—you can't go home again, as Wolfe's namesake Thomas Wolfe once proclaimed in a novel by that name:

> Charlotte *wanted* to cry when she said goodbye to them, but she was parched with a fear of the unknown that went far beyond the nervousness she suffered the first time she set out from the Blue Ridge Mountains for—that place. One thing the trip home had shown her: She could never make Allegheny County home again; nor any other place either—least of all, Du—the college to which she was heading. The bus was home; and let the trip be interminable.[27]

Here's Turgenev's generation gap, but without a showdown—only a forlorn bus winding through blue hills to a college whose name she can't even get herself to utter in secret, mental dumb-speak. Haunted by the prospect of failure yet unable to admit defeat, she returns to college with her innocence lost, travelling without the hope of a horizon, a conscious little projectile hurtling into peril, morosely feeling sorry for herself.

The accumulated guilt is such that she returns a basket case, collapsing into the arms of Adam, the nicest character in the novel, helplessly in love with Charlotte. Charlotte's six-week nervous breakdown in the care of Adam is well drawn, yet her gratitude appears scant—in terms of her previously limned character and in terms of any believable response from anyone. Her eventual and sudden recovery,

"I *am* Charlotte Simmons again, but a Charlotte Simmons who has walked over the coals and through the flames,"[28] breathes new life into the novel. She confides in Adam: "I felt like I was caught in a . . . in like the maelstrom of the Edgar Allan Poe story, and there was no way I could get out of it."[29] This refers to Poe's romantic maritime story "The Descent into the Maelstrom." A story within a story, it tells of a man who survived a shipwreck by noticing that larger objects sank into a whirlpool faster than smaller objects: He decides to jump ship in an effort to avoid the whirlpool, while his brother stays aboard the ship and drowns. As a story of survival, the hapless teller doesn't expect anyone to believe the tale because it is based on a reasonable observation of how physical objects behave—since people are habitually irrational in their "thinking," why should anyone believe his tall tale? He's a kind of oddball Odysseus whose story has become irrelevant in an urban culture focused upon bland notions of conformity.

Charlotte continues to be incoherent about the loss of her virginity or why it happened, but she is a survivor, and the reader knows the reasons for her loss—conformity and status-seeking. Wolfe probably uses the allusion to Poe because of the pseudo-etymological pun: Male-storm—Charlotte had descended into the sexual male-storm and survived to tell the tale, but some of her peers may not. The now effervescent Charlotte has her social radar up-and-running and retooled for *Star Wars* when she is with Adam, then Jojo in the cafeteria. From her chrysalis of collapse, Charlotte emerges as a Southern belle butterfly that soars to entertain Mr. Starling's neuroscience class with humorous down-home phrases that teach the class in a more effective manner than Prof. Starling can. There's a touch of Ava Gardner, North Carolina's most famous backwoods character, to her performance, although Charlotte displays a modesty that Gardner never knew.[30]

At the other end of the emotional spectrum, Adam finds himself humiliatingly "hung" by Professor Quat (the name is lifted from "Radical Chic" where Leon Quat is a black-power radical). In a moment of weakness based upon faith tribal and religious identity as well as a general sense of humanity and common sense, Adam imprudently confesses the truth about his ghosting the history paper on the psychology of George III for Jojo to the V-neck Q. The satire on a bitter, aging radical comes across as insouciantly amusing; the portrayal of Quat as an insensitive dork belongs to the realm of melodramatic comedy more than any kind of natural realism, yet it works quite well. While it's clear that Adam doesn't know anything about the outdated and imaginary wars Quat wants to fight, it is also clear that Quat hasn't the faintest idea of what Adam means when he refers to the young idealism contained in Balzac's *Lost Illusions*. By the end of the chapter, Adam resembles his bookish hero Lucien. We have just witnessed a clash of generations in the manner of Turgenev's *Fathers and Sons*, which recalls the debate and subsequent duel between Arkady's friend Bazarov and Arkady's uncle Piotr. The ages of the antagonists are about the same in both novels, but the political orientation in Wolfe finds itself reversed: Adam is the Romantic interested in the older and more traditional learning of Balzac and secret learned societies while Quat (like Bazarov) is all contemporary politics (ironic, too, that he's a history professor) and he wants to manipulate the vehicle of media publicity for his own ends. Once again Wolfe uses a literary template to run his counterpoint motif, in this case, like Turgenev, to make a point about contemporary university education.

Quat resembles the Marxist rabble-rouser Leo Duffy of Malamud's *A New Life* (1961) who was "a nuisance of the 32 degree"[31] and failed half of his students, yet the contrast with Duffy is that Quat *ultimately* makes no trouble, thus indicating the diminished sociological effectiveness of Marxists on the contemporary college campus. Unlike Duffy, Quat is not fired and the reader identifies with the president's saintly forbearance of Quat. And unlike Quat, Duffy had the respect of his peers, while his suicide is perceived as tragic; the pressure Quat lowers on Adam nearly drives him to suicide. By the way, professors rarely ever fail students today because students usually pay so much tuition that the customer is always right principle customarily prevails at universities.

The use of the college newspaper with its shocking boldface headlines recalls the innovative use of newspaper headlines by Dos Passos in his *U.S.A.* (1938) trilogy where the bold social headlines contrast with the interior personal stories of the novel's characters; Wolfe's humorous counterpointing is that there is *no* contrast between the consciousness of the students and the headlines—rather than think the headlines are alarming, possibly misleading, or announce social corruption, the students perceive the headlines as a reification of their own distorted values with regard to what they consider stylishly cool, either in vocabulary or content.

There's another literary allusion in the next chapter when Adam embraces Charlotte: "He embraced her, causing the blanket to fall to the floor. It wasn't the embrace a boy gives to a girl. It was the one Studs Lonigan gave his mother in the doorway when he came home to die, as best Charlotte could remember the book."[32] The counterpoint here, unlike in the 1920s, indicates that it has become socially acceptable for young women to pursue a life of decadence immersed in drink, sex, and drugs. Yet unlike the drink and drugs that Studs has succumbed to and not felt guilty about, Charlotte suffers badly from an old-fashioned guilt complex. In contrast to Studs, she is more independent yet depends on another man (not her mother or another female) to help her in her difficulties during her breakdown; unlike Studs, she recovers.[33]

One more literary counterpoint to the episode of Adam nursing Charlotte through her breakdown resides with Steinbeck's *Grapes of Wrath* (1939) in the shocking climactic scene where Rose of Sharon, who has had a stillborn baby, physically breastfeeds a starving man with her milk; the scene both becomes a personal act confirming communal hope and displays the possibility of social survival through cohesion. This scene is physical, graphic, and contains a subliminal sexual nuance. The sexual role reversal with Adam and Charlotte indicates diminished stereotyped roles based upon sex, but the greater point is that Americans in the early twenty-first century are more likely to be psychologically damaged than physically starving as people were in the Great Depression. Also, there is no subliminal sexual context: Adam remains all too aware of his sexual attraction to Charlotte, which is not reciprocated. In terms of time, the Steinbeck scene is brief while Adam nurses Charlotte for several weeks. Steinbeck's ideal of a larger communal identity finds itself replaced by the discretion of independent individuality when Adam rejects the idea of bringing Charlotte to a hospital, the place of healing and romance in Hemingway's tragic novel *A Farewell to Arms* (1929). While many reviewers were disturbed by the realistic use of student obscenity in Wolfe's novel, Steinbeck's Oakies provide much more obscenity.

The various plot lines suddenly arrive at a climactic junction and Adam's secret source, the Deep Throat informer, turns out to be I. P., whom Hoyt had clearly tagged as the fraternity's "mistake." This deep informer spy aspect displays good plotting that is reminiscent of Deep Throat from the Nixon Watergate scandal, but I think I. P.'s family connections inside Pierce & Pierce presents a credibility gap, both in that it is vaguely probable that such a connection could exist or that even if such a connection did exist I. P.'s parents would take such a legal risk on behalf of improving their son's social status at college by doing something that is questionable in terms of morals or legality as well as the willingness of these unseen and hence magical parents to intervene nearly anonymously in both politics and campus life. This angle of the plot invokes the creaky *deus ex machina* device that links Adam's triumph to the national coverage on Atlanta's CNN television network. Such magical revenge through a national medium is more akin to the romance of *The Count of Monte Cristo* (1848–50) or Woodward and Bernstein's *All the President's Men* (1974) than it is to any brand of realism in a college novel. Yet melodramatic revenge is sweet whether on the national stage or on campus when it is justified. Adam and I. P. revel in it, especially Adam when Quat, somewhat improbably, lets Adam off the hook as he becomes a national celebrity for exposing a right-wing presidential candidate whom Quat loathes. Charlotte and Jojo turn into a public item of gossip; being on her string revivifies Jojo's basketball career as well as his academics, and Charlotte even succeeds in developing a chaste courtship. In the last epiloguelike chapter it is appropriate that the older and more innocent Beatles' tune of "I Want to Hold Your Hand" accompanies their chaste courtship; divested of his crippling narcissism, Jojo becomes a leading star of college basketball. The allusion to the Beatles brings back the resonance of Jojo's name: As in the song "Get Back," Jojo has gotten "back to the place where you once belonged" while his girl Charlotte cheers him on. Kesey had employed the "Get Back" musical motif of the Beatles for the conclusion of his essay on the death of Neal Cassady.[34]

The courtship of Charlotte by Jojo, a romance that runs counter to the prevailing college culture, began in earnest at one of the school cafeterias. Jojo has enrolled in a nineteenth century French poetry course taught in French; he begs Charlotte to help him. He wants to tape the class and have her translate the tape for him. Jojo says: "'Right now we're reading Victor Hugo. That old dude—the world must have been different back in the day'" Charlotte innocently replies: "'Victor Hugo? I didn't even know he wrote poetry.'"[35] This frank admission of her limitations in French comes as comic relief to both Jojo and the reader, since Victor Hugo is traditionally considered the greatest of all French poets, although some dissenters might propose Verlaine or Valery. Hugo's most charming poems are about his family.

Charlotte, who arrived at college with a great burning ambition to *be* Charlotte Simmons of intellectual achievement, has a serious but silent self-examination with herself amid the roar of the crowd. She finally finds some peace of mind in accepting herself for who she is: a student who will be able to get by and shine in the social stratosphere not because of wealth, brilliance, or determination, but because of her down-home honesty and emotional discretion. With her ambition and virginity dusted off, the world is her blank map to explore. The novel has no closure for her: She sits in the stands at the basketball court on her own little Dariénlike status peak as the band plays on. Emma Bovary was an ordinary girl who lived through extraordinary events for her time, while in counterpoint Charlotte Simmons is an extraordinary girl who lives through the ordinary events of growing up. The title of the novel works throughout the novel as if it is a lyrical refrain in a ballad, a good ballad in which the repetition of the refrain reveals a new and different meaning to the very same words, and a technique that Wolfe imitates from Ken Kesey's novel *Sometimes a Great Notion*.

Writing a novel from the point of view of the opposite sex has always been considered the highest achievement of a novelist because it reveals a skill that goes beyond the confines of the author's consciousness. Flaubert's success with this unusual approach led others to attempt a similar *tour-de-force*. Notable successes with reverse-sex stream of consciousness, following in Flaubert's footsteps, include such masterpieces as Turgenev's *On the Eve* (1860), Tolstoy's *Anna Karenina* (1877), James' *Portrait of a Lady* (1881), Moore's *Esther Waters* (1894), Cather's *My Antonia* (1918), Joyce's last chapter of *Ulysses*, (1922) and Mauriac's *Thérèse Desqueyroux* (1927). More recently, there's William Styron's *Sophie's Choice* (1979), J. M. Coetzee's *Age of Iron* (1990), and Jostein Gaarder's *Sophie's World* (1994). Wolfe's novel joins that eminent list.

I Am Charlotte Simmons manages to transcend the genre of the college novel and is ultimately a *bildungsroman* (a coming-of-age novel) like Goethe's *Wilhelm Meister's Apprenticeship* (1796), a genre characterized by its commonly comic conclusion. American novels in this vein include Melville's *Redburn* (1849), Hawthorne's *The Blithedale Romance* (1852), Crane's *The Red Badge of Courage* (1895), Twain's *The Adventures of Huckleberry Finn* (1884), Dos Passos' *Three Soldiers* (1921), Farrell's *Studs Lonigan* (1935), Russell Banks's *Rule of the Bone* (1995), and Jerome Charyn's *Johnny One-Eye* (2008). In scope, sweep, and excellence, Wolfe's only contemporary rival remains Mary McCarthy's *The Group* (1963), another novel of sociological realism, yet its focus remains on adult lives as it traces the roots of individuals with tragic problems back to their formative college years. Pete Hamill's *Loving Women* (1989), by far his best novel, belongs to this coming-of-age genre.

In writing a superior literary novel with deep characterization and serious cultural critique, Wolfe's achievement was not the smashing economic success he anticipated. According to BookScan, *I Am Charlotte Simmons* sold 431,000 hardcover and paperback copies with a first printing of 1.5 million hardcover

copies.[36] In "My Three Stooges," Wolfe quotes an Updike interview in a pejorative context, bemoaning Updike's defensive attitude about the sales of literary
novels: "People read less, they're less comfortable with the written word. They're
less comfortable with novels. They don't have a backward frame of reference that
would enable them to appreciate things like irony and allusions."[37] Wolfe pro-
ceeded to rebuke Updike: Great writers like Dickens, Dostoevsky, Tolstoy, Zola,
and Twain managed to overcome this. But as readers we should bear in mind
that not all of their books were bestsellers. But what about great writers like
Flaubert, Turgenev, Melville, Joyce, Bulgakov, and a host of others who did not
achieve commercial success?

In many ways, but from a conservative point of view and during a very different
zeitgeist, Wolfe's novel presents a dramatic and more humorous updating of
Richard Hofstadter's classic study, *Anti-Intellectualism in American Life* (1963),[38]
which from a utilitarian point of view attacked small-town Puritan morality and
traditional virtues that created an egalitarian leveling of achievement through
the Puritan sensibility of not displaying one's own pride. Hofstadter blamed
the educational system for fostering a similar distrust of intellectual pursuits as
not being practical or as leading to immorality; Wolfe attacks the permissive
ambiance of student life that colleges have adopted as big corporate business,
its nonjudgmental orthodoxy of political correctness as it relates to evaluating
mores, and the idolization of sexuality as the psychological key to both one's
identity and social status. Sociological concerns have undergone a dramatic shift
in mores and manners over the past fifty years.

Coming from opposite ends of the political spectrum, both Hofstadter and
Wolfe agree that American intellectuals aloofly oppose their fellow Americans.
This quandary about popular culture and our common intellectual history is not
new, but many of the current problems are fairly new, since the Puritan dispensation has long since vanished and the pendulum has swung toward hedonism.
Despite the pessimism contained in Wolfe's satiric caricatures, the upbeat comic
ending indicates that the prospect of a good education endures at universities for
those students who pursue it. In that sense, the more things change, the more
they remain the same, for when was that ever not so?

Wolfe locates the culture of anti-intellectualism in American universities in
two locales: The frat and sorority system and the cult of sports. These tribal
structures echo a consumer status that dominates the culture at large. At the
lower rung of the status pecking pole lurk the nerds who take their education
seriously, yet even lower are those who have limited sexual experiences. Campus
jocks sit at the apex of the status pyramid and women get in line to score
with jocks to enhance their social status. Yet back in the time of Balzac, a
woman's fancy "invested all men of genius with haloes."[39] The perception of
status has changed: In the Romantic era young educated women were drawn to
men's intellects, while in America today women lust after celebrities. When Jojo
perplexedly asks a groupie why she goes to bed with basketball players, she's
incredulous at the question, replying: "'Every girl wants to . . . fuck . . . a star.' She
said it in the same sweet, sincere voice she said everything else. 'Any girl who

says she doesn't is lying. Any girl.'"[40] In the Romantic era the imagination of women was stimulated by poetry and novels, while in our contemporary era the imagination of women find stimulation in tabloid television and graphic movies, thus providing an illustration of Marshall McLuhan's prophetic message about the medium being the message.

What separates Wolfe's novel from the common herd of novels about campus life remains his psychological drama that one's social status on campus is intimately linked to one's sex life. Such tribal patterns of conspicuous consumption display the kind of consumer niche status that Veblen considers in *The Theory of the Leisure Class* (1912). Considerations of status float like a cartoon cloud above the heads of students while "the academic culture of the university is largely irrelevant to the daily lives of most of the students."[41] The fishbowl gossip mill sorts all this out one way or another and one's reputation among one's peers depends not upon intellectual pursuits but on social climbing through sexual affairs. Wolfe obviously does not approve of this barbaric "system" that has no rational basis—he sees it as Kurtzlike tribal madness that revolves around the worship of the alpha male or female who defines their superior social status through sexual promiscuity, the conspicuous display of money, fashionable clothing, gym grooming, and the ability to consume large quantities of alcohol. All these things combined to excess may ascend into the immortal divinity of legend, a kind of informal pagan canonization, as with Hoyt's campus reputation. At the conclusion of the novel Charlotte's sublimated courtship of Jojo operates as an ideal restoration of cultural values outside the current mainstream, reverting back to the social mores of Americans in the 1950s. The fact that Charlotte becomes the dominant partner in the relationship indicates that much has changed since the 1950s—women now have new opportunities to use their independence more wisely, although most do not.

There have always been and always will be frat boys like Hoyt and Julian or sorority girls like Beverly or Nicole who waste their time, their parents' money, and their professors' time. And there will always be overly nerdy and irrelevant professors like Professor Quat who take their jobs too seriously. But colleges that have Charlottes, Jojos, Adams, Starlings, and even Buster Roths will continue to teach students how to be human and succeed in life's long and difficult journey. I have to wonder whether some Americans have just lost their sense of humor when the novel received such irregular and cranky reviews. Or perhaps Wolfe's Zolaesque stance of "I'm different and above you" has laurelled him with the public image of a mischievous curmudgeon. On the other hand, the voluminous and competitive output in the college novel genre had hit a peak of superfluous frenzy in the few years that preceded Wolfe's novel, an observation hinted at in my opening paragraph. The popular appeal of Wolfe's many successful books partly lay in the fact that the books address social aspects that other writers have not treated with comic aplomb—the satiric college novel inhabits a well-trodden grove.

CHAPTER 10

VROOM! WOLFE'S STATUS IN AMERICAN LITERATURE

> Tom Wolfe led the way, brilliantly, in pushing the contest between nonfiction
> and the novel into the public's consciousness.
> —Norman Sims, *True Stories: A Century of Literary Journalism*

Wolfe has written a body of interesting and provocative journalism centered upon the theme of how status operates in various aspects of American society. Two of his longer journalistic works, *The Electric Kool-Aid Acid Test* and *The Right Stuff*, endure as historical testaments that explore and explain two fascinating American subcultures, the hippie movement and the cult of military heroism in fighter pilots. These books profiled two aspects of the culture wars that radically split America along a polarizing political divide that still exists nearly fifty years later. The first-person presence of the writer in The New Journalism movement plays an even greater role today than when it was controversial, while the tag itself has fallen by the wayside as Wolfe had predicted.[1] Wolfe's later journalism moves into various intellectual arenas from painting and architecture to evolution and neuroscience as he employs his prankish wit to alert the reader to misleading perceptions among intellectual gatekeepers in various disciplines. Wolfe has functioned as a Socratic gadfly, attacking received notions of literature and art, and more recently science.

As an essayist of cultural trends, he advocated cultural heroes like Marshall McLuhan, Teilhard de Chardin, Frederick Hart, and others. His later essays address the history of ideas in the scientific community. The ability to present complex ideas in a clear manner often finds dramatization in a Manichean manner. While Wolfe was most willing to argue elegantly a new theory on journalistic freedom to defend what he did in *The Electric Kool-Aid Acid Test*, he later attacked aspects of modernism and postmodernism that he thought had become dogmatic and ineffective. He then took the plunge to state a thesis rather than theory about the strengths of the American novel. He has been a stimulating commentator with both a historical and sociological perspective.

Wolfe's later work concentrates on what he calls the realistic novel which attempts to paint a sweeping portrait of American society in the tradition of Flaubert and Zola who had exerted an enormous influence on the best of American writing, influencing novelists like Henry James, Edith Wharton, John Dos Passos, James T. Farrell, Sinclair Lewis, John Steinbeck, Russell Banks, and Louis Auchincloss. Favoring the sociological aspects of the novel because it is rooted in the observation of how life is actually lived, Wolfe dismisses the modern and especially postmodern preoccupation with imaginative creativity and strategic gimmicks that have the vain surface appeal of originality. Furthermore, he finds a programmatic political bias in modern and postmodern writing which he views as distorted and so he has revived the sociological novel with a political twist, adapting it to satire while arguing that he writes in the realistic tradition.

Modernism evolved out of the realism of Zola and Ibsen; the first real European modernist was Anton Chekhov. Because of the political repression leading up to World War I and the horrors of the war itself, Modernism became dogmatically antistate, antireligious, and antisocial as it proclaimed the virtue of the individual over any group. Due to the horrors of World War II, Postmodernism became ethnically politically correct and sought to discover a new tolerance for religion, politics, and social freedom, but it imposed a new ideology in art that welcomed any and all experiments in creativity as long as they severed any roots with representational art which was demonized as the source of ignorant conformity, intolerance, and naïve cliché. Wolfe thinks that such emphasis on creativity and imagination resulted in a second-rate literature of solipsistic narcissism that is irrelevant, anarchically self-indulgent, and out of touch with the general populace—its removal from the great public traditions of art that flowered in the *polis* of classical Athens that laid the foundations for Western art constitutes a great loss to the public good. Wolfe thinks that the international outlook of postmodern art has led American writers to neglect the sociological aspects of American society. Wolfe's solution was to revive the great sociological novel through realism as it connects to social status.

A careful examination of Wolfe's novels reveals that what he writes is not realism in the manner of Flaubert or Zola, although the sociological outlook of Wolfe's novels possesses an *ad hoc* sociological affinity to the novels of Dos Passos, Farrell, and Lewis. Despite Wolfe's nostalgia for late nineteenth century writers like Zola, Nietzsche, and Weber, Wolfe lives within the postmodern age and his writing, though influenced by nineteenth-century thinkers, breathes with a postmodern spirit of creativity while it defies the limits of postmodern orthodoxy. Although Wolfe employs a sociological perspective, he rejects the neo-Marxist brand of sociological analysis advocated by the Frankfurt School, just as he rejects the more recent French philosophical and sociological analysts. He roots his sociological approach in Weber. While the role of status in his journalism was paramount, it also remains so in his novels, as Wolfe bluntly admits: "In my opinion all stories have to do with status."[2]

The past can always be an inspiration, but the past can't be a reproduction that the present invokes. Wolfe's call for the revival of realism remains a rallying cry for his own brand of maverick postmodernism. Although Wolfe eschews the popular indulgence in metafiction in which so many postmodern writers indulge, like other postmodern writers Wolfe employs self-conscious literary references to past art: Thackeray, Fielding, Poe, Flaubert, Zola, Cather, Conrad, Dos Passos, Fitzgerald, Faulkner, Farrell, Lewis, and Steinbeck. In most postmodern writing such literary references commonly consist of self-indulgent showmanship on the part of writers, but in Wolfe's practice the use of literary referents pointedly displays significant sociological changes and such referents operate either by counterpoint or irony, an artistic perspective that reaches as far back as Homer. Like the Athenians, Wolfe conceives of all important art as public art.

The critical inclination to label anything and everything has both its uses and limits. I would call what Wolfe writes in his novels *hyper satiric realism*. Although Wolfe has written only three novels, these novels are large in scope and ambition. They are all excellent and very different novels, and while I have objected to what I think are some flaws in the novels, I consider my criticisms to be minor cavils; I regard these novels as great literary achievements. The strain of Wolfe's humor resembles the satiric mentality on display in the liberal novels of Mark Twain, but in Wolfe's case the political orientation veers toward conservatism. I think that Wolfe's insistence on inserting his neoconservative political orientation on occasion mars his art. *Bonfire of the Vanities* succeeds as both entertainment and literature—it should endure as a successful comic novel that depicts the snobbish elitism and racial divide in New York City during a difficult period in the city's history. Although I think that the two major characters in *A Man in Full* are painted thinly, I judge it to be a stimulating thematic novel, Wolfe's most ambitious novel in originality and sociological scope. *I Am Charlotte Simmons* displays great depth in character development, vigorous intellectual themes, and such expert montage cutting and pacing of plot that it presents a superior novel yet suffers in its excellence merely from its limited focus of a few months in the life of an adolescent. *I Am Charlotte Simmons* is, I think, a masterpiece, but only time, distance, and more analysis will tell, especially with a novel that makes the academic community uncomfortable.[3]

The Electric Kool-Aid Acid Test is generally considered to be Wolfe's uncontested masterpiece, which is why I devoted more space to that work. It endures as one of the most successful examples of the New Journalism,[4] a postmodern development of journalism that appropriates the artistic freedoms postmodern critics also claimed as their right. The reasons that this work should be regarded as an uncontested masterpiece are threefold: It employs a superior *reversal* to those in Wolfe's novels as it avoids the *deus ex machina* devices that appear in all of Wolfe's novels; it remains the only work in which the reader experiences what Aristotle identifies as *catharsis* whereby the reader identifies so closely with

Kesey the protagonist—the writer himself also doing this at one point—that it alters the perceptions of the reader about the psychology and humor of everyday life, just as Kesey altered much of American society's perceptions of itself and its *zeitgeist*; the book is written as a tragedy and nearly everyone since Aristotle's *Poetics* regards tragedy as the greater description of life because its realistic roots derive from the perception that defeat and death reveal the limits of life and art. As part novel and part sociological journalism as well as intellectual history, *The Electric Kool-Aid Acid Test* defies categorization or imitation while it captures a moment in American history and literature that no one else, with the exception of Kesey in his great novel, *One Flew Over the Cuckoo's Nest* (1962), had been able to wrestle into significant artistic format.

While Wolfe's theories may appear to be a willfully cranky defiance of his own practice, one need not take them too seriously. Like his idol Zola, he doesn't strictly practice the theories he exalts, and if he did, his writing would be archaic and probably irrelevant rubbish. Wolfe's surface style blithely sails along in a prankish manner and because of that many who should know better miss his boat in the coastal fog and refuse to take a second look—by then he's gone and sailing in a different direction.

Wolfe's Zolaesque stance of "I'm right and there may be a dozen or two other people in the world who are not fools or stooges" certainly strikes a tiresome pose that makes enemies everywhere. Like fighter pilots, writers are notorious egomaniacs who wrestle like Jacob or Odysseus with angels or gods. Wrestling with the gods remains as dangerous an occupation as it ever has been.

Wolfe's claim to be the only realist writing with breadth remains as much hot air as challenging boast. Realism has not died yet it's no longer the mighty Mississippi but the tributary stream running through the small town or the city that is not much noticed by the inhabitants, and it remains true that academics have removed the realistic novel from the college curriculum, allowing it to be relegated it to a special course in late nineteenth-century fiction. Realism began with Homer's description of battle in *The Iliad* (c.740 B.C.) and was cogently analyzed by Aristotle in his *Poetics* (c.340 B.C.); after a sustained lapse to romantic epic in the Middle Ages, the *Poetics* continued to occupy the mainstream of Western writing up until the early 1900s; despite a bewildering variety of postmodern innovations, it continues to be practiced today, although in diminished significance. Wolfe's dismissal of modern and postmodern writing squats preposterous in its self-defensiveness, yet he rests on firm ground in declaring realism to be the main strain of Western writing. There's nothing unsound in being a postmodern practitioner of realism when the writing soars with excellence. In Wolfe's case the writing is both superior and controversial, but all good writing is controversial—otherwise it wouldn't be interesting.

Wolfe's fundamental approach to critical thinking displays an anchor with two prongs: his use of literary counterpointing graphically displays the changes in American social mores over time as if in a flow chart. On the other side, he employs tools of status analysis in perceiving and evaluating social or personal distinctions based upon status, both real and imagined; he examines the symbolic accoutrements of status and analyzes how it functions in the mental processes of various groups; he scrutinizes how status operates in the lives of individuals as well. In many ways Wolfe's roving, skeptical eye raises the question as to whether such perceptions of status are grounded in social realities or operate as vain worldly illusions deserving of social ridicule. Much of Wolfe's satiric humor produces a dialectic that divides people into heroes and villains, or heroes and fools. This kind of populist approach runs parallel to the populist cartoon sensibility of Ken Kesey and many threads of American culture, yet its prankish results have a different political direction than either what one finds in Kesey or Fishwick, and to understand Wolfe's politics one must look to his Southern roots and conservative education at Yale.

The critical approach I have taken toward Wolfe's novels concentrates on explicating his use of literary antecedents. There are two reasons for this approach: Serious critical evaluations of Wolfe's work remain in infancy and we need to know what Wolfe attempts to do in the novels before we can arrive at any judgments about resonance or performance. Secondly, I have thought of my audience as college students or readers of Wolfe who want to know more about what he's up to. In places I have not fully developed some observations or ideas in the hope of stimulating readers or students into further thinking about Wolfe's writing. I have brought dusty but trustworthy Aristotle into play, yet I don't share or identify with Wolfe's views, neither his neoconservative politics nor his atheism. I do think Wolfe's writing holds a vital place in the dialogue of American letters. Despite Wolfe's quasi-atheism,[5] he exhibits a deep moral view of American life that is blithely optimistic and like most accomplished artists he raises more questions than he can definitively answer, although he makes a great effort to arrive at the definitive in a somewhat self-righteous manner that many intellectuals find arrogant.

On the one hand, Wolfe's probing skepticism permits him to mock foolish behavior and to ridicule dogmatic thinking through his Nietzsche-inspired pessimism. On the other hand, his buoyant optimism in language achieves a corrective counterbalance in his quest to uncover and hail heroes who are role models for Americans to emulate in spirit and in dedication. Throughout both procedures he has taken the approach of the mischievous prankster-bystander who juggles approaches in an entertaining manner without becoming the rube clown. He poses as a populist who desires a wide audience as he snobbishly demeans liberals whom he jestingly labels as "intellectuals," yet below the surface of his hyperbolically kinetic prose lurks intellectual arguments, invective, irony, and counterpointing literary allusions that appeal only to the very intellectuals he consistently debunks. Wolfe appears as a man of paradox fond of invoking paradox. Some prominent intellectuals have asserted that he should be banned from the symposium of American letters, and Wolfe replies with a dismissive laugh that such a vindictive response merely proves his point about hypocrisy in the current trend of political correctness that grips the intellectual and academic world.

Over two hundred years ago de Tocqueville looked for the strength of America in her material resources and found that strength in America's churches, concluding that when America ceased to be good, she would cease to be strong. While Wolfe sees America's churches as merely social and political organizations and he himself has no personal interest in them, he locates the strength of America in its disparate individuals. One aspect of his writing is to locate and celebrate those heroic individuals. He began with a boxer named Cassius Clay (Muhammad Ali) and went on to discover heroes in bootleggers, a custom car designer, an art speculator, a jailed great writer, fighter pilots and astronauts, spiritual visionaries and media prophets, cops, lawyers, and judges, a working-class stiff searching for religious meaning in life, and finally college students who represent America's future in his second masterpiece.

When people are not heroes, Wolfe judges them as fools, and so he has attacked surfer gangs, playboys, strippers, student audiences, narrow dogmatists in art and architecture, political meddlers, Wall Street speculators, self-interested lawyers, empty-headed and selfish socialites, opportunistic bankers, artists interested in selfishness rather than the common good, athletes who are predators, politicians who are puppets, scientists and intellectuals who seek egotistically to aggrandize their expertise into other fields or employ skepticism to silence rational debate, cynical television manipulators, builders more interested in building their own empire than in contributing to the common good of society, students who are devotedly anti-intellectual. Wolfe employs his hop-scotching dialectic across the sociological sweep of the country in a pranksterlike fashion that entertains, confuses, and sometimes annoys people, but his goal consists of presenting moral models and to flog the sinners with embarrassment and hoots of laughter.

There is a palpable Manichean duality to Wolfe's mentality and such Manichean dialectics in postmodern fiction stem from the horror of World War II; it continues as a persistent theme in writers like Samuel Beckett, Norman Mailer, and Tom Wolfe, as well as numerous others. No one wants to be pilloried in Wolfe's Puritan town square, and as readers we must ask ourselves whether this Nietzsche-inspired Grand Inquisitor is just or not, and whether his own attempts at high art achieve success as art.

There is no debate that in the arena of journalism Wolfe's methods shifted the direction of journalism and that his influence still remains as an enduring contribution to both journalism and American culture. Anyone who has written two masterpieces, *The Electric Kool-Aid Acid Test* and *I Am Charlotte Simmons,* as well as three excellent books—*The Right Stuff, The Bonfire of the Vanities,* and *A Man in Full*—has a secure perch on "Parnassus."

In his novels Wolfe has no imitators or school of followers because his hybrid blends of satire, irony, humor, literary jokes, and documentary realism remain difficult to achieve, much less duplicate. His novelistic approach with its sociological bias remains quite distinctive while well rooted in the history of American and French literature. Wolfe's various poses—from off-stage millionaire dandy to intellectual populist to political curmudgeon—may alienate or annoy other writers, yet his contribution to the panorama of American literature achieves both humor and distinction. Popular culture in America continues to be addicted to childlike fantasies, an observation that Wolfe shared with Kesey. Wolfe's efforts at introducing his particular brand of postmodern neorealism into American popular culture should be applauded as therapeutic, yet I remain slightly puzzled as to why it persists in being misunderstood, unless it can be easily explained by willful prejudice on the part of academics reviling Wolfe's neoconservative politics.

The liberal critic John Leonard once dismissively tagged Wolfe a "neoconservative Warhol."[6] Many great artists employ doubling motifs: Warhol's series of ice cream paintings present behind their surface a suggestive allegory about sex, while other quasi-realistic paintings reveal an oblique satiric layer about our society, especially in Warhol's motif of serial repetition. In like manner there are literary allusions in Wolfe's novels that reveal a double layer presenting a realistic assessment of how American society has changed over time—usually for the worse in mores and manners. Like Warhol, Wolfe champions the use of a documentary realism, but Wolfe's realism derives from broad sociological observations. Both Warhol and Wolfe satirize bourgeois notions of art, the official "dogmas" of current art, and attempt to woo both a popular and lucrative following disguised with a prankish humor. We need not subscribe to the political or social views of either to recognize that both have made significant critiques and immense contributions to American arts and letters. Nor should we let their mutual pose of attacking the establishment erect a barrier to understanding their art or message. Like Warhol, Wolfe's place in American culture will continue to be both controversial and secure.

In writing this book I've dined on a surfeit of splitting ideas and identifying unsettling sociological changes to American society. I'd like to conclude with an iconic image of unity: The black-and-white photo self-portrait of Andy Warhol wrapped in the American flag with paintbrush in hand and a daub of paint on the flag where he smiles in his hometown Pittsburgh museum may stand not only for him, but also for people as diverse as Tom Wolfe, John Glenn, Leonard Bernstein, Fred Hampton, Sinclair Lewis, and Ken Kesey, as well as any reader of this book.

NOTES

Chapter 1: The Manhattan Virginian

1. McKeen, William. *Tom Wolfe* (Boston: Twayne, 1995), 4.

2. Applebome, Peter, "A Man in Tune with his Heritage," *NYT*, November 11, 1988.

3. See www.vanityfair.com/culture/bestdressed. Accessed 10/01/08.

4. Gorner, Peter, "Tom Wolfe: In Big League as a Writer." *Chicago Tribune*, December 7, 1976.

5. Thompson, Toby, "The Evolution of Dandy Tom," *Vanity Fair*, October, 1987.

6. Ibid.

7. McKeen, *Tom Wolfe*, 5.

8. Fishwick, Marshall, "Conversations with Scholars of American Popular Culture," *Americana: The Journal of American Popular Culture*, Fall, 2003.

9. Thompson, Ibid.

10. Grossman, Lev. "Mind and Body Happiness," *Time*, October 31, 2004.

11. See Chapter Two, Adams, Henry, *The Education of Henry Adams* (Boston: Houghton Mifflin, 1973, reprint of 1918).

12. Elliott, Jean, Obituary, *Virginia Tech News*, May 24, 2006.

13. Jacobs, Erica, "Picturing America," *San Francisco Examiner*, March 3, 2008.

14. McKeen, *Tom Wolfe*, 6.

15. Ragen, Brian Abel, *Tom Wolfe: A Critical Companion* (Westport: Greenwood Press, 2002), 9.

16. Wolfe, "In the Land of Rococo Marxists," *Hooking Up* (New York: Farrar Strauss Giroux, 2000), 113–130.

17. Ragen, Ibid., 11. For more on Wolfe, Breslin, and the *Tribune* see Kluger, Richard. *The Paper: The Life and Death of the Herald Tribune* (New York: Knopf, 1986).

18. *Time*, Dec 28, 1998–Jan 4, 1999.

19. Wolfe, Tom, in *American Writers*, Supplement II, Part 2 (New York: Charles Scriber's Sons, 1991).

20. Wolfe, Tom, "Tales of Felker," *The New York Observer*, July 7–14, 2008.

21. *Contemporary Authors 9* (Detroit: Gale, 1983), 538.

22. *Contemporary Authors 70* (Detroit: Gale, 1983), 443.

23. www.brown.edu/Administration/George_Street_Journal/v20/v20n24/wolfe. html. Accessed 10/01/08.

24. "Interview with Tom Wolfe," *Paris Review*, No. 118, Spring, 1991.

25. Applebome, Ibid.

26. Thompson, Ibid.

27. Grossman, "Mind and Body Happiness."

28. Salomon, Julie, *The Devil's Candy*: The Bonfire of the Vanities *goes to Hollywood* (Boston: Houghton Mifflin, 1991), 408.

29. There's lots of fun for Thompson fans at www.gonzo.org.

30. McGrath, Charles, "Wolfe's World," *NYT*, October 31, 2004.

Chapter 2: Journalism and Hyperbole

1. Capouya, Emile, "True Facts and Artifacts," *Saturday Review*, July 31, 1965.

2. Wolfe, Tom, *The Kandy-Kolored Tangerine-Flake Streamline Baby* (New York: Farrar Straus Giroux, 1968), x.

3. Wolfe, Tom, *The New Journalism*, ed. with E.W. Johnson (New York: Harper & Row, 1973), 28–29.

4. Ibid., 32.

5. Ibid., 33.

6. Wolfe, Tom, *The Kandy-Kolored*, 220.

7. Ibid., 287.

8. Ibid., 293.

9. Ibid., 291.

10. Wolfe, Tom, *The New Journalism*, 33.

11. Wolfe, Tom, *The Kandy-Kolored*, 75.

12. Mewborn in Scura, Dorothy, ed. *Conversations with Tom Wolfe* (Jackson: University Press of Mississippi, 1990), 237.

13. For an amusing article about Spector, John Lennon, and leveled guns see Anson, Robert Sam, "Legend with a Bullet." *Vanity Fair*, June, 2003.

14. *Yale Alumni Magazine*, Summer, 2003. An alternative explanation appears in *The New Journalism*, 35–36.

15. Kasack, Wolfgang, *Dictionary of Russian Literature since 1917* (New York: Columbia University Press, 1988), 354.

16. Wolfe, Tom, *The Kandy-Kolored*, 288.

17. Ibid., 326.

18. Wolfe, Tom, NEH Jefferson Lecture, 2006, at www.neh.gov/whoweare/wolfe/lecture.html. Accessed 9/01/08.

19. Wolfe, Tom, *The New Journalism*, 34.

20. Wakefield, Dan, *The Atlantic*, "The Personal Voice and the Impersonal Eye," June, 1966.

21. *Yale Alumni Magazine*, December, 2000.

22. My summary of Wolfe's March 20, 2008 *NYT* interview; a more detailed description is available in *The New Journalism*, 46–47.

23. For a discerning read on the origin and varieties of The New Journalism see Sims, Norman, *True Lies: A Century of Literary Journalism* (Evanston: Northwestern Univ. Press, 2007), 219–62.

24. Weingarten, Marc, *The Gang That Wouldn't Shoot Straight: Wolfe, Thompson, Didion, and the New Journalism Revolution* (New York: Crown, 2006), 213.

25. Wolfe, NEH Jefferson Lecture.

26. Ibid.

27. Wolfe, Tom, *The Pump-House Gang* (New York: Farrar Straus Giroux, 1975), 142.

28. Ibid., 154.

29. Ibid., 77.

30. Ibid., 71.

31. "Interview with Tom Wolfe," *NYT*, March, 2008.

Chapter 3: Prankster Riddles

1. Wolfe, Tom, *The New Journalism*, ed. with E.W. Johnson (New York: Harper & Row, 1973), 45.

2. Wolfe, Tom, *The Electric Kool-Aid Acid Test* (New York: Farrar Straus Giroux, 1968), 263.

3. Plummer, William, *The Holy Goof: A Biography of Neal Cassady* (New York: Da Capo Press, 2004), 149.

4. Weingarten, Marc, *The Gang That Wouldn't Shoot Straight: Wolfe, Thompson, Didion, and the New Journalism Revolution* (New York: Crown, 2006), 101–7.

5. McClanahan, Ed, Introduction to *Kesey's Jail Journal* (New York: Viking, 2003).

6. Major, Clarence, *Juba to Jive: A Dictionary of African-American Slang* (New York: Viking, 1994), 234.

7. Kesey's novel contains a valorization of popular culture through folksongs and diction, a theme Wolfe was probably attracted to, as well as the main character who defied a union.

8. Wolfe, Tom, *The Electric Kool-Aid Acid Test* (New York: Farrar Straus Giroux, 1968), 19.

9. Ibid.

10. Nietzsche, Friedrich, *Thus Spake Zarathustra* in *The Philosophy of Nietzsche* (New York: The Modern Library, 1947), 31.

11. Scott, Chloe, "No Furthur," *Spit in the Ocean #7*, ed. Ed McClanahan (New York: Viking, 2003), 76.

12. See the beginning of Chapter Six for Wolfe's earlier use of this metaphor.

13. Nietzsche, Friedrich, *"Beyond Good and Evil"* in *The Philosophy of Nietzsche* (New York: The Modern Library, 1947), 60–72.

14. Ibid.

15. Wolfe, Tom, *The Electric Kool-Aid Acid Test* (New York: Farrar Straus Giroux, 1968), 31.

16. Ibid., 25.

17. Ibid., 31–32.

18. Ibid., 55.

19. Brightman, Carol, *Sweet Chaos: The Grateful Dead's American Adventure* (New York: Simon & Schuster, 1998), 45.

20. I have often wondered if it was in imitation of Wolfe's running gag that the balladeer motif in the Mel Brooks' Western comedy *Blazing Saddles* (1974) was inspired by Wolfe's book.

21. Hesse, Hermann. *The Journey to the East*, trans. Hilda Rosner (New York: Noonday press, 1957), 149.

22. Ibid., 28.

23. McMurtry, Larry, "Bus Story#3: Stark Naked Gets off the Bus," *Spit in the Ocean #7* (New York: Viking, 2003), 104–06.

24. Wolfe's acknowledgement of this appears on page 434.

25. Brightman, Carol, 78.

26. De St Joree, John, *Venus Bound* (New York: Random House, 1994), 68.

27. Leary provides a slightly different account in his memoir *Flashbacks* (1983). See Greenfield, Robert. *Timothy Leary: A Biography* (New York: Harcourt, 2006), 220–23. In any case, they all became friendly counterculture allies.

28. Wolfe, Tom, *The Electric Kool-Aid Acid Test* (New York: Farrar Strauss Giroux, 1968), 132. See also, Leland, John, "Psychodelia's Middle-Aged Head Trip," *NYT*, November 18, 2001.

29. Berkovitch, Sacvan, *The Puritan Origins of the American Self* (New Haven: Yale, 1977), 113.

30. Stevens, Jay, *Storming Heaven: LSD and the American Dream* (New York: Harper & Row, 1987), iv.

31. Smith, Craig E., "Albert Hofmann, the Father of LSD, Dies at 102," *NYT* April 30, 2008. See also Hofmann, Albert, *LSD: My Problem Child*, trans. Jonathon Ott (New York: McGraw-Hill, 1980).

32. Stone, Robert, *Prime Green* (New York: Ecco Press, 2007), 94–95.

33. Wolfe, Tom, *Spit in the Ocean #7*, "In the Pudding," 121–24.

34. With regard to the problem of genre, David Stanford, Ken Kesey's editor at Viking, says in a letter to me, "I'd say the main interest in his [Kesey's] life was in Making Things Happen. Getting involved in something in real time and seeing where you can take it and it can take you."

35. Wolfe, Tom, *The Electric Kool-Aid Acid Test* (New York: Farrar Straus Giroux, 1968), 147.

36. Kesey probably got the term *kairos* from reading the theologian Paul Tillich.

37. Wolfe, Tom, *The Electric Kool-Aid Acid Test* (New York: Farrar Straus Giroux, 1968), 149.

38. Ibid., 154.

39. Quoted from the BBC documentary, *The Beyond Within: The Rise and Fall of LSD*, 1987.

40. Wolfe, Tom, *The Electric Kool-Aid Acid Test* (New York: Farrar Strauss Giroux, 1968), 156.

41. Ibid.

42. Ibid., 183.

43. Lehmann-Haupt, Obituary, *NYT*, Nov. 11, 2001.

44. Thompson, Hunter S., "Walking with the King," *Spit in the Ocean# 7*, 80.

45. Wolfe, Tom, *The Electric Kool-Aid Acid Test* (New York: Farrar Strauss Giroux, 1968), 184.

46. Weingarten, 114.

47. Wolfe, Tom. "As Gonzo in Life as in His Work," *Wall Street Journal*, Feb. 22, 2005.

48. According to Brightman, 40, they had a rather lengthy affair.

49. Wolfe, Tom, *The Electric Kool-Aid Acid Test* (New York: Farrar Straus Giroux, 1968), 193.

50. Ibid., 200.

51. Kesey, Ken, *Demon Box* (New York: Viking, 1986), 56–90.

52. Thompson, Toby, "The Evolution of Dandy Tom," *Vanity Fair* 50, October, 1987.

53. Wolfe, Tom, *The Bonfire of the Vanities* (New York: Bantam, 1987), 164, 523.

54. For the theme of Jesus as wonderworker see Smith, Morton, *Jesus the Magician* (New York: Harper & Row, 1978).

55. Wolfe, Tom, *The Electric Kool-Aid Acid Test* (New York: Farrar Straus Giroux, 1968), 247–48.

56. Sixteen years later, Allen Ginsberg told me the same thing about the conflict in Northern Ireland without knowing the slightest iota about the history of Ireland, nor having ever been there. He confidently said that if the United Nations or a philanthropist sent him over *he* could end the conflict in a couple of weeks. He was surprised to hear that Catholics had just gotten a full vote in Northern Ireland in 1971 and confided to me that as a poet he had never been asked to read in Ireland. (I later discovered he had been invited many times by different groups and had declined to go.) From reputation and my own experience, Ginsberg was fonder of hearing himself rant than engaging in mutual dialogue—he appeared constitutionally oblivious to respecting an alternative point of view.

57. Wolfe, Tom, *The Electric Kool-Aid Acid Test* (New York: Farrar Straus Giroux, 1968), 257.

58. Brightman, 4–6.

59. The page can be viewed at the Grateful Dead's website: www.dead.net/features/dictionary-page-where-grateful-deads-name-came. Accessed 10/01/08.

60. Brightman, 4–6.

61. Wolfe, Tom, *The Electric Kool-Aid Acid Test* (New York: Farrar Straus Giroux, 1968), 263.

62. Brightman, 101.

63. Ibid., 297.

64. Brightman 105–07, 170–73.

65. Wolfe, Tom, *The Electric Kool-Aid Acid Test* (New York: Farrar Straus Giroux, 1968), 304.

66. Wolfe, Tom, *The New Journalism*, ed. with E.W. Johnson (New York: Harper & Row, 1973), 228.

67. At Intrepidtrips.com there is a free (grainy and orange) video clip of Cassady matter-of-factly handing out elaborate calligraphic diplomas.

68. Wolfe, Tom, *The Electric Kool-Aid Acid Test* (New York: Farrar Straus Giroux, 1968), 341.

69. Ibid., 414–16.

70. Brightman, 92.

Chapter 4: From Reporting to Politics

1. Wolfe, Tom, *The New Journalism*, ed. with E.W. Johnson (New York: Harper & Row, 1973), 412.

2. Wolfe, Tom, *Radical Chic & Mau-Mauing the Flak Catchers* (New York: Farrar Straus Giroux, 1970), 15.

3. Dean, John, "Is Barack Obama Truly Too Elite To Be Elected?" http://www.smirkingchimp.com/thread/14666. Accessed 10/01/08.

4. Wolfe, Tom, *Mauve Gloves & Madmen, Clutter & Vine* (Farrar Straus Giroux, 1976), 200.

5. Toby Thompson notes the "Chinese yellow" drapes decorating Wolfe's study in his article "The Evolution of Dandy Tom," *Vanity Fair* 50, December, 1987.

6. Wolfe, Tom, *Radical Chic*, 14.

7. Mann, Thomas, *Stories of Three Decades*, trans. H.T. Lowe-Porter (New York: Modern Library, 1936), 173–80.

8. Wolfe, Tom, Foreword, *New York Stories* (New York: Random House, 2008), xxv.

9. Wolfe, Tom, *Radical Chic*, 40.

10. Ibid., 41.

11. Ibid., 42–43.

12. Walker, Pamela, Letter to *NYT*, June 21, 1987.

13. De Vries in Scura, Dorothy, ed., Conversations with Tom Wolfe (Jackson: University Press of Mississippi, 1990), 243.

14. Thackeray, William Makepeace, *The Book of Snobs* (New York: Penguin, 1993), 101.

15. Ibid., 106.

16. Wolfe, Tom, *Radical Chic*, 87–84.

17. See Rosenmeyer, Thomas G., *The Green Cabinet: Theocritus and the European Pastoral Lyric* (Berkeley: University of California Press, 1969) and Doody, Margaret Anne. *The True Story of the Novel* (New Brunswick: Rutgers University Press, 1997).

18. Blumenthal, Ralph, "Files Detail Years of Spying on Bernstein," *NYT*, July 29, 1994.

19. Blumenthal, Ralph, "Bernstein was Monitored as Late as 70's," *NYT*, May 17, 1995.

20. Blumenthal, Ralph, "Files Detail Years of Spying on Bernstein," *NYT*, July 29, 1994.

21. Bernard, Sydney, *Witnessing: The Seventies* (New York: Horizon Press, 1977), 5–8.

22. http://www.youtube.com/watch?v=TrlYRWD_tnA&feature. Accessed 10/01/08.

23. See Gray, Mike & Associates, *The Murder of Fred Hampton* (Chicago: Facets Multimedia, 2007).

24. Foster, R.F., *Modern Ireland: 1600–1972* (New York: Viking, 1988), 587.

25. Monje, Scott C., *The Central Intellignece Agency: A Documentary History* (Westport: Greenwood Press, 2008, 400.

26. Mills, C. Wright, *The Power Elite* (New York: Oxford University Press, 1956), 89. For an excellent introductory article on Mills, see Wolfe, Alan, "Gonzo Sociology," *The New Republic*, Oct. 8, 2008.

27. Ibid., 90.

28. Henahan, Donal, Obituary, *NYT*, Oct. 15, 1990.

29. In contrast, note the humorous 1970 send-up of the Black Panthers that Kesey provoked as described by Ed McClanahan in *Famous People I Have Known* (New York: Farrar Straus Giroux, 1985), 89–111.

30. See Blakeley, William, "2500 Students at Mass Meeting," *Yale Daily News*, April 30, 1970 and Bigart, Homer, "Comments on Moratorium at Yale," *NYT*, April 30, 1970 and Bigart, Homer, "Education; Another Spring of Revolt on the Campus," *NYT*, May 2, 1970; also the *NYT* Obituary of Kingman Brewster, Jr. by Eric Page, Nov. 8, 1988.

31. Wolfe, Tom, Foreword, *New York Stories*, xxvii.

32. Hess, Thomas B., "Mauve Gloves and Madmen, Clutter & Vine," *NYT*, Dec. 26, 1976.

33. Wolfe, Tom, *Mauve Gloves*, 45.
34. Ibid., 32–33.
35. Ibid., 40.
36. Ibid., 43.
37. Ibid.
38. Ibid., 42–46.
39. Ibid., 55.
40. Twain, Mark, *Life on the Mississippi* (New York: Oxford University Press, 1966), 468–70.
41. Wolfe, *Mauve Gloves*, 153.
42. Miller, Perry, *The Life of the American Mind* (London: Victor Gollancz, 1966), 90.
43. Ivy League schools have always prized de Tocqueville and there is a particular connection with Yale since the head librarian there, Daniel Gilman, once published an edition of *Democracy in America* in 1898. Mancinci, Matthew. *Alexis de Tocqueville and American Intellectuals* (New York: Rowman and Littlefield, 2006), 111.
44. Wolfe, Tom, *Mauve Gloves*, 166–67.
45. Schlesinger, Arthur, "The Amazing Success Story of 'Spiro Who?'" *NYT*, July 26, 1970.
46. *In-Depth with Tom Wolfe* (Washington, D.C.: C-Span Video Library, Dec. 5, 2004). Wolfe replied to the first caller who enjoyed his early books saying that his first two collections of essays had "a juvenile spirit that you can't beat."
47. Wolfe, Tom, *The New Journalism*, 37.
48. "When a piece of Clyde's head is blown away by a bullet [in *Bonnie and Clyde*], [Director Arthur] Penn wanted it to remind audiences of the Kennedy assassination." Biskind, Peter, Easy Riders, Raging Bulls (New York: Simon & Schuster, 1999), 19.
49. Personal communication, 1987. The book, published by Harcourt, had been sponsored by Columbia University. Gallagher submitted the manuscript for approval as his contract required. Nobody objected, but when the book was published there was an outcry from Administration which thought the book did nothing to further the reputation of the school. A truck pulled up before the building near Columbia where Gallagher lived and unloaded the whole printing on the sidewalk, which Gallagher then stored in the building basement. There were no reviews of this excellent book.

Chapter 5: Historian at Edge City

1. Wolfe, Tom, *The Right Stuff* (New York: Bantam, 1979), 17.
2. Ibid., 24.
3. Ibid., 19.
4. Ibid., 28.
5. Ibid., 28–30.
6. Ibid., 35–57, 54–55.
7. Ibid., 364–67.
8. Ibid., 61
9. Ibid., 64.
10. Ibid., 72.
11. Ibid, 97.
12. Ibid, 100–01.

13. Weingarten, Marc, "A 'Mad Hulking Carnival' of American Life" at http://www. neh.gov/whoweare/wolfe/appreciation.html. Accessed 10/1/01.

14. Wolfe, Tom, NEH Jefferson Lecture, 2006 at http://www.neh.gov/whoweare/wolfe/appreciation.html. Accessed 10/1/01.

15. Wolfe, *The Right Stuff*, 102–03. President Reagan tried to change this.

16. Ibid., 103.

17. Ibid., 104.

18. Ibid., 104–05.

19. Ibid., 117–18.

20. Ibid., 118.

21. Ibid., 130–31.

22. Ibid., 149.

23. Menzies, Gavin, *1421: The Year China Discovered America* (New York: William Morrow, 2002), 62.

24. The Mercury Astronauts, *We Seven* (New York: Simon & Schuster, 1962), 183.

25. For all of the astronauts, except Shepard, these delays were the most agonizing aspect of the project. Ibid., 185.

26. Wolfe, *The Right Stuff*, 209.

27. Ibid., 265.

28. Ibid., 214–19.

29. Ibid., 220–23.

30. Ibid., 225.

31. Mailer, Norman, *Of a Fire on the Moon* (Boston: Little Brown, 1970), 25–28.

32. Collins, Michael, *Carrying the Fire: An Astronauts' Journeys* (New York: Farrar Straus Giroux, 1974), 59. Collins didn't enjoy PR work and regularly declined speaking engagements; he said it was because he didn't enjoy the lifestyle that such engagements demanded, 95.

33. Wilford, John Noble, *We Reach the Moon* (New York: Bantam, 1969), 80.

34. Gagarin, Yuri, *The First Man in Space* (New York: Crosscurrents Press, 1960), 41–2.

35. Wilford, 37–38.

36. Dickson, Paul, *Sputnik: The Shock of the Century* (New York: Walker, 2001), 216.

37. Wolfe, *The Right Stuff*, 228.

38. Ibid., 231.

39. Ibid., 243

40. Ibid., 249.

41. Ibid., 258–63.

42. Ibid., 289.

43. Ibid., 294. Just like Senator Edward Kennedy's speech at the Denver Democratic National Convention in August, 2008.

44. Brightman, Carol, *Sweet Chaos: The Grateful Dead's American Adventure* (New York: Crown, 1998), 1.

45. Wolfe, Tom, *The Right Stuff*, 291–93.

46. Wolfe, Tom, *The Electric Kool-Aid Acid Test* (New York: Farrar Straus Giroux, 1968), 263.

47. Wolfe, Tom, *The Right Stuff*, 318.

48. See Kristeller, Paul Oskar, *Eight Philosophers of the Renaissance* (Stanford: Stanford University Press, 1964), 1–18.

49. Wolfe, Tom, *The Right Stuff*, 343.

50. Ibid., 355.

51. Yeager, Chuck with Leo Janos, *Yeager: An Autobiography* (New York: Bantam, 1985), 407–08.

52. Wolfe, Tom, *Mauve Gloves and Madmen, Clutter & Vine* (New York: Farrar Straus Giroux), 58.

53. Sims, Norman. *True Stories: A Century of Literary Journalism* (Evanston: Northwestern Univ. Press, 2007), 235.

54. Brightman, *Sweet Chaos*, 3.

55. Ibid., 36.

56. Ibid., 20.

57. *Contemporary Authors* 9, 538.

Chapter 6: Iconoclastic Culture Shredding

1. Wolfe, Tom, "Tiny Mummies!" *Hooking Up* (New York: Farrar Straus Giroux, 2000), 259.

2. Krim, Seymour, *Shake It for the World, Smartass* (New York: Dial Press, 1970), 173.

3. Streitfeld, David, "Tom Wolfe Collection has the Wrong Stuff," *San Francisco Chronicle*, December 22, 2000. For those who want to pursue this controversy in more detail see John Hersey, "The Legend on the License," *Yale Review*, autumn 1980 and Ben Yagoda, *About Town: The New Yorker and the World It Made* (New York: Scribner, 2000).

4. Wolfe, Ibid., 271.

5. Sims, Norman, *True Stories: A Century of Literary Journalism* (Evanston: Illinois University Press, 2007), 233.

6. Wolfe, Tom, *The Painted Word* (New York: Bantam, 1975), 75.

7. Ibid., 94.

8. Heaney, Seamus, *Seamus Heaney: Poems and a Memoir* (New York: Limited Editions Book Club, 1982).

9. Heydarpour, Roja, Pearson Obituary, *NYT*, December 18, 2006; Glueck, Grace, "Henry Pearson—'Selected Drawings 1959–69,'" *NYT*, May 16, 2003; McGrady, Patrick J., *Henry Pearson: The Poetry of Line* (University Park: Palmer Museum, Pennsylvania State, 2001).

10. See Jordan Obituary by Palermo, Sara, *Pine Plains Register*, Dec 8, 2008.

11. Smith, Bernard, ed., *The Antipodean manifesto: essays in art and history* (Melbourne: Oxford University Press, 1975).

12. Wolfe, Tom, *Hooking Up*, 131–39.

13. See the architecture critic Benjamin Forgey in the *Washington Post Book World*, Nov. 15, 1981.

14. Lehmann-Haupt, Christopher, "From Bauhaus to Our House," *NYT*, Oct 9, 1981.

15. Goldberger, Paul, "In the Bird's Nest," *The New Yorker*, June 2. 2008.

16. Ouroussoff, Nicolai, "In Changing Face of Bejing," *NYT*, July 13, 2008.

17. Wolfe, Tom, "Stalking the Billion-Footed Beast," *Harper's*, November, 1989.

Chapter 7: Vanity Rags

1. Vladimir Nabokov is a good example yet he has the lame excuse that Russians have always distrusted German thinkers.

2. Lemann, Nicholas, "New York in the Eighties," *The Atlantic*, Dec 1987, 106.

3. Erlanger, Steve, "Bonfire in Bronx!!! Wolfe Catches Flak!!!" *NYT*, March 11, 1988.

4. Margolick, David, "The Law; At the Bar," *NYT*, Feb, 5, 1988.

5. Wolfe, Tom, *The Bonfire of the Vanities* (New York: Bantam, 1988), 125.

6. Ibid., 131.

7. Margolick, David, *NYT*, Feb, 5, 1988.

8. DeVries in Scura, Dorothy, ed., *Conversations with Tom Wolfe* (Jackson: University Press of Mississippi, 1990), 243.

9. Margolick, "The Law; At the Bar."

10. Taylor, D.J., *Thackeray: The Life of a Literary Man* (New York: Carroll & Graf, 1999), 241.

11. Margolick, "The Law; At the Bar."

12. Troyat, Henri, *Turgenev* (New York: Dutton, 1988), 82–84.

13. Spike Lee was outraged that the movie script was changed, allowing Lamb to live; he was also dismayed to learn that Wolfe had never read the movie script, nor cared to get involved in the film. See Salomon, Julie, *The Devil's Candy: The Bonfire of the Vanities goes to Hollywood* (Boston: Houghton Mifflin, 1991), 191.

14. Wolfe, *Bonfire*, 140.

15. Ibid., 141.

16. Ibid., 163.

17. Lemann, Nicholas, "New York in the Eighties," *The Atlantic*, Dec. 1987.

18. Wolfe, *Bonfire*, 169–70.

19. Bloomfield, Morton W. and Leonard Newmark, *A Linguistic Introduction to the History of English* (New York: Knopf, 1963), 225–87.

20. Wolfe, *Bonfire*, 230–31.

21. Ibid., 252.

22. Douglas, Martin, "Seeking the Soul of the City's Summer," *NYT*, May 9, 1999.

23. Wolfe, *Bonfire*, 264.

24. Ibid., 351.

25. In "Radical Chic" at the Leonard Bernstein party the opera *Cavalleria Rusticana* was cited—for many decades it appeared on a double bill with *Pagliacci*, due both to their brevity and the shared theme of a jealous love-murder. So this party is the second half of Wolfe's double bill celebrity gathering.

26. Wolfe, *Bonfire*, 371.

27. Ibid., 383.

28. Ibid., 398.

29. Ibid., 403.

30. For example, Putnam, Robert D., "The Prosperous Community: Social Community and Public Life," *The American Prospect*, March 21, 1993.

31. Wolfe, *Bonfire*, 486.

32. Ibid., 470.

33. For a recent nautical nightmare adventure along Conrad's Congo river, I recommend Jeffrey Tayler's *Facing the Congo: A Modern-Day Journey into the Heart of Darkness* (New York: Three Rivers Press, 2000).

34. *Bonfire*, 573.

35. Ibid., 599.

36. Ibid., 525.

37. Ibid., 579.

Chapter 8: Cultural Drift

1. Frantz Fanon was the author of the most intellectually stimulating treatise on revolution, *The Wretched of the Earth* (1961), which delineated the psychological anthropology of colonial domination against indigenous peoples. The name (with its pun on freak) mocks the intellect of the athlete as well as intellectuals who find Frantz Fanon a brilliant analyst of imperialism. A fanon is a double cloak worn only by the Roman pope.

2. Cather, Willa, *My Antonia* (New York: Signet Classic, 1994), 67.

3. Wolfe, Tom, *A Man in Full* (New York: Farrar Straus Giroux, 1998), 89.

4. Ibid., 227.

5. Balzac, Honoré, *Lost Illusions*, trans. by Kathleen Raine (New York: Modern Library, 1967), 44–50.

6. Wolfe, *A Man in Full.* 196.

7. Richardson, Joanna, *Verlaine* (New York: Viking, 1971), 89ff.

8. Wolfe, 380.

9. Ibid., 371.

10. This comic novel's sexual themes resemble yet differ from a popular French comedy of the day, *Le Cocu magnifique* (1920), by Fernand Crommelynck, later made into an opera by Berthold Goldschmidt in 1930. While Joyce, according to Richard Ellman in *James Joyce* (London: Oxford University Press, 1982, 498), knew Crommelynck's play, the personal parallel antedates Joyce's Paris days and relates to the painter Frank Budgeon's declining an affair with Nora Joyce in Zurich. See Budgen, Frank, *Myselves When Young* (London: Oxford University Press, 1970), 181–204.

11. Greek drama had its roots in public recitations of Homer, notwithstanding Aristotle's fanciful anthropological explanation. In his *Poetics*, Aristotle (or a student of his) argues for the superiority of the single plot as against the double plot. He thinks that the single plot contains more power because it is undivided and in this way remains more convincingly powerful. Using Sophocles' *Oedipus Rex* as the standard of excellence, he measures all plays by that play. It is clear that the tradition of main plot and sub-plot that had descended from Homer (although Homer really had a bifurcated plot) was the dominant practice of Greek tragedy and Aristotle was arguing against that practice. Later on in England, Marlowe and Jonson championed the single plot, while Shakespeare preferred the double plot in comedy and the single plot in tragedy.

12. Wolfe, 285.

13. Ibid., 307.

14. Ibid., 310.

15. Fishwick, Marshall, "Conversations with Scholars of American Popular Culture," *Americana: The Journal of American Popular Culture*, fall, 2003.

16. Faulkner, William, *The Hamlet* (New York: Random House, 1940), 309–421. This episode appears in the *The Long, Hot Summer* (1958) starring Paul Newman as the mercurial Quick.

17. Wolfe, "Digibabble," *Hooking Up* (New York: Farrar Straus Giroux), 78.

18. Wolfe, *A Man in Full*, 419.

19. Ibid., 193.

20. Wolfe, Tom, "My Three Stooges," *Hooking Up*, 146.

21. Wolfe, *A Man in Full*, 428.

22. Wolfe, "My Three Stooges," *Hooking Up*, 148.

23. Leonard, John, *Lonesome Rangers* (New York: New Press, 2002), 89.

24. Michel Foucault's *Les mots et les chose* (*Words and Things,* 1966) was influenced by the American critic Wylie Sypher who had an encyclopedic knowledge of literature, music, and especially painting from the Italian Renaissance to World War II. Like Wolfe, he failed to grasp or rejected postmodernism. Sypher was one of the greatest non-stop teacher-talkers who ever walked the globe yet he only spoke to students—if he discovered that you had a doctorate, he would treat you like the local village idiot and would not speak to you. Sypher's lectures were a witty parody of doctoral oral exams.

25. This doctrine goes back to the Egyptians, Plato, St. Paul, and Rousseau. Without a grounding in Rousseau, Voltaire, and French history, it remains difficult for Americans to understand the sociological and historical sensibility behind Foucault's writings.

26. Balzac, Honoré, *Lost Illusions,* 90–112.

27. Wolfe, *A Man in Full,* 425.

28. Ibid., 534.

29. Ibid., 582–83.

30. My translation. Book IV, 219–232. While Egyptian doctors receive an advertisement for their superior healing skills, Homer claims they learned these skills from the Greek god of healing (*Iliad* V, 401, 899).

31. Wolfe, *A Man in Full,* 617.

32. In *Tom Wolfe: A Critical Companion* (Westport: Greenwood Press, 2002), 174, Brian Abel Ragen briefly discusses the theme of Stoicism in the life of author Admiral James Stockdale who discovered Epictetus in a North Vietnamese prison.

33. Wolfe, *A Man in Full,* 682–87. The meaning and derivation of Ogygia remains uncertain, but ancient scholars understood it to mean "primeval," as in Hesiod; the sound value is terrific. See Huebeck et al., *A Commentary on Homer's Odyssey,* vol. 1 (Oxford: Clarendon Press, 1990), 85.

34. Ibid., 710.

35. Applebome, Peter, "A Man in Tune with his Heritage." *NYT,* November 11, 1988.

36. Lewis, Sinclair, *Arrowsmith, Elmer Gantry, Dodsworth* (Library of America, 2002), 762.

37. At the conclusion of Zola's great novel *The Ladies' Paradise* there is a similar capitulation on the part of the main character Mouret before the inevitable; also, there emerges a new (satiric) religious sensibility emanating from capitalistic hedonism—in contrast to Wolfe's Stoicism.

38. Arthur, Anthony, *Literary Feuds: A Century of Celebrated Quarrels—from Mark Twain to Tom Wolfe* (New York: St. Martin's Press, 2002), 206–07.

39. Wolfe, *Hooking Up,* 169–71.

40. Ibid, 148.

41. As the Tsar's Inquisitor judge of religious intolerance, Illych remains responsible for the breakup of thousands of families, even though he prides his liberal sensibility for not having conducted mass executions like many of his colleagues.

42. Ibid., 147.

43. Ibid., 236.

44. Begley, Adam, "Ambush at Fort Brag," *The New York Observer,* October 29, 2000.

45. Lottman, Herbert, *Flaubert: A Biography* (Boston: Little Brown), 1989, 242–43.

Chapter 9: The Ivory Tower in Ruins?

1. See Kramer, Jr., John E., *The American College Novel: An Annotated Bibliography* (Lanham: Scarecrow Press, 2003); also, Showalter, Elaine, *Faculty Towers* (Philadelphia: Univ. of Pennsylvania Press, 2005).

2. Flaubert never found lasting happiness in love, though he might not have wanted it for fear it would destroy his art. Flaubert had seduced Louise Colet in a carriage ride (such a scene appears in Flaubert's novel), but was apparently impotent in the bouncing carriage, the only time he claimed to have had that problem. They became lovers for almost two years and their letters from this period are some of the most-sought after letters in the history of literature, both for literary value and intimate anatomical frankness. Flaubert, whom Colet described in a poem as "an untamed buffalo of the American desert, / Vigorous and superb in your athletic strength," was divided by his maddening lust for Louise and his dutiful devotion to his mother with whom he lived. Flaubert secretly relished a pair of Louise's slippers, stained with her menstrual blood and stuff snugly in a draw, a relic of their first night of love-making. When the married Colet proclaimed her desire for a love-child, Flaubert became suicidal. Although she had many lovers, this affair appears to be the great frustration of Colet's life—it became the autobiographical experience that Flaubert alchemized into *Madame Bovary*. Lottman, Herbert, *Flaubert: A Biography* (Boston: Little Brown, 1989) 42–44, 69–82.

3. Wolfe, Tom, *Hooking Up* (New York: Farrar Straus Giroux, 2000), 6.

4. In *Madame Bovary* Charles Bovary was "brought up in a school of Spartan austerity." Flaubert, Gustave, *Madame Bovary* translated by Gerard Hopkins (Oxford: Oxford World Classics, 1994), 5. Wolfe also employs the tree metaphor (*I Am Charlotte Simmons*, 35) that Flaubert uses (*Madame Bovary*, 6) to describe the future male lover in their novels.

5. For a short background interview on the novel see http://www.nerve.com/screeningroom/books/interview_tomwolfe. Accessed 10/01/08.

6. Wolfe, Tom, *I Am Charlotte Simmons* (New York: Picador, 2005), 94. All citations are to this paperback edition, since Wolfe revised the novel for the paper printing.

7. Twain, Mark, *The American Claimant* (New York: Charles L Webster & Co., 1892), especially chapters XV and XXIII. In the novel a spectacular hotel burns down; it is called the Gadsby.

8. Houllebecq is the leading French satirical novelist.

9. Wolfe, *I Am Charlotte Simmons*, 157.

10. Ibid., 249.

11. Ibid., 196.

12. Bowden, Mark, "I Am Charlotte Simmons," *The Atlantic Monthly*, December, 2004.

13. Wolfe, *I Am Charlotte Simmons*, 308.

14. The attentive reader might recall Wolfe's use of Rudyard Kipling's poetry in his essay "The Luther of Columbus Circle." In the current context God becomes a metaphor for the intellectual and moral life.

Recessional

June 22, 1897

God of our father, known of old,
  Lord of our far-flung battle-line,
Beneath whose awful Hand we hold
  Dominion over palm and pine—
Lord God of Hosts, be with us yet,
Lest we forget—lest we forget!

The tumult and the shouting dies;
  The Captains and the Kings depart:
Still stands thine ancient sacrifice,

An humble and contrite heart.
Lord God of Hosts, be with us yet,
Lest we forget—lest we forget!

Far-called, our navies melt away;
    On dune and headland sinks the fire,
Lo all our pomp of yesterday
    Is one with Nineveh and Tyre!
Judge of the Nations, spare us yet,
Lest we forget—lest we forget!

If, drunk with sight of power, we loose
    Wild tongues that have not thee in awe,
Such boastings as the Gentiles use,
    Or lesser breeds without the Law—
Lord God of Hosts, be with us yet,
Lest we forget—lest we forget!

For heathen heart that puts her trust
    In reeking tube and iron shard,
All valiant dust that builds on dust,
    And guarding, calls not thee to guard,
For frantic boast and foolish word—
Thy mercy on thy People, Lord!

15. See Popkin, Richard H., *The History of Scepticism: From Erasmus to Descartes* (New York: Harper & Row, 1964).

16. Wolfe, Tom, *I Am Charlotte Simmons*, 308.

17. Ibid., 321.

18. Ibid., 370.

19. Ibid., 376. The stricter association between the owl and Athena is a post-Homeric development.

20. Ibid., 381.

21. Ibid., 486.

22. Ibid., 427. Note the feminine pronoun—Charlotte's feminist cast of mind is natural and not self-conscious.

23. Ibid.

24. Lewis, Sinclair, *Arrowsmith, Elmer Gantry, Dodsworth* (Library of America, 2002), 665–68. Lewis' scene may have been inspired by the concluding pages of Zola's *The Ladies' Paradise* with its powerful poetic symbolism.

25. Wolfe, Tom, *I Am Charlotte Simmons*, 527.

26. Ibid., 543.

27. Ibid., 607.

28. Ibid., 668.

29. Ibid., 669.

30. In his anthology *The New Journalism* Wolfe included Rex Reed's amusing article on Ava Gardner, "Do You Sleep in the Nude?"

31. Malamud, Bernard, *A New Life* (New York: Farrar Straus Giroux, 1961), 42.

32. Wolfe, Tom, *I Am Charlotte Simmons*, 698.

33. James T. Farrell's *Studs Lonigan* (1932) would be an accessible and wonderful novel for high school students to read; perhaps Wolfe subtlety advocates that it *should* be in the high school curriculum (if only one could get students to read a book of more than three hundred pages).

34. *Demon Box*, 89–90.

35. Wolfe, Tom, *I Am Charlotte Simmons*, 681.

36. Bodwell, Joshua, "Such Sweet Sorrow," *Poets & Writers Magazine*, May/June, 2008.

37. Wolfe, Tom, *Hooking Up*, 158.

38. Hofstadter, Richard, *Anti-Intellectualism in American Life* (New York: Knopf, 1963).

39. Balzac, Honoré, *Lost Illusions*, trans. Kathleen Raine (New York: Modern Library, 1967), 53.

40. Wolfe, *I Am Charlotte Simmons*, 647.

41. Holland, Dorothy C. and Margaret A. Eisenhart. *Educated in Romance* (Chicago: Univ. of Chicago Press, 1990), ix.

Chapter 10: Vroom! Wolfe's Status in American Literature

1. Sims, Norman, *True Stories: A Century of Literary Journalism* (Evanston: Northwestern Univ. Press, 2007), 262.

2. "Tom Wolfe+ Michael Gazzaniga," www.seedmagazine.com/news/2008/07/tom_wolfe_michael_gazzaniga.php.

3. An influential minority, both liberal and conservative, support Wolfe's critique of academia—evidence of this is that Wolfe was chosen to pen the foreword to *Declining by degrees: Higher education at risk* (New York: Palgrave Macmillan, 2005). Wolfe also participated in making the PBS companion video.

4. Important elements of the New Journalism can be found in the proletarian Japanese writer Hayashi Fumiko (1904–51), but there is no evidence American writers were familiar with her work.

5. Wolfe locates the notion of God in humankind's invention of language as a speaking animal. In his Jefferson Lecture he cites the beginning of St. John's Gospel, "In the beginning was the Word," as his central tenet. By doing so, he discards the negativity of atheism and embraces hope through language that contains a moral charge.

6. Leonard, John, *Lonesome Rangers* (New York: New Press, 2002), 89.

BIBLIOGRAPHY

Books by Tom Wolfe (in chronological order)

The Kandy-Kolored Tangerine-Flake Streamline Baby. New York: Farrar Straus Giroux, 1965; Bantam, 1968.

The Pump House Gang. New York: Farrar Straus Giroux, 1968; Bantam, 1969.

The Electric Kool-Aid Acid Test. New York: Farrar Straus Giroux, 1968; Bantam, 1969.

Radical Chic & Mau-Mauing the Flak Catchers. New York: Farrar Straus Giroux, 1970; Bantam, 1971.

The Painted Word. New York: Farrar Straus Giroux, 1975; Bantam, 1976.

Mauve Gloves & Madmen, Clutter and Vine. New York: Farrar Straus Giroux, 1976; Bantam, 1977.

The Right Stuff. New York: Farrar Straus Giroux, 1979; Bantam, 1980.

In Our Time. New York: Farrar Straus Giroux, 1980; Bantam, 1999.

From Bauhaus to Our House. New York: Farrar Straus Giroux, 1981; Bantam, 1982.

The Purple Decades: A Reader. New York: Farrar Straus Giroux, 1982; Bantam, 1983.

The Bonfire of the Vanities. New York: Farrar, Straus Giroux, 1987; Bantam, 1988.

A Man in Full. New York: Farrar Straus Giroux, 1998; Bantam, 1999.

Hooking Up. New York: Farrar Straus Giroux, 2000.

I Am Charlotte Simmons. New York: Farrar Straus Giroux, 2004; Picador, 2005.

Note: Picador has recently reprinted all of Tom Wolfe's books in paperback.

Books Cited

This is a list of books cited; it does not include all books referred to or many of the books I have read in writing this book. This is by no means a bibliography on Wolfe, about whom many more books will be written.

Adams, Henry. *The Education of Henry* Adams. Boston: Houghton Mifflin, 1973, reprint of 1918.

Arthur, Anthony. *Literary Feuds: A Century of Celebrated Quarrels—from Mark Twain to Tom Wolfe.* New York: St. Martin's Press, 2002.

Balzac, Honoré. *Lost Illusions,* trans. by Kathleen Raine. New York: Modern Library, 1967.

Biskind, Peter. *Easy Riders, Raging Bulls.* New York: Simon & Schuster, 1999.

Bloomfield, Morton W. and Leonard Newmark. A *Linguistic Introduction to the History of English.* New York: Knopf, 1963.

Berkovitch, Sacvan. *The Puritan Origins of the American Self.* New Haven: Yale, 1977.

Brightman, Carol. *Sweet Chaos: The Grateful Dead's American Adventure.* New York: Simon & Schuster, 1998.

Budgen, Frank. *Myselves When Young.* London: Oxford University Press, 1970.

Cather, Willa. *My Antonia.* New York: Signet Classic, 1994.

Collins, Michael. *Carrying the Fire: An Astronauts' Journeys.* New York: Farrar Straus Giroux, 1974.

De St Joree, John. *Venus Bound.* New York: Random House, 1994.

Dickson, Paul. *Sputnik: The Shock of the Century.* New York: Walker, 2001.

Doody, Margaret Anne. *The True Story of the* Novel. New Brunswick: Rutgers University Press, 1997.

Ellman, Richard. *James Joyce.* London: Oxford University Press, 1982.

Faulkner, William. *The Hamlet.* New York: Random House, 1940.

Flaubert, Gustave. *Madame Bovary* translated by Gerard Hopkins. Oxford: Oxford World Classics, 1994.

Gagarin, Yuri, *The First Man in Space.* New York: Crosscurrents Press, 1960.

Grateful Dead's website: www.dead.net/features/dictionary-page-where-grateful-deads-name-came.

Greenfield, Robert. *Timothy Leary: A Biography.* New York: Harcourt, 2006.

Heaney, Seamus. *Seamus Heaney: Poems and a Memoir.* New York: Limited Editions Book Club, 1982.

Hersh, Richard H. and John Morrow. *Declining by degrees: Higher education at Risk.* Foreword by Tom Wolfe. New York: Palgrave Macmillan, 2005.

Hesse, Hermann. *The Journey to the East,* trans. Hilda Rosner. New York: Noonday Press, 1957.

Hofmann, Albert. *LSD: My Problem Child,* trans. Jonathon Ott. New York: McGraw-Hill, 1980.

Hofstadter, Richard. *Anti-Intellectualism in American* Life. New York: Knopf, 1963.

Holland, Dorothy C. and Margaret A. Eisenhart. *Educated in Romance.* Chicago: University of Chicago Press, 1990.

Huebeck et al., *A Commentary on Homer's Odyssey,* vol. 1. Oxford: Clarendon Press, 1990.

Kasack, Wolfgang. *Dictionary of Russian Literature since 1917.* New York: Columbia University Press, 1988.

Kesey, Ken. *Demon Box.* New York: Viking, 1986.

———. *Jail Journal.* New York: Viking, 2003.

Kluger, Richard. *The Paper: The Life and Death of the Herald Tribune.* New York: Knopf, 1986.

Kramer, Jr., John E. *The American College Novel: An Annotated Bibliography.* Lanham: Scarecrow Press, 2003.

Krim, Seymour. *Shake it for the World, Smartass.* New York: Dial Press, 1970.

Kristeller, Paul Oskar. *Eight Philosophers of the Renaissance.* Stanford: Stanford University Press, 1964.

Leonard, John. *Lonesome Rangers.* New York: New Press, 2002.

Lewis, Sinclair. *Arrowsmith, Elmer Gantry, Dodsworth.* Library of America, 2002.

Lottman, Herbert. *Flaubert: A Biography.* Boston: Little Brown, 1989.

McGrady, Patrick J. *Henry Pearson: The Poetry of Line.* University Park: Palmer Museum, Pennsylvania State, 2001.

Mailer, Norman. *Of a Fire on the Moon.* Boston: Little Brown, 1970.

Major, Clarence. *Juba to Jive: A Dictionary of African-American Slang.* New York: Viking, 1994.

Malamud, Bernard. *A New Life.* New York: Farrar Straus Giroux, 1961.

Mancinci, Matthew. *Alexis de Tocqueville and American Intellectuals.* New York: Rowman and Littlefield, 2006.

Mann, Thomas. *Stories of Three Decades*, trans. H.T. Lowe-Porter. New York: Modern Library, 1936.

McClanahan, Ed. *Famous People I Have Known.* New York: Farrar Strauss Giroux, 1985.

McClanahan, Ed, ed., *Spit in the Ocean #7.* New York: Viking, 2003.

McKeen, William. *Tom Wolfe.* Boston: Twayne, 1995.

Menzies, Gavin. *1421: The Year China Discovered America.* New York: William Morrow, 2002.

The Mercury Astronauts. *We Seven.* New York: Simon & Schuster, 1962.

Miller, Perry. *The Life of the American Mind.* London: Victor Gollancz, 1966.

Monje, Scott C., *The Central Intelligence Agency: A Documentary History.* Westport: Greenwood Press, 2008.

Nietzsche, Friedrich. *The Philosophy of Nietzsche.* New York: The Modern Library, 1947.

Plummer, William. *The Holy Goof: A Biography of Neal Cassady.* New York: Da Capo Press, 2004.

Popkin, Richard H. *The History of Scepticism: From Erasmus to Descartes.* New York: Harper & Row, 1964.

Ragen, Brian Abel. *Tom Wolfe: A Critical Companion.* Westport: Greenwood Press, 2002.

Richardson, Joanna. *Verlaine.* New York: Viking, 1971.

Rosenmeyer, Thomas G. *The Green Cabinet: Theocritus and the European Pastoral Lyric.* Berkeley: University of California Press, 1969.

Salomon, Julie. *The Devil's Candy:* The Bonfire of the Vanities *Goes to Hollywood.* Boston: Houghton Mifflin, 1991.

Scura, Dorothy, ed. *Conversations with Tom Wolfe.* Jackson: University Press of Mississippi, 1990.

Showalter, Elaine. *Faculty Towers.* Philadelphia: Univ. of Pennsylvania Press, 2005.

Sims, Norman. *True Stories: A Century of Literary Journalism.* Evanston: Northwestern Univ. Press, 2007.

Smith, Bernard. ed. *The Antipodean Manifesto: Essays in Art and History.* Melbourne: Oxford University Press, 1975.

Smith, Morton. *Jesus the Magician.* New York: Harper & Row, 1978.

Stevens, Jay. *Storming Heaven: LSD and the American Dream.* New York: Harper & Row, 1987.

Stone, Robert. *Prime Green.* New York: Ecco Press, 2007.

Tayler, Jeffrey. *Facing the Congo: A Modern-Day Journey into the Heart of Darkness.* New York: Three Rivers Press, 2000.

Taylor, D. J. *Thackeray: The Life of a Literary Man.* New York: Carroll & Graf, 1999.

Thackeray, William Makepeace. *The Book of Snobs.* New York: Penguin, 1993.

Troyat, Henri. *Turgenev.* New York: Dutton, 1988.

Turgenev, Ivan. *Fathers and Sons.* Trans. Rosemary Edmonds. New York: Penguin, 1975.

Twain, Mark, *The American Claimant.* New York: Charles L Webster & Co., 1892.
———. *Life on the Mississippi.* New York: Oxford University Press, 1966.
Weingarten, Marc. *The Gang That Wouldn't Shoot Straight: Wolfe, Thompson, Didion, and the New Journalism Revolution.* New York: Crown. 2006.
Wilford, John Noble. *We Reach the Moon.* New York: Bantam, 1969.
Wolfe, Tom. Foreword. *New York Stories.* New York: Random House, 2008.
Yagoda, Ben. *About Town: The New Yorker and the World it Made.* New York: Scribner, 2000.
Zola, Emile. *The Ladies' Paradise.* Trans. Brian Nelson. New York: Penguin, 1995.

Articles Cited

Abbreviations: *NYT, New York Times*

Anson, Robert Sam. "Legend with a Bullet." *Vanity Fair*, June, 2003.
Applebome, Peter. "A Man in Tune with his Heritage." *NYT*, November 11, 1988.
Begley, Adam. "Ambush at Fort Bragg." *The New York Observer*, October 29, 2000.
Bigart, Homer. "Comments on Moratorium at Yale." *NYT*, April 30, 1970.
Bigart, Homer. "Education; Another Spring of Revolt on the Campus." *NYT*, May 2, 1970.
Blakeley, William. "2500 Students at Mass Meeting." *Yale Daily News*, April 30, 1970.
Blumenthal, Ralph. "Files Detail Years of Spying on Bernstein." *NYT*, July 29, 1994.
Blumenthal, Ralph. "Bernstein was Monitored as Late as 70's." *NYT*, May 17, 1995.
Bodwell, Joshua. "Such Sweet Sorrow." *Poets & Writers Magazine*, May/June, 2008.
Bowden, Mark. "I Am Charlotte Simmons." *The Atlantic Monthly*, December, 2004.
Capouya, Emile. "True Facts and Artifacts." *Saturday Review*, July 31, 1965.
Dean, John. "Is Barack Obama Truly too Elite to be Elected?" http://www.smirkingchimp.com/thread/14666. Accessed 10/01/08.
Douglas, Martin. "Seeking the Soul of the City's Summer." *NYT*, May 9, 1999.
Elliott, Jean. Marshall Fishwick Obituary. *Virginia Tech News*, May 24, 2006.
Erlanger, Steve. "Bonfire in Bronx!!! Wolfe Catches Flak!!!" *NYT*, March 11, 1988.
Fishwick, Marshall. "Conversations with Scholars of American Popular Culture." *Americana: The Journal of American Popular Culture*, Fall, 2003.
Glueck, Grace. "Henry Pearson—'Selected Drawings 1959–69.'" *NYT*, May 16, 2003.
Goldberger, Paul. "In the Bird's Nest." *The New Yorker*, June 2. 2008.
Gorner, Peter. "Tom Wolfe: In Big League as a Writer." *Chicago Tribune*, December 7, 1976.
Grossman, Lev. "Mind and Body Happiness." *Time*, October 31, 2004.
Hersey, John. "The Legend on the License." *Yale Review*, autumn, 1980.
Hess, Thomas B. "Mauve Gloves and Madmen, Clutter & Vine." *NYT*, December 26, 1976.
Heydarpour, Roja. Henry Pearson Obituary. *NYT*, December 18, 2006.
"Interview with Tom Wolfe." *NYT*, March, 2008.
"Interview with Tom Wolfe." *Paris Review*, spring, 1991.
"Interview with Tom Wolfe." *Yale Alumni Magazine*, December, 2000; summer, 2003.
Jacobs, Erica. "Picturing America." *San Francisco Examiner*, March 3, 2008.
Lemann, Nicholas. "New York in the Eighties." *The Atlantic*, December 1987.
Lehmann-Haupt, Christopher. "From Bauhaus to Our House." *NYT*, October 9, 1981.
———. Kesey Obituary. *NYT*, November 11, 2001.
Leland, John. "Psychodelia's Middle-Aged Head Trip." *NYT*, November 18, 2001.

Margolick, David. "The Law; At the Bar." *NYT*, February 5, 1988.

McClanahan, Ed. *Famous People I Have Known*. New York: Farrar Straus Giroux, 1985.

———, ed. *Spit in the Ocean #7*. New York: Viking, 2003.

McGrath, Charles. "Wolfe's World." *NYT*, October 31, 2004.

Ouroussoff, Nicolai. "In Changing Face of Bejing." *NYT*, July 13, 2008.

Page, Eric. Kingman Brewster, Jr. Obituary. *NYT*, November 8, 1988.

Palermo, Sara. Henry Pearson Obituary. *Pine Plains Register*, December 8, 2008.

Putnam, Robert D. "The Prosperous Community: Social Community and Public Life." *The American Prospect*, March 21, 1993.

Schlesinger, Arthur. "The Amazing Success Story of 'Spiro Who?'" *NYT*, July 26, 1970.

Smith, Craig E. "Albert Hofmann, the Father of LSD, Dies at 102." *NYT* April 30, 2008.

Streitfeld, David. "Tom Wolfe Collection has the Wrong Stuff." *San Francisco Chronicle*, December 22, 2000.

Thompson, Toby. "The Evolution of Dandy Tom." *Vanity Fair* 50, October, 1987.

"Tom Wolfe+ Michael Gazzaniga." www.seedmagazine.com/news/2008/07/tom_wolfe_michael_gazzaniga.php. Accessed 10/01/08.

Walker, Pamela. "Letter to the Editor." *NYT*, June 21, 1987.

Wakefield, Dan. *The Atlantic*. "The Personal Voice and the Impersonal Eye," June, 1966.

Weingarten, Marc. "A 'Mad Hulking Carnival' of American Life." http://www.neh.gov/whoweare/wolfe/appreciation.html. Accessed 10/1/08.

Wolfe, Alan. "Gonzo Sociology." *The New Republic*, October 8, 2008.

Wolfe, Tom. "As Gonzo in Life as in His Work." *Wall Street Journal*, February 22, 2005.

Wolfe, Tom, "Stalking the Billion-Footed Beast," *Harper's*, November, 1989.

"Wolfe, Tom." In *American Writers*, Supplement II, Part 2. New York: Charles Scriber's Sons, 1991.

"Wolfe, Tom." In *Contemporary Authors 9 and 70*. Detroit: Gale, 1983.

Wolfe, Tom, NEH Jefferson Lecture, 2006. www.neh.gov/whoweare/wolfe/lecture.html. Accessed 10/01/08.

Wolfe, Tom. "The Nerve Interview." www.nerve.com/screeningroom/books/interview_tomwolfe. Accessed 10/01/08.

Wolfe, Tom. "Tales of Felker." *The New York Observer*, July 7–14, 2008.

DVDs

Gray, Mike & Associates. *The Murder of Fred Hampton*. Chicago: Facets Multimedia, 2007.

Green, Sam and Bill Siegel. *Weather Underground*. New York: Distributed by New Video, 2004.

Hersh, Richard H. and John Morrow. *Declining by degrees: Higher education at Risk*. Washington: PBS Home Video, 2005.

Lamb, Brian. *In-Depth with Tom Wolfe*. Washington: C-Span Video Library, 2004.

The Merry Band of Pranksters Look for a Kool Place #1 and #2. Pleasant Hill: Key-Z productions, 2005.

Suggested Further Reading

Bloom, Harold, ed. *Tom Wolfe: Modern Critical Views*. Broomall: Chelsea House, 2000.

Brown, Frederick. *Zola: A Life*. Baltimore: Johns Hopkins University Press, 1995.

Glenn, John with Nick Taylor. *John Glenn: A Memoir*. New York: Bantam, 1999.

Kesey, Ken. *Sometimes a Great Notion*. New York: Viking, 1964.

Mills, C. Wright, ed. John Summers. *The Politics of Truth: Selected Writings of C. Wright Mills*. Oxford: Oxford University Press, 2008.

Perry, Paul. *On the Bus: The Complete Guide to the Legendary Trip of Ken Kesey and the Merry Pranksters and the Birth of the Counterculture*. New York: Thunder's Mouth Press, 1990.

Shomette, Doug, ed. *The Critical Response to Tom Wolfe*. Westport: Greenwood, 1992.

Thompson, Hunter. *Hell's Angels: A Strange and Terrible Saga*. New York: Ballantine, 1967.

Veblen, Thorstein. *Theory of the Leisure Class*. New York: Macmillan, 1912; 1943.

Weber, Max, ed. Richard Swedberg. *Essays in Economic Sociology*. Princeton: Princeton University Press, 1999.

Weber, Max, ed. Sam Whimster. *The Essential Weber: A Reader*. New York: Routledge, 2004.

Wolfe's Official Website: www.tomwolfe.com.

INDEX

194 Index

Warhol, Andy, 7, 13, 169
Weber, Max, 4, 11, 19–20, 22, 23, 33, 56, 69, 75, 164
Weingarten, Marc, 41, 79
Wenner, Jann, 7
Wharton, Edith, 104, 164
Whitman, Walt, 16, 17, 34, 48
Willson, Dixie, 29
Wilson, Edmund, 23
Wolfe, Thomas, 155

Wordsworth, William, 16, 43, 60, 61

Yale University, 2–4, 15, 17–19, 27, 33, 37, 39, 44, 64–68, 98, 109, 117, 167
Yeager, Chuck, 75–77, 79, 81, 90–91

Zamyatin, Evgeny, 16
Zola, Emile, 123, 128, 132–33, 140–42, 151–52, 161, 164, 165, 166
Zoroaster, 29, 33, 52

About the Author

KEVIN T. McENEANEY is the author of two books, *The Enclosed Garden* and *Longing*, which has been translated into French and Japanese. He has published over 50 encyclopedia articles and is the coeditor of *The Irish Literary Supplement*. He teaches at Marist Aquinas College in Poughkeepsie, New York.